GW00836275

# A Concise History of Malta

# A Concise History of Malta

## Carmel Cassar

Mireva
Publications

First published in 2000
by Mireva Publications of
Tower Street, Msida, Malta. MSD 06.
(Mireva and logo are Registered Trade Marks. [Malta] Reg. No. 17998.)
Typeset and paged on
MirevaNewCenturySchoolBook 10/12 by
MirevaSet, Msida, Malta.
Produced by Evan Cumbo.
Cover design by Evan Cumbo.
Printed and bound by
Gutenberg Press
Gudja Road, Tarxien, Malta. PLA 19


International Standard Book Number

1-870579-52-6

All rights reserved. No part of this publication may be produced or
transmitted in any form or by any means electronical, mechanical,
photocopying, recording or otherwise, or stored in any retrieval system of any nature without the written permission of the copyright
holder and the publisher, application for which shall be made to the
publisher.

© *A Concise History of Malta* – Carmel Cassar – Mireva Publications – 2000

*to the memory
of my grandfathers:
Carmelo Cassar and
Saverio Fenech*

# Table of Contents

# List of Illustrations

# List of Figures

# Preface

In a concise history of a country one is compelled to compress thousands of years of a highly complex history into a brief volume. It is an attempt which will, in all probability, provoke disapproval from most specialists, who see their own particular patches of historical interest constrained, misrepresented, perhaps distorted, or even ignored altogether. Yet a brief history on such a large topic can make no attempt at comprehensiveness and can at best hope to provide guidance into the main traits of the rich historical past of the country in question – in this case, Malta.

Malta consists of a miniscule central Mediterranean archipelago whose geographical isolation made possible the development of peculiar characteristics which started from prehistoric times. The same cultural influences from neighbouring southern European and North African states continued to be integrated into the socio-cultural fabric of Malta. This may be particularly said of Italy of the pre-unification days, and more specifically of nearby Sicily.

Chapter one is intended mainly to provide the general geographical and historical backgrounds that are so fundamental in a proper understanding of the socio-cultural traits of Malta. Chapter two is a cursory general overview of the history of the country from prehistoric times to the Middle Ages. The next chapter discusses the main issues and impact of the Order of St John. Finally chapters four, five and six discuss the development of Maltese political aspirations, in the nineteenth and twentieth centuries, and raise arguments about the difficulties encountered when trying to integrate an island with a varied cultural background into the British imperial set-up. The epilogue comes right down to the present and attempts to give a feeling of the moral and political crisis Malta is facing at the dawn of the twenty-first century. This makes any conclusion risky beyond need, and may, at times, sound rather pessimistic.

This book discussing such a wide period relies heavily on researches undertaken by others. It was, above all, my concern to represent a synthesis of existing knowledge – based, as it is, on quite conflicting views – and to develop a coherent overall account. While conscious of gaps and inadequacies it is hoped that this book may stimulate the reader for subsequent more detailed exploration of particular aspects discussed here. It may also help the general reader to locate the existing knowledge and interests on Malta within a broad Mediterranean framework.

I am grateful to colleagues and friends who have read and commented on parts of the manuscript. I would in particular like to thank Paul Sant-Cassia and Dominic Cutajar for their painstaking efforts to improve the text. They have been constant friends over many years. I also wish to thank Evan Cumbo who first set me the challenge to write this book. The choice of appropriate illustrations was a difficult task and raised many problems of selection, interpretation and omission. Readers may notice that the publisher and myself have tried to keep illustrations to a minimum and have generally preferred the representation of broad themes.

My grandfathers, to whom this book is dedicated, each has in his own very special way, nurtured in me a love for history. I will always remember my childhood weekly visits to heritage sites with my paternal grandfather, a master-baker proud of his trade, and madly in love with all that makes us Maltese. On the other hand, the vivid descriptions which my maternal grandfather used to give me of his travels around the world – as soldier, sailor and emigrant – during the first decades of the twentieth century, will forever remain indelibile. Finally, while admitting that very little would have been achieved hadn't it not been for the encouragement and support given by my father and my mother, I cherish my main sources of inspiration – Susan my wife, and Marc'Andrea my son, both of whom I have robbed many an hour, rightfully theirs. I can never thank them enough.

*Carmel Cassar*
*27th June 2000*
*University of Wales, Lampeter.*

# *1*

# The Land and its People

## A. *The Geographical Determinants of Maltese Culture*

(i) Geographic Position and the Climate

The Maltese archipelago, together with the islands of Pantelleria, Lampedusa and Linosa, lie in the narrow channel which separates Sicily from North Africa. If we try to locate Malta in the marine topography of the central Mediterranean, we find that it has been described as lying 'off the beaten track', away from the coast-hugging trade routes. Until the advent of the steamship, the Mediterranean was an immensity of water... where shipping was only active along the coastline. Even so, documentary evidence seems to suggest that vessels travelling from East to West usually preferred to pass through the straits of Messina while shipping from north to south very often by-passed the Maltese islands.

The geographical position of the islands affected Malta's cultural tradition, since this tended to develop in relative isolation. Such a situation explains why it was possible for a unique megalithic culture to flourish during Chalcolithic times. Nevertheless, from the Roman period until 1530, Malta was ruled jointly with Sicily. Sicily, the largest and most populous island in the Mediterranean, is moreover ideally situated to dominate the sea. Malta thus became no more than an auxiliary base,

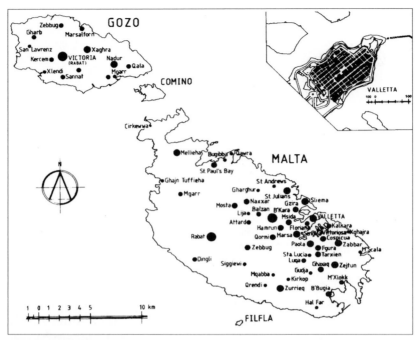

Map of the Maltese Islands.

as a Sicilian overlord had no interest in doing anything with Malta, other than keeping it out of the hands of a hostile power.

This explains why the Apostle Paul reached Roman Malta only after having been shipwrecked. The history of the Maltese islands was to change dramatically only with the advent of the Order of St John.

Malta was essentially a self-contained island with its own language, customs and archaic economy and for centuries, it managed to preserve its own form of civilization.

In striking contrast with this isolation, an accidental change of rule in the sixteenth century brought to Malta's shores an entirely different civilization and a new way of life. Malta became integrated into the shipping routes of the central Mediterranean and even its culture was transformed.

Lying in the centre of the Mediterranean region, the climate of the Maltese islands is dominated by the breath of two external

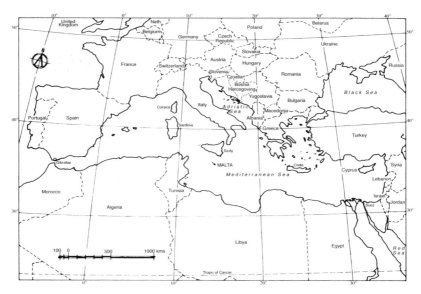

Map of the Mediterranean.

forces: the Atlantic ocean, the sea's neighbour to the west, and the Sahara desert, its neighbour to the south. Within this open-ended area, two natural factors are at work. The Sahara brings dry air, clear intense daylight and vast blue skies. The Atlantic sends in an abundance of grey mist and moist air which induces the mild rainy winters which have always been a fact of life in the central Mediterranean.

Winter lasts from September to April while summer usually starts in May till the end of August. Torrid summer reigns un-contested between the end of June and early September when the sea is usually astonishingly calm. No wonder that the summer season was the best time for shipping, piracy and war during a time when sailing ships plied the Mediterranean.

The vegetation of the Maltese islands, as in the rest of the Mediterranean, includes mostly drought-tolerant evergreen shrubs and trees together with winter-charged annuals producing a healthy maquis and a beautiful garigue. The eminent French historian Fernand Braudel claims that one can find 'the same eternal trinity' consisting of wheat, olives and vines throughout the Mediterranean region. This means that the different parts of the sea, produced identical agricultural products rather than complementing each other. Thus the states bordering the region had the same granaries, wine-cellars, and oil presses, the same tools, flocks and herds and often the same agrarian traditions and daily preoccupations. It therefore follows that similar goods can be found and produced in any country bordering the sea. The Mediterranean countries should hence have been in direct competition with each other. Yet until the advent of industrialization, especially until the mid 19th century, the total volume of exchange was small and distances travelled short.

(ii) The Economy, Food Production and Commerce

Written information about the economy and food production on Malta dates back to the High Middle Ages. The presence of extensive areas of karstic table-lands suitable mainly for rough grazing provide evidence that animal husbandry was an important activity. The tenth century Arab chronicler Ibn Hauqal devoted a few lines to Malta which, according to him, was inhabited only by savage donkeys, numerous sheep, and bees. Visitors, presumably from Sicily, did come, bringing their own provisions, to collect honey and hunt the sheep, which were scarcely marketable, and the donkeys which were exported and sold.

It might follow that Malta was largely, or even wholly, depopulated after the upheavals of 871. Later, in the eleventh century it could have been resettled with Arab speaking Muslims, slaves and Christian captives. Al Idrisi, the Arab geographer of the Norman King Roger II, gives some reliable facts about the economy of Malta in the twelfth century. Admittedly the conditions relate to Norman times but are still certainly relevant for the proper Islamic period of Maltese history. Al Idrisi explains:

Away from the island of Pantelleria at a distance of one hundred miles towards the east one finds the island of Gozzo with a secure port. From Gozzo one goes to a small isle named Kamuna. From there going eastwards one finds the island of Malta. It is large and has a sheltered port on the east side. Malta has a town and abounds in pasture, sheep, fruit and honey.

It would seem therefore that animal husbandry was supplemented mainly by horticulture and bee-keeping. The Arabs appear to have introduced the growing of cotton to Sicily and from there eventually to Malta, together with new types of fruit like oranges. And it seems likely that by this period the growing of olives and the production of oil from the local olive crop – apparently one of the mainstays of Maltese agriculture in classical times – had almost come to an end.

The most important account is contained in the letter sent by the Emperor Frederick II in reply to Gilibertus Abate, his agent in Malta, around 1241. Gilibertus points out that there were two castles in Malta – Mdina and the *castrum maris* (castle by the sea) – and the Gozo Citadel. The garrison numbered some 220 (twenty-five of whom were sailors) besides seventy wives. The report indicated an economy based on the royal estates, cereal-producing *latifundia* worked by *villani* (serf / labourers). Each of these workers received a ration of around two-and-a-half tumoli of wheat, besides cheese, meat, butter and other foodstuffs. Furthermore there were eighty-four *servi* from Djerba working in the *massarie* (farmsteads); sixty *servi* and *ancille* (male and female slaves) in the service of the *curia* (local government); fifty-five cowherds; ten shepherds; and others who consumed barley bread. These were listed along with a number of beasts of burden.

It is evident that special importance was attached to the consumption of grain. There was lack of local wine and potable water although the locals drank large quantities of wine, as did the Muslim inhabitants. One may presume that wine was imported from Sicily. There are indications that cheese and honey were produced in relatively large quantities and presumably consumed locally. Thus we are told that bread was often accompanied by cheese. By 1394 a visitor to Malta commented about the prosperous state of the island, and mentioned amongst others, the production of cotton, cumin, wine and meat.

Descriptions of Malta dating from the sixteenth and seventeenth centuries, starting with the Knights' Commissions' Report of 1524, tend to concur on the fact that Malta was a 'land of hunger', sterile, treeless, and mostly dependent on Sicily for its food supply. The sterility of the land was a hazard which worried all Grand Masters right up to the end of the Order's rule in 1798. This is elicited in the official correspondence to other Heads of State, to Secretaries of State and ambassadors all over Europe. These usually referred to Malta as a *sterilissima isola* (most sterile island), owing to the shortage of grain and foodstuffs. On one occasion, Grand Master Perellos y Roccaful (1697-1720) even refused permission to the Carmelite friars to refound a friary in Vittoriosa, on the pretext, that the island could not sustain any extra mouths.

Early modern Malta depended, above anything else, on agricultural produce. It was the type of society where food, especially bread, (which the Italian food historian Piero Camporesi calls, 'that stuff of life which is the symbol of survival'), dominated both private and public, official and unofficial cultures, in the Mediterranean and all over Europe.

It is worth noting therefore, that cereal cultivation in Sicily expanded during the sixteenth century. This increase in produce

The hamlet of Mtahleb in the north of Malta with terracing and troglodytic dwellings.

is attributed to the fact that Sicily was growing grains of three varieties, namely:

i. *tunimunia* or *timilia* which was harvested in spring;
ii. *roccella* or *maiorca* which was used for the white bread of the town, but which was difficult to export as it could turn bad;
iii. *grano forte* which could be stored for a long time and was therefore preferred both for cultivation and export.

However, in reality, during the same period Malta did not produce enough grain to feed its own inhabitants. For example, it is recorded that in 1590, only 3,879 *salme* and nine *tumoli* (measure) of grain were produced on the island. Most of this produce was barley. Fifty per cent of the Maltese grain came from the countryside around the villages of Birkirkara, Naxxar, Siġġiewi and Żebbuġ. Between them, these villages produced a total of 1,975 *salme* and 10 *tumoli* of grain.

The importation of duty-free grain from Sicily to the Maltese islands continued, with great difficulty, throughout the rule of the Order of St John. This was sustained even in years of poor harvests. However during the early 1590s and early 1600s, Sicily was struck by bad harvests, plague, and famine, and this made exportation from this land impossible. Thus, although no grain was exported from Sicily after the harvest failures of 1606, 1607 and 1608, an exception for duty-free quotas was made in the case of Malta. It seems that this consistent provisioning was instigated by concern over the problem of food shortages on the island. A further increase in duty-free quotas, in 1622 and 1632, helped to alleviate further the food shortage. In the meantime the Maltese had devised other means of procuring grain to feed themselves.

In 1654 the Inquisitor, later cardinal-archbishop of Milan, Federico Borromeo, informed the Holy See that Malta produced enough grain to last for six months of the year, while the rest was bought duty free from Sicily. He added however, that, in case of food shortages, it was customary for the Maltese galley squadron to raid North African vessels, (and sometimes even

Christian ones), laden with grain. The officers-in-charge were then forced to sell their merchandise to the Maltese authorities.

It has been pointed out that, in Sicily, toll exemptions were granted only to towns belonging to the *regio demanio* (royal demesne), and this very often in return for political support or loyalty. Since such allowances involved some loss of income for the crown, requests for exemptions were sometimes refused. Thus when Malta was still directly under the royal control of Sicily, the *Università* in Malta received its required supplies of grain free of charge. The situation changed with the arrival of the Order of St John. Then, the crown often found difficulty in maintaining its earlier promises, particularly when the Order continued to strengthen its position on the island.

Each Sicilian town had its own *municipium* or *Università*. In the late sixteenth century, the importance of municipal territory was very clear to the Sicilians even though boundaries seem to have been frequently a matter of local dispute. Town officials called *giurati* (jurats) were expected to secure adequate food supplies from the territory they controlled. They also had to seek the assent of the Royal Patrimony, the institution responsible for Sicily's financial administration, if obliged to buy grain from other municipalities. The jurats were entitled to buy the necessary grain supplies for their town from the municipal territory at the established price of the *meta* (price fixing by the authorities).

The *meta* was not the market price, but a rate which was fixed every year in each town to reflect the state of the harvest within its territory. Grain prices, like all other commodities, were fixed by *mete* from the *Università* all over Sicily and ratified by the Viceroy. On the whole, prices did not differ much from one area of Sicily to another, since the local market depended on foreign agrarian credit. The system of *mete* had been progressively unified by the middle of the sixteenth century in line with the selling prices of the *carricatori* (large harbour stores). Prices were until then lower on the south coast (Sciacca, Girgenti, Licata and Terranova), and they were higher on the northern coast at the *carricatori* of Castellamare and Termini. The difference was however minimal, ranging from two to three *tarì*, and corresponded to the prices obtained at Palermo and Genoa. *Mete* often increased and decreased in relation to transport costs.

Bearing these circumstances in mind, one understands why Jean Quintin d'Autun, writing in 1536, described Malta as 'fortunate'. This, he said, is because of the proximity of Malta to Sicily, a proximity which makes access to shipping routes easy enabling the Maltese islands to afford the luxury of a grain trade. Henri Bresc points out that in the early 1400s, regular and massive imports of grain were necessary for the island's survival. By 1530 the local yields were so low that Malta imported some 9,000 *salme* (measure) of grain per year from Sicily. Following the advent of the Order of St John, Malta required between 14,000 and 28,000 *salme* of grain per year, or their equivalent in barley or maslin (barley mixed with wheat). The secretary of the Papal envoy, Mgr. Visconti, writing in 1582 reports that, 'the greater part of the people eat *pane misturato*, (bread made of a mixture of barley and wheat) vegetables, and *latticini* (cheeses)'. During the latter part of the eighteenth century, Malta was still importing the greater part of its food supplies from Sicily.

One cannot however fail to admit that the standard of living improved steadily between the early sixteenth and late eighteenth century. During his visit to Malta, Jean Quintin D'Autun observed that the Maltese 'have a Sicilian character, with a mixture of African... The people are very devoted to their religion... [which] is wonderfully practiced in the whole island'. Apart from Mdina 'and some houses in the suburb', the Maltese live in make-shift houses with tiles or reeds, 'which one would take for African huts'. Above all, the Maltese depended heavily on Sicily for their grain supplies and used thistles and cow dung for fuel, as timber had to be imported. 'The people, conscious of their country's sterility, live a very frugal life' points out Quintin D'Autun.

By the late eighteenth century, Malta was described as a country of growing material prosperity. The Order's rule had brought law and order, security and prosperity to the Maltese. The new boost of activities must be seen within the context of demographic growth, witnessed throughout the period of the Order's rule. A large number of Maltese men were engaged in the Order's navy, state- or privately-owned merchant shipping, as well as in corsairing (piracy against Muslim shipping) activities. The latter was fast becoming a very profitable enterprise. The essence of local men and the heavy influx of foreigners may suggest why Maltese females from the Harbour area tended to marry foreigners at a time when nearly a third of the population of Malta was based in the Harbour towns. Thus from an economy which was largely dependent on agricultural produce Malta came to possess a highly commercialized economy depending on trade.

These drastic and continual changes led to the rise of a new class on which the ruling Order of St John relied heavily for the running of its bureaucratic machine. At the same time the *Università*, consisting of members of the old landowning class, depended on this new class for the provision of commodities. The new class was made up of a mixture of descendants of original Rhodiotes, who first settled in Malta on the Order's arrival, and Maltese country dwellers who were lured to the Harbour towns in search of better work opportunities. Others hailed from various parts of Europe especially Sicily, Greece, Italy and southern France. These established themselves in Malta with a view to career advancement, a good salary, or maybe, in the case of a some northern Europeans, to avoid persecution at home. From the middle of the sixteenth century onwards the highly responsible jobs were entrusted to members of this class, from which the leading entrepreneurs of the period were also elicited. One may safely assume that trading families became the keystone of Malta's expanding trade in the post-siege years.

Furthermore, it has to be emphasized that the Order drew Malta nearer to Europe simply because the country happened to lie nearer the communication-lane running along the southern coast of the continent. From the onset the Order realized that seaward communications were vital for their prolonged presence in Malta. On the other hand, the emergent Harbour élite reflected the new socio-economic order, which was perfectly in line with the Order's policies of creating a new genre of entre-preneurship. This new business élite was entrusted with the highly responsible task of enhancing the development of a town/ country dichotomy which was to spread its roots to all levels of Maltese society, right from the start of the Order's rule. There-fore the stronger the position of the Order in Malta became, the greater was the success of urbanization. This new outlook of an expanding economy helped to enhance the position of the Harbour area which became a focus of economic dynamism and a centre of mercantile development. All this was made possible by the creation of a strong political and administrative system.

In a society which depended heavily on transactions of low value and bulky commodities, political intervention was vital for the survival and growth of trade. Under such circumstances, the institution had to be flexible, continually adapting to new economic conditions. While the market expanded and became more integrated at the regional level, the Order's government continually encouraged the emergence of a new entrepreneur-ial class, which could be employed in its service. The Maltese experience tends to suggest that changes in the economy helped to transform society, and ultimately its values and ideas. Var-ious schools of thought have developed very different views on the topic.

More recently, the trend has been to see the middle-class as a rising element in the early modern social structure. There was a field of compatibility between the programme of the abso-lutist state, which fundamentally represented an apparatus for the protection of aristocratic property or privileges, but simul-taneously assured the basic interests of the nascent mercan-tile and manufacturing classes. The early modern entrepre-neurial Maltese family seems to have formed part of a self-interest group which lacked any class consciousness, although members from this group may have been allowed to join the lower ranks of the Order of St John. However their closest attachment remained primarily to their urban environment. As townsmen they were, without any doubt, consciously keen on belonging to their particular community, but they had little regional (let alone national) awareness.

It is within this context that the community of trustworthy *padroni* (boat-owners) should be considered. They could be relied upon to fulfil a large number of contacts with continental Europe, whether of a diplomatic nature, economic – such as the collection of remittances from Europe – or the importation of basic commodities and trade transactions. They contributed to the shift from a rural to an urban environment in the social and cultural climate of the Harbour area, where new forms of economic life, industry and commerce gained the upper hand.

The Order of St John did much to stabilize economic conditions and to bring about economic welfare in Malta. This was largely possible since the Order intervened directly to stimulate the economic life of the country. In fact there was a degree of economic prosperity throughout the seventeenth and eighteenth centuries. By the late eighteenth century, thanks to the geographic position of the islands, Malta served as a transit depot for French goods in the central Mediterranean. The Order had paved the way for economic expansion, particularly since it had transformed Malta into its own naval base and had thus provided employment in the war industry, while attracting trade to the Harbour area and developing local agriculture. It also encouraged local manufacturers by taking protective measures and by stimulating maritime activities which indulged mainly in corsairing activities and legitimate trade.

At the same time the amount of capital put into the building of fortifications was large and kept a substantial number of men employed in the building industry throughout the rule of the Order of St John. In addition the administration of the *commende* (commanderies) afforded the Order of St John a steady annual income which sustained the economy of Malta in very much the same way as the infusion of foreign grants sustain the economy of Third World countries in our days. Of course occasional food shortages, wars, and plague left their negative imprint on Maltese economic life but the general stability created by the Order had many compensations. Economic prosperity grew largely thanks to the mercantilist and expansionist policies of the Order.

As a result of this approach, agriculture experienced rapid development during the seventeenth and eighteenth centuries. It is worth pointing out that during this same period, agriculture was marked by a steady modification of existing crop patterns, which was brought about by economic pressures. During this period economic efforts were directed to the production of cotton as a cash crop, so there was a large increase in the acreage occupied by the cotton plant. It left a handsome profit with which the island could easily procure its grain supplies. Since grain arrived from Sicily duty free, the Maltese cotton trade redeemed the expenses for the grain.

The cotton plant seemed to have enjoyed a high popularity for its durability. It grew so well, that, by the end of the eighteenth century, most of the available land in Malta and Gozo had been given over to cotton production. The crop was cultivated at the expense of grain, legumes, as well as the hitherto extensively produced cumin which continued to be exported in smaller quantities. Recent research has shown that, both in Malta and in Gozo, much farmland was devoted to the cultivation of cotton, and this included localities such as Siġġiewi and Żebbuġ which were previously well known for the production of grain. Most of the land on which cotton was cultivated, belonged to the Church, to the municipal authorities, and to the large landowners, while very little was owned by small landholders.

However the importance of the cotton industry was already on the decline by the time the British gained control of the Maltese islands. When in 1801 the British declared Malta a free port, the manufacturing industries, especially the production of cotton, were badly affected. The cotton industry which served as a a cash crop since the Middle Ages, had now lost its importance as an industry. Egypt was experiencing its economic boom and the importation of vast amounts of cheap cotton from this country, or from America, gave the final *coup de grâce* to a once healthy industry. By the 1840s the manufacture of cotton had ceased.

During the first half of the nineteenth century, industrial activity was so low that the main form of employment remained agriculture while external commerce fared badly except during war time. A characteristic feature of British economic thought was the emphasis on private enterprise. According to Arthur G. Clare, the British imposition of a *laissez-faire* policy meant:

> that the Maltese individual had to seek out his own economic salvation; second, that the Maltese... should not expect heavy financial commitments from British sources except by way of defence spending; third, that the island had to survive on its own taxes. While this state of affairs might have had some measure of success in a country endowed with rich resources in terms of both men and materials, in Malta's case it retarded economic growth.

Malta's non-agricultural activity was heavily dependent on foreign trade, which was usually carried out with other Mediterranean states. But foreign trade in the early nineteenth century Mediterranean was unstable and subject to a variety of influences. This was coupled with Malta's inability to widen its industrial structure since there was a lack of raw materials and natural resources essential for an adequate capitalist development.

Other industries included the production of cigars. This industry, according to the British traveller Thomas MacGill, was 'a most profitable branch of trade...' which 'gives employment to many thousands of poor families'. By 1856, it provided work for 1,500 workers and exported cigars to all parts of the Mediterranean. But the industry was doing very badly by the end of the nineteenth century. In the latter part of that century, Malta had such a weak commercial performance that even the island's highly valued oranges were being exported only on a small scale. In 1890, 127,000 dozen oranges were shipped, but by 1899 the figure went down to a mere 9,000 dozen.

As early as 1839, Thomas MacGill had already suggested the extension of the ship-building industry, predicting that by the building of a drydock, 'this branch would become one of the most extensive and important of the island'. The drydocks, were inaugurated in 1848 and continued to expand until the Second World War and immediately proved to be one of the island's main source of employment, the other being the opportunities provided by the British services. The dockyard catered mainly for the Royal Navy, which had its Mediterranean fleet based in Malta. The dockyard proved to be the most important industrial development of the British period since the yard saw a rapid increase in its work-force between the 1890s and 1940s.

Steamships were to help in the growth of this major industry. The first steamship called at Malta in July 1825. Up to the 1850s merchant vessels were still mainly sail-powered. However, according to the *Malta Mail* of 13th January, 1854 the introduction of steamships had by then raised Malta 'as a commercial depot from comparative insignificance to one of the utmost importance'. There must have been some truth in this assertion since the overall tonnage of shipping calling on the island had increased from 500,000 tons in 1850 to 5.2 million by 1880, decreasing sharply after 1890 to 3.5 million tons. Commercial pursuits were further enhanced after the opening of the Suez Canal in 1869 as this placed Malta in the centre of an increased traffic between Europe and the Levant. Arthur G. Clare asserts that:

> The economic uplift which this event engendered was of a longer duration than previous booms and it was destined to effect a structural change in the economy.

This explains why there was a general drift away from agricultural employment into occupations related to harbour activities in the late nineteenth century. Thus non-agricultural employment was becoming increasingly important at the time.

Small business links with North African ports, where many Maltese migrants had settled, were established during the first part of the nineteenth century. These Maltese businessmen trafficking in cloth, tobacco, wine, oil, skins, beasts of burden and farm animals made good profits. The advent of the British regiments further enhanced this kind of commercial activity as

Idyllic life in the Malta harbour area during the inter-war period.

the local traders began to supply provisions to the Armed Forces – a very profitable business known as ship-chandling. A number of Maltese families became well established in the supply of provisions to the British Forces by the end of the First World War. These business families shifted from ship-chandling to other enterprises with the advent of NAAFI (Navy, Army and Air Force Institutes) in 1919. Such enterprises included the importation of cars and the development of a scheduled bus service.

Work connected with the British navy had by the early part of the twentieth century become vital to the Maltese economy. When, in the beginning of the twentieth century, the Mediterranean fleet was reduced by six battleships, the commercial activity of the island was greatly effected, so much so that the 1911 Royal Commission could not help but note that business was revived once the fleet entered the Maltese harbours. Employment with the services was to decrease only after the Second World War although in 1957, as much as twenty-seven per cent of the work-force was still gainfully employed in colonial establishments. Many Maltese had become dependent on the British in various ways. The Armed Forces employed a large force, not only as sailors, but on all sorts of odd jobs such as waiters, cooks, barbers, businessmen, washer-women, coal-heavers, servants, clerks, nurses, and even fishermen and farmers. All classes of Maltese were involved in the maintenance of the Island-Fortress.

It was only after the independence of the country in 1964 that the economy of the Maltese islands started to diversify and diminish its dependence on the British services. By the late 1970s the British services withdrew entirely from the country. Malta now has an economy which is mainly based on the manufacturing industries and tourism. Malta's economy in the two decades after independence was largely dominated by an increasing demand for labour, improved standard of living and an improved system of social and health services. Naturally such improvements led to a rise in the cost of living, and so cheap labour – one of the main advantages Malta had enjoyed – disappeared. As a market, the country can now only boast of a skilled labour force. In more recent years Malta is reconsidering its financial position and there have been efforts to control inflation. It has also legislated and devised plans to control the use of land. Agricultural productivity has increased especially in the sphere of market gardening. The tourist industry has a more professional approach and industry is slowly being directed towards exportation. The legislation of the country is also being constantly reshaped to be in line and in full conformity with the European Union.

(iii) Food Consumption: 1530-1990

Religion surrounded food with rules, rituals, and prohibitions. Food itself was eaten partly on the Church's orders. People ate fat or lean according to the dictates of the Catholic Church. In 1582 Inquisitor Federico Cefalotto defined what the Church meant by fasting.

It is illicit to eat prohibited foods, that is meat and dairy products in Lent, the *quatuor temporum vigilii*, and other days on which the Holy Church prohibits us.

Inquisitor Fabio Chigi (1634-1639) – later elected as Pope Alexander VII – described his Lenten meals to a close relative. He declared that he avoided salted meats. His meals consisted mainly of vegetable soups, a little fish, dates, dried figs, olives and other small food items, besides of course his usual sweet orange drink and wine.

Fasting usually meant a proscription against the consumption of meat. Eating meat on prohibited days was thus a serious offence particularly at a time when the Roman Inquisition Tribunal started to implement the more rigorous post-Tridentine principles. Anyone who transgressed was immediately reported to the Holy office. The Inquisition kept very strict rules over this issue so that meat, eggs, and poultry could not be sold during the forty days of Lent, Fridays, and other prohibited days. Invalids had to produce two certificates, one from their doctor and one from a priest, in order to be exempted. Anyone who pretended to be sick risked getting into trouble and be reported to the Inquisition. The number of days on which meat and dairy products were prohibited led to a large demand for fish, salted or smoked. However, fish in Malta was not always plentiful. Fishermen were few, although they were scattered all over the island. Moreover, fishing was restricted during the winter, due to weather conditions and rough seas. For these reasons it was common to import fish from abroad.

Diet remained pretty much the same over the centuries, particularly for the lower classes. The Maltese ate little meat, cheap fish, and poor-quality cheese. Bread was the staple commodity and remained so at least until the early twentieth century. Society was heavily dependent on agricultural produce. Yet it was rare for a harvest to escape all the dangers that threatened it. Fields were relatively small and there was always the fear of famine. A few changes in temperature and a shortage of rainfall could have a disastrous effect. Indeed, throughout the Mediterranean, no major wars were fought during harvest time, while the only detail of everyday life that regularly found its way in diplomatic correspondence concerned harvest. Malta was no exception to the rule, and the continuous droughts made it 'a land of hunger'. The island depended so heavily on the importation of grain from Sicily that this business activity provided a strong initiative to entrepreneurs and became the *raison d' être* of the *Università* of Malta and Gozo. This in part explains why land continued to be the most coveted of possessions. It was the safest capital, and agriculture the greatest source of revenue.

Vegetables were a side dish and for most people meat or fresh fish was an occasional luxury. Maltese society tended to rely on one or two staples for the bulk of its food. In Malta the mass of the population consumed large quantities of bread and wine, supplemented by oil, cheese, vegetables, and very little fish or meat. A condition which seems to apply to any other pre-industrial state of the Mediterranean.

In the early British period the general standard of living of the Maltese deteriorated particularly after the plague of 1813 when the islands began to experience enormous economic difficulties. The British often attributed the misery of the Maltese to their lack of initiative and reckless birth rate. But one must add that the Maltese had a very low income which induced a very low standard of living throughout the British rule. It was only after the Second World War that the standard of living began to compare favourably with that of other countries in Southern Europe.

Nowhere was this better reflected than in the food the Maltese consumed. Visitors to Malta from the 1830s onwards agree that both breakfast and dinner were of the most frugal type. Both meals consisted mainly of barley bread, cheese, olives, onions, garlic, dried fruit, salted dried fish, oil, and similar foods. In season they ate freely of melons, prickly pears, and raw vegetables. They also drank a moderate amount of wine and enjoyed cooked vegetables (*minestra*) after a day's work. In 1839 Thomas MacGill exclaimed that in spite of such a poor diet the Maltese 'are a strong and healthy people'.

Meat was so rarely tasted that in 1842, another British visitor John Davy remarked that in Gozo

only one bullock was killed weekly for the market, and that was sufficient for the whole population, including a detachment of British troops who used a considerable proportion of it.

In many ways the standard of living of the 1870s and 1880s remained quite similar to that of forty years before. The Maltese working class still consumed very little meat and not much more vegetables, cheese, oil, pasta, or wine. There was a marked difference, however, in bread consumption. The 1836 Royal Commissioners had reported that a field labourer ate two pounds of bread per day. Francis Rowsell, a British Commissioner investigating the matter forty years later, concluded that in 1877 the same person ate from four to five pounds of bread per day. Furthermore bread was now being made from good quality wheat, although its price was twice that of the 1830s.

Bread remained the staple food for the masses to the extent that in 1919 the Lieutenant Governor, William Robertson, opined that a rise in the price of bread could easily lead to riot. Due to complete interruption of the Russian grain trade after 1914, the price of bread had in fact gone up from $2^1/_2$ pence to $7^1/_2$ pence per rotolo – a 300 per cent increase. Indeed this situation was the main reason for the Sette Giugno (7 June) riots of 1919 in which several Maltese were killed or wounded by the British troops.

Living conditions improved after 1919 and continued to do so up to the outbreak of the Second World War. The diet of the rural and urban poor only differed in that, while the latter used various forms of pasta, the former began to make use of potatoes. A very striking difference existed in the diet of the well-off classes. Ever since the early nineteenth century, these had adopted a South Italian diet, distinguished from that of the poor by the inclusion of macaroni, meat and good quality wine which was often imported from Italy and Greece.

During the war the British introduced the 'Victory Kitchen' which provided meagre meals that prevented the Maltese from starving at a time of acute food shortages. But the most humiliating aspect was perhaps the queuing up for the *gaxin*, the surplus of army and navy rations, a common practice still in use in the immediate post-war years, especially in the Harbour area where most military activity was centred. The poor and the idle used to do their utmost to get the choice pieces of meat and other left-overs.

In the 1950s, Maltese cooking was described as 'sub-Italian, monotonous, and drab'. It included a high amount of starch which adversely affected the figure of the majority of Maltese by their mid-twenties. British-style food, such as fried eggs, bacon, and chips, had become very popular and quickly spread all over the island. Up to the late 1950s, and indeed until independence, a visitor from Britain, Christopher Kininmonth, had in mind only one place where one could eat in style – the Hotel Phoenicia. However he added that the Valletta market had a wide variety of food, indicating that in the city there were people who ate well at home.

In more recent years the language of cookery has become to a certain extent uniform and homogeneous. Under the pressure of commercial standardization of foods especially concerning production and sales techniques, American and northern European habits have conquered Malta as has happened in other southern European countries. The market has now become inundated with a multiform cascade of packaged, frozen and tinned foods. Along with the benefits of cheap prices and convenience Malta has, in recent years, been invaded by foods alien to its economy.

(iv) Communications and Internal Means of Transport

Since time immemorial the Maltese islands were heavily dependent on the importation of food from abroad. This was carried by means of seaward communications. Thus, until modern times inland transport played second fiddle and was for a long time neglected by various administrations ruling the islands.

Perhaps the best example can be elicited from the period during which the Order of St John ruled over Malta. On its advent in Malta, in 1530, the Order hastened to create an efficient maritime communication system thanks to which, the fast developing Harbour area was kept *au courant* of events in Europe. The net result was the creation of two separate mentalities. While the Harbour towns developed into a veritable centre of activity which could be compared to any other south European coastal urban centre, the countryside – often referred to as the *campagna* – remained cut-off from European cross-currents.

But the bad state of roads and the primitive means of transport continued to hamper every kind of human activity at least until the advent of the Industrial Revolution. The state of roads was so precarious that the eighteenth century economist Adam Smith commented that 'to travel on horseback, mules are the only conveyance which can safely be trusted'. The only means of internal transport consisted of travelling by mule, donkey or cart. Indeed, distance was the main problem faced by travellers even in a tiny state the size of Malta where already in the late fifteenth century those arriving at the Malta Harbour from abroad could hire donkeys for their journey up to Mdina, eight miles inland. In winter time travel by mule, donkey and carriage must have been particularly difficult. By the early eighteenth century, it was still normal to travel by donkey from Valletta to Mdina but by the end of that century the *kaless* (a horse- or mule-drawn carriage) came into use.

The communication system did not help to improve the disparity between the Harbour area and the countryside, as the conditions of the roads were deplorable. These usually consisted of numerous, uneven, and dusty paths and lanes that turned into mud with the first rain, making them impossible to use in winter time. In the sixteenth century the bad state of roads and the primitive means of transport, made it difficult for the Rabat parish priest to travel to nearby Dingli during the winter months. Often it was impossible for him to attend to his duties, such as the anointing of the sick.

The shortage of horses was a major preoccupation until at least the seventeenth century. In 1640 Grand Master Lascaris even issued an edict in which he proclaimed that horses should not be exported without a licence. In fact official documentation for the period 1589-1611 reports how only a negligible number of horses were exported out of the island during that period. The edict issued under Lascaris indirectly confirms that pack animals were, without any doubt, the regular means of inland transport. Probably their popularity lay in the fact that they were cheaper in price and easy to maintain.

Throughout the Mediterranean, mules, in particular, were especially in demand due to their sturdy nature. Thus, we are told that they were widely used for agriculture in Spain, Languedoc and elsewhere in Europe. These animals were excellent for the use of 'large transports' on the Alps and became so popular that she-mules are recorded to have been sent from Sicily for the works being carried out at La Goulette, in Tunisia, in 1592. Apart from being an agricultural aid, the mule is a marvellous pack animal distinguished for its strength and docility. The sixteenth century French writer François Rabelais, described the mule as, 'a more powerful less delicate beast than any other, and one capable of harder work'. The great seaport of Genoa is reported to have owed her existence not only to ships but also to the mule-trains which, inside the city, even had brick paths reserved for them. Mule-trains were also very important as part of the traffic passing through Messina and the Sicilian channel. Mule traffic, although apparently small in volume, or value, was decisive for communication in the Mediterranean world.

The British period saw the appearance of the steamship, the railway, telegraphy, and the telephone. Nonetheless, early in the nineteenth century, the communication system was still poor and the condition of roads remained bad. The internal communication system developed gradually under the British rule. Some roads were improved for military purposes, while others were constructed to serve new settlements. But by and large the system of tracks, which the island had acquired over the centuries, was adapted to modern needs.

In the early years of British rule internal transport continued to be dominated by the *kaless*. In 1853 there were 278 *kalessi*, 14 of which were in Gozo. The *kaless* remained in use until the 1870s but it was an expensive means of transport which only a few could afford. The introduction of the horse-drawn omnibus in 1856 was beneficial to most of the population. At first it only travelled between Valletta and Lija and carried 16 passengers. However a year later, when the service was extended to several villages, vehicles with a capacity of 24 passengers were ordered. From 1859 onwards the omnibus company was also entrusted to carry mail, and this marked a general improvement in the postal service. However, during the 1890s the popularity of the omnibus began to wane until it stopped functioning completely owing to competition from other means of transport. By this time the *karozzin* (cab), a modern version of the *kaless* became an ideal means of transport for those who wanted to visit places not reached by the omnibus. The bicycle was also introduced around 1870. It was at first restricted to British military officers, but by the 1890s its use became commonplace among civilians.

A new means of transport was the railway. It was the transport everybody could afford. Introduced in 1883, it ran between Valletta and Mdina and at first it was thought that the Railway Company could create considerable employment on the island. Yet although it was originally planned to fan out into most of the inhabited parts of the island, only the original line was actually laid. After experiencing financial losses, the railway became government property in 1892, and for a time it prospered.

In 1903, the Electric Tram Company was established. This secured a more practical means of transport than the railway. Originally the tram was planned to provide a U-shaped route around the southern end of the Grand Harbour, but changes were made even before track-laying began. The tram proved popular to such an extent that it was strongly opposed by cab drivers whose livelihood depended on the number of passengers they carried. Like the railway, the tram soon found itself in financial straits. By 1929, the tram too was taken over by the state but the company was allowed to continue to operate the Upper Barracca lifts, which were installed at the beginning of the twentieth century and remained popular until the 1960s. By the 1930s both the tram and railway companies were facing financial losses and the authorities decided to close them down.

Communication between Malta and Gozo had been ensured by boats which carried passengers and goods on a daily basis from Gozo to Valletta and vice-versa since the early days of the Order of St John. Another boat service dating back to the times of the knights was that between Valletta and the Three Cities. This service was further extended to Sliema by the British. Boatmen had a monopoly of transport in the Harbour area and in 1856 there were 42 licensed boats. These boatmen had to face strong competition with the setting up of the Motor Ferry Service in 1881. At first ferries operated from Valletta (Marsamxett) to Sliema and, although harassed by protests from boatmen, it proved to be the best and cheapest means of transport on the island. A trip to or from Valletta cost only half a penny. The ferry boats continued to function until August 1959.

Though the ferry service proved to be of great convenience to the growing urban centre around Marsamxett, the need was felt for an even more efficient system of transport. By 1905, this was partly solved with the introduction of the Scheduled Bus Service. Transport facilities were to develop further after 1918

The ferry-boat plying between Senglea Wharf and Valletta in the early years of the twentieth century.

when the British services sold their lorries and trucks to private individuals, who immediately adapted them for civilian use. By the 1920s the bodies of such vehicles were being built in Malta. In the 1930s the bus service was extended to remote parts of the island like Żurrieq. At first buses could only carry 20 persons who had to sit on two long wooden benches. Later, greater passenger capacity and more comfortable seats were introduced. In 1974 routes were amalgamated and the number of companies reduced to three, and later on, to one, making the system easier to operate.

Up to this time, goods were still being transported by the *karettun* (cart) even when goods belonged to the British services. Motor lorries came into use for the first time in the 1920s. But a major transformation in the transport system was brought about by the introduction of private cars early in the twentieth century. The car replaced the horse-drawn carriages, like the *karozella* or the *parilja*, used by the wealthier classes. In 1906 there was only one registered car in Malta, but the number increased steadily so that by the 1920s there must have been a reasonable number of cars. In 1926 a foreigner exclaimed that Malta was 'full of cars, chiefly of American and Italian makes'. Nevertheless it was only in the late 1960s that private ownership began to increase dramatically.

## B. *Population and Development*

### (i) Migration

As in other small island societies of the Mediterranean food and work in Malta were less assured than anywhere else. Such islands could rarely provide their own food and were normally governed by a perpetual shifting of inhabitants so that human mobility was one of the great social features of such societies. It was men who travelled while the womenfolk usually stayed at the home base.

Malta's geographical position, coupled with dependence on Sicily for its grain, led to the creation of very strong bonds between the populations of the two islands. The oldest reference to these bonds is given by Cicero, who in his indictment of Caius Verres refers to Diodorus Melitensis, an inhabitant of Malta, who migrated to Lilybaeum (modern Marsala), where he enjoyed great fame. In the Verrine orations we hear time and time again of people moving from one Sicilian town to another. Thus people in the Roman province were in the habit of travelling from one part to another, without let or hindrance, in search of better job opportunities or otherwise. According to the local classicist Joseph Busuttil,

> Cicero relates a story of a person who like other Sicilians had a Greek name. Like other Sicilians he could move from one part of the province of Sicily to another. He was, like other Sicilians, under the patronage of powerful individuals in Rome.

In later times, Malta retained its ties with Sicily. It formed part of Muslim Sicily, and together with Sicily, was conquered by the Normans. After Count Roger's *razzia* of 1091, the Arabs were permitted to stay in Malta. However, in 1127, Roger's son, King Roger I reconquered the islands and immediately established a Christian administration, which largely arrived from Sicily, and which by time continued to grow. In 1398 Malta and Gozo came to form part of the royal domain or *regio demanio*, thus passing to the direct administration of the crown. Fear of a Muslim 'invasion', besides being of great pressure to the local defence system, always led to a great number of Maltese to flee to Sicily. At that time large scale migration to Sicily was such a great worry to Palermo that, in May 1437, the Maltese residents of Sicily were compelled to return to Malta.

It should therefore come as no surprise that the Maltese found it so natural to settle in the various Sicilian communes and fuse with ease with the inhabitants of mainland Sicily. It seems that such a state of affairs had persisted in the late Middle Ages. Godfrey Wettinger puts forth this notion in the case study of the prominent Maltese Jew, Abraham Safaradi. In 1450 Abraham Safaradi was described as a 'Jew of the walled town and island of Gozo because he was married there and had a major part of his goods (that is, his immovable property) in the said island of Gozo'. He also paid his taxes in that island.

Whatever the pattern in any given instance, town and state were then conceived as a single unit. The whole was bound together not merely by economics, or by force, but also psychologically. The members of any particular community fostered among them a feeling of unity which was sustained by a common cult and by a tradition best described in the mythical and traditional sense. Hence Safaradi's allegiances primarily revolved round the Gozitan Jewish community of which he formed part. Maltese identity rarely meant much more than a purely and narrowly geographical expression.

A similar situation could be applied to the non-Jewish Maltese, who were practically all Christians and who, above anything else, strongly felt the need to identify with Christianity. They were forcefully motivated to think in these terms on account of Malta's proximity to Muslim North Africa. Such clear-cut notions of identity became even more clear after the expulsion of the Jews in 1492. The *conversos* seemingly formed less than one per cent of the total population. In Wettinger's opinion, 'the new Christians were unwilling, unable perhaps, to organize themselves in any way separately from the other inhabitants'. They were thus easily absorbed by the Christian population.

Until the advent of the Order of St John in 1530, Malta was considered as one of the many communes of Sicily. This state of affairs was not altered in the first part of the sixteenth century. This explains why in 1536, Jean Quintin d'Autun, a priest and a French member of the Order of St John, described Malta as a

> part of Sicily and has its same customs, Malta became Roman along with Sicily, and since that time it has always had the same rights and the same government.

At the end of the sixteenth century the official historian of the Order, Iacomo Bosio, could still recall a practice common in the kingdom of Sicily, and indeed the Italian peninsula – that of honouring towns with a title. In accordance with this custom, Palermo was called *Felice*, Messina *Nobilissima*, Syracuse *Fedelissima*, and Catania *Chiarissima*. Bosio points out that it was in the spirit of this tradition, then prevalent in the Kingdom of

Sicily, that Mdina, the seat of the Maltese municipality, was called *Notabile*. The custom of giving honorific titles to towns prevailed even in the late sixteenth century and it was for this reason that the Council of Government of the Order decided to honour the new city named after Grand Master La Valette with the title of *Umilissima*. This was done in order to remind Christian Europe of Malta's role as the bulwark of Christianity in defence against the Ottoman Turks.

The advent of the Hospitallers accelerated this movement – that is, of Maltese migration to Sicily and of foreigners settling in Malta – even further, partly due to the aggressive policies of the Order *vis-à-vis* the neighbouring Muslims, and partly on account of the cosmopolitan atmosphere created in the Harbour area. Such a state of affairs led to the development of drastic changes, to the extent that by the middle of the seventeenth century, G.F. Abela could point out that apart from being over populated, Malta was frequented by a multitude of foreigners who eventually settled on the island. These settlers often declared themselves to be citizens of Valletta or inhabitants of Malta, suggesting that early modern Malta was a haven teeming with foreigners.

Meanwhile, many Maltese, attracted by the good work opportunities, the abundance of food, and the relative safety from Turkish incursions of nearby Sicily, were induced to settle there before and after the siege of 1565. This tendency often verged on mass migration, especially in times of danger, and it was only during the reign of Grand Master Lascaris (1636-1657) that special measures to check the outflow were enacted. Lascaris decreed that a special licence had to be sought by those intending to emigrate from Malta. The Grand Master even enacted regulations prohibiting Maltese living abroad with no intention of returning to Malta, to continue owning immovable property in the country. Yet this phenomenon of native Maltese leaving their island home was more than compensated for by the uninterrupted inflow of foreigners and returning migrants.

When the Hospitaller Order of St John set up their convent in Malta, it found a population who considered the Sicilian communes as sister-entities. Therefore it was natural for the Maltese to set up home there if they so desired. At the time, the majority of individuals viewed their commune with a loose transferable sense of loyalty. This attitude facilitated the movement of people to and out of Sicily. It seems that, even until the early seventeenth century, there was little feeling among the Maltese themselves that their commune was in any way distinct or unique from others in Sicily. Malta kept its representatives or consuls in the principal Sicilian towns. Their job was to ensure a regular supply of goods to the island, paying particular attention to commodities. On the other hand, Sicilian businessmen had their representatives in Malta, and artisans were engaged side by side in all activities.

Although with the arrival of the Order, administrative 'independence' from Sicily became more tangible, it had to take many generations before the Maltese could feel different from the Sicilians, or indeed from the Italians, at the individual human level. Some Maltese intellectuals, like the eighteenth century musician, Gerolamo Abos, though born in Malta, was sent to be educated in Naples and never returned to his island-home. Joseph Vella points out that the case of Gerolamo Abos reflects the Maltese eighteenth century frame of mind and artistic inclinations. Abos, not only made Italian culture his own, but he came to be considered as one of the important Neapolitan composers of that century. On its part the Order's government discouraged this kind of behaviour, considering these tendencies a threat to the Order's sovereignty. Notwithstanding all this, the Maltese continued to consider themselves and their island-home as an extension of Sicily. Proof of this is the fact that up till the late seventeenth century, Maltese citizens were still joining, as full members, the Archconfraternity of the Sicilians in Rome.

Nonetheless, human mobility entailed personal sacrifices on the part of migrants. They usually left behind close relatives, friends and familiar situations that had afforded them a measure of security. Despite such losses, however, most migrants fully committed themselves to a new lifestyle in order to achieve some of the personal goals they had set for themselves. In the case of Maltese emigrants, they sometimes returned merely to convey their close relatives to their new home base. Often new migrants settled in towns and thus acted as catalysts in the urbanization process.

Foreigners often tended to merge completely with the Maltese community of which they eventually came to form an integral part. Evidence for this kind of integration is eloquently borne out by the Greek refugee community from Rhodes which originally numbered around 5,000 in 1530. Most of them had in fact settled in Birgu and came to form three Greek parishes there. By 1574, the three parishes them catered for 74 households within the city which was renamed Vittoriosa after the Great Siege. By 1587, the most important of these parishes, the one dedicated to Our Lady of Damascus, was transferred to Valletta. By 1617 the other two parishes had ceased to function.

Human traffic continued to flow into Malta from Mediterranean Europe. Enforced settlers or slaves also came to Malta throughout the Order's rule. Slaves were captured in warring and corsairing activities, mostly during swift raids carried on the coasts of North Africa, and came to form an important labour force, employed especially as builders, stone-carriers, galley-rowers, and domestic servants. Slaves were relatively free to mix with all strata of Maltese and resident society and were allowed to take part-time jobs in order to gain money for their eventual redemption. Yet, it was not uncommon for some of these slaves to accept Christianity, marry locally and in their turn become integrated within Maltese society.

Economic reasons remained the principal factors behind the phenomenon of migration in the nineteenth century. Periods of poverty at home often drove the Maltese overseas. At times, boom conditions induced them to seek their fortune elsewhere in the Mediterranean. A considerable number of Maltese settled in North Africa, notably after the French conquest of Algiers in 1830. By 1842 there were 20,000 Maltese emigrants in Mediterranean countries. Of these the majority settled in North Africa, mainly in Tunisia, Algeria, Tripoli and Egypt.

During the Crimean War, not even prosperity at home could counteract the cotton and building boom in Egypt and emigration to that country rose to record heights. The end of the Egyptian boom coincided with a widespread depression in North Africa which induced many Maltese to return to their home-base. Indeed the number of returned migrants was higher than the number of emigrants who left in the 1850s and 1860s. Emigration to the North African shores, then increased again during the 1870s.

It appears that the Maltese found it hard to travel beyond the shores of the Mediterranean. Although the British government tried to encourage them to settle in other parts of the Empire, all these attempts failed and the majority of those who did try to settle in such places was unsuccessful. The first attempt was to establish Maltese plantation settlements in Guiana and Granada between 1831-1841. Other attempts to settle colonies in Australia and the Americas failed. As a result nineteenth century migration continued to be directed towards the coasts of North Africa and the Levant. According to Charles A. Price writing in the mid-1950s this restricted scope of choice was largely influenced by three economic factors:

> the belief that America and Australia were the permanent homes of strange and deadly diseases; the belief that it was necessary to settle in a country near enough to Malta to enable easy and frequent return to the beloved homeland; the belief that similarity of language and customs marked out North Africa the divinely appointed region for Maltese settlement abroad... it was not until the widespread distress which preceded and followed the war of 1914-18 that significant numbers turned their attention to the continents of the outer world.

Migration towards America, particularly the United States, and the Anglophone parts of the British Empire, began to develop in the early twentieth century. However in the early 1930s the various quota schemes introduced by the USA, Canada and Australia reduced the inflow of emigrants from Europe and thus even from Malta. At this point the Maltese began to find it convenient to emigrate to the United Kingdom where Maltese status as British subjects ensured preferential treatment.

The hardships, insecurity and population boom of the post-war times induced many to migrate to USA, Canada, Britain, Australia and other English-speaking countries. Thus outward movement reached a climax between 1948 and 1966 when it rarely fell below the 5,000 mark annually.

## (ii) Demographic Growth

Approximate Estimates of Population Growth: 1241-1990

| Year | Malta | Gozo | Others | Total |
|---|---|---|---|---|
| 1241 | 1,753 | 366 | | 2,119(a) |
| 1419 | 8,335(b) | not available | | c.10,000 |
| 1480s | 9,829(b) | not available | | ? |
| 1535 | 22,000 | 6,500 | | 28,500 |
| 1590 | 27,000 | 1,864 | 3,426 | 32,290 |
| 1632 | 49,866 | 1,884 | 3,648 | 51,750 |
| 1670 | | | | 50,790 |
| 1736/40 | 58,435 | 7,929 | | 66,364 |
| 1798 | 90,000 | 8,000 | | 98,000 |
| 1813 | 96,403 | 14,400 | | 110,803 |
| 1842 | 97,535 | 14,330 | | 113,864 |
| 1871 | 182,000 | 18,000 | | 200,000 |
| 1931 | 220,940 | 24,700 | | 245,640 |
| 1948 | | | | 304,991 |
| 1990 | 328,910 | 27,000 | | 355,910 |

(a) These figures could represent the number of hearths rather than the total population for Malta and Gozo.
(b) Established population figures.

The first census available to us is the one prepared by Gilibertus Abate in about 1241. Unfortunately the document has been recopied several times and may be incorrect. The population was divided by religion into Christians, Muslims and Jews and reached a total of 2119. Anthony Luttrell suggests that instead of representing the total population of Malta the census represents hearths. If each hearth is taken to consist of approximately five members then the total population of Malta would rise to about 10,000. We know that around 1250 the Kingdom of Sicily was purged of all Muslims who were exiled to the Apulian town of Lucera. There is evidence that Muslims hailing from Malta were exiled to Lucera but the purge may not have had a drastic impact on the Maltese islands. It is probable that in the late thirteenth century there were massive conversions to Christianity so that by the fifteenth century the Maltese population vaunted their allegiance to Christianity as witnessed in the militia and *angara* lists.

In 1530, the arrival of the Knights Hospitallers, with their entourage and a substantial contingent of Rhodiot refugees, led to the complete transformation of the area around Birgu, where the seat of administration was set up. Still this initial impact had only a limited effect on the general demography of the island. The report of the Knights' Commissioners gives the 1524 population of Malta as 17,000. By 1530, it had risen to 25,000, twenty per cent of which consisted of professed members of the Order, their retinues, and the refugees from Rhodes.

The pattern of the progressive growth of the population was however reversed in the 1550s and 1560s. Once again, another decline was experienced after the ravages of the great famine of 1591 and the plague which followed. Such reversals had the tendency to act as a repeated exogenous brake on the population, primarily by reducing it rapidly and drastically, and then by keeping it at a suppressed level.

In spite of such severe checks, the programme of urbanization was successfully achieved in the first half of the seventeenth century. By 1614 the population had already climbed to over 41,000. By 1632, this had gone up to 52,000, if one excludes 5,000-strong retinue of the Order. The population remained stable until 1676, when another severe outbreak of the plague wrought the greatest havoc inside the Harbour towns, where well over a third of the inhabitants lived.

The seventeenth century chronicler and historian of the Order of St John, Bartholomeo Dal Pozzo assures us that, before the

St Gregory intercedes for the plague-stricken of 1813. Oil on canvas by Salvatore Busuttil (1798-1854).

plague of 1676, the population stood at 60,000. Then, there followed a drop, and it declined to 49,500 in 1680. However, in 1693 it climbed again to 60,000. In 1798 the total population of the Maltese islands had nearly reached the 100,000 mark. Malta's population decreased slightly between 1798 and 1800. This came about as a consequence of the uprising against the French, together with food shortages and the spread of disease. But after 1800 there was a gradual increase in the population of the islands. The plague of 1813 once again checked this growth by claiming 4,600 lives. Nevertheless by 1828 the population was again on the rise. There was an upward trend in Maltese demography throughout the British period in spite of the fact that, in 1837, cholera brought about the untimely death of some 4,000 people. The population increase during the second half of the nineteenth century can be attributed to the advances in medicine, sanitation and the slight improvement in the standard of living. In fact from just over 100,000 in the early nineteenth century, the population surpassed a quarter of a million in the years following the Second World War and rose to over 355,000 by 1990.

### (iii) The Language, Religion, and Cultural Values.

Joseph Aquilina points out that the Normans introduced Sicilian, which, together with Latin, became the official language of Malta by the fifteenth century. Italian in its Tuscan form, had established itself as *lingua franca* around the mid-sixteenth century, thirty years or so after the advent of the Order. Thus, throughout the Order's rule, it remained entrenched among the cultural élite. This was evident in the seventeenth century, and especially in the eighteenth century. This situation is expressively manifested by Dr Francesco Saverio Farrugia, a Councillor of the Supreme Tribunal of Justice, who not only wrote in Italian, but even referred to this language as *la lingua materna*.

In the course of the seventeenth century, Tuscan Italian had firmly established itself as the literary language of the Italian peninsula. Since culturally Malta was under Italy's domain, it became more urgent for the élite groups to acquire the dominant language. In this way, Italian continued to spread its importance more and more, until it infiltrated the smooth running of the duties and functions of everyday life. The widespread use of romance European languages, instead of Maltese, is stressed by the French traveller Sieur Du Mont, who stopped in Malta for few days in June 1690;

> There are three languages spoken in the city; French, Spanish and Italian. The last of these is authoriz'd by the Government and used in publik Writings. The peasants in the country speak a corrupt dialect of the Arabic...

The Maltese language was less used in the Harbour area which was also the cultural, administrative, and business centre of the island. This was partly due to the ever-growing presence of immigrants who married and established themselves there. However, another reason was that there was the presence of a large mercantile class, as well as an administrative class, and both classes knew very little Maltese.

Agius De Soldanis observed that the Maltese people living in Valletta and in the Harbour area spoke Maltese amongst themselves, but Italian was the current language they used in communicating with foreigners. On the other hand, in the villages, or *casali*, the *nazionali* (nationals) used Maltese throughout. This is the language they learnt from their parents. Inspired by the revival of interest in Etruscan, Agius de Soldanis justified his eagerness in establishing an alphabet for Maltese. He did this partly to enable scholars to learn ancient Punic, and partly to serve as a grammar for the *nazionali*, as well as for the *forastieri* (foreigners), particularly the professed Knights of St John.

'Italian' was then the language of trade in the Mediterranean, and in the Maltese Harbour towns, this language spread at the expense of Maltese, which was in turn reduced to the status of a local dialect spoken by servants, peasants and the lower orders of society. By the late eighteenth century, this jargon seems to have developed into what Mikiel Anton Vassalli labelled, *dialetto della città* (city dialect). He considered this as the most corrupt dialect of Maltese, due to the large number of foreign words it contained. The presence of a great number of foreigners, as well as the use of foreign languages, notably Sicilian, Italian, French and other European languages, led to the *barbarizzare l'idioma nativo* ('barbarization' of the native idiom).

As a result of all this, in 1796, Vassalli began to insist on the social need to cultivate *la lingua nazionale* (the national language). Vassalli reflected upon the attitudes of his times and admitted that Maltese seemed undignified and abounding in 'barbarisms' which, he concluded, were the result of the long neglect of the language. Vassalli's ideal perspective of a defined Maltese culture and language, was to take root more than a century after his death. His dream of Maltese consciousness could only materialize with the widespread use of literacy.

Wettinger and Fsadni produce enough evidence to show that in the fifteenth and sixteenth centuries, notaries were continually translating contracts from the original Latin, Sicilian and later Italian for the illiterate majority. Typical of agrarian-based societies, writing had endowed its practitioners with high status, a social situation already firmly entrenched among the ancient Egyptians. The hegemony of the notarial class was somewhat restricted in the Harbour area, owing to the presence of the Order's administrators, the multitude of foreign entrepreneurs, and other Maltese professionals who were able to read and write. But in the Maltese countryside, where life was centred around Mdina, and to a lesser extent in the larger villages, notaries often acted as power holders, participating in the running of the *Università*, and were by far the most respectable and influential group after the clergy.

The power of writing created an ambivalent situation. On the one hand, it evoked a persistent aura of hostility to its dissemination. This hostility is best shown in the Maltese retaliation against the imposition of new taxes by the French revolutionary regime, barely three months after their occupation of Malta in 1798. On 3 September of that year, the peasants from the countryside surrounding Mdina, attacked the old town, massacred the small French garrison and immediately stormed the administrative offices and burned the archives of the Mdina *Università*, as well as tax registers, feeling that new excise taxes threatened their livelihood. Mob action of the kind was surely motivated by the peasants' deep-seated resentment against written documentation.

The differentiation into high culture (written) and low culture (oral) was not simply a cultural division, but it also manifested a distinction between two kinds of work. Administrative, academic and professional work could only be aspired to through the acquisition of a literary education; manual work required considerable experience in the craft performed. Thus writing created a radical distinction between the literate and illiterate elements of society.

Furthermore a substantial part of the population considered literacy as a sacred and powerful weapon used primarily in the form of talismans and amulets for protection against the evil-eye, as well as for love charms, healing and divination.

Another influential literate group were the clergy. They had long been expected to be literate in order to celebrate mass, since this oral performance was in fact a public reading from the service book, the Missal. The clergy were obliged, or at least expected, to recite other daily prayers, mostly readings from the Breviary. They had to keep themselves up to date in their pastoral care by reading other books as well be they theological, devotional, or practical.

The union of the various strata of the population was thus made possible through the profound ties of the inhabitants to the Catholic Church. Religion seeped deeply into all sections of society with the clergy serving as the focus of social organization. They even combined teaching and other advisory duties with their spiritual role, acting also as the main link between the common folk and the power-holders.

In medieval times, the Maltese were not so much aware of being Maltese. Rather they derived great pride in their being Catholic. The belief attached to the sites concerning St Paul's stay on the island was of utmost importance. A chapel stood at St Paul's Bay in remembrance of the Apostle's shipwreck of AD 60. A 1441 reference to the chapel indicates, that due to the ravages of time, the Cathedral Chapter of Mdina decided to rebuild it and endow it with a pious benefice. J. Quintin d'Autun asserts that 'the people believe as firmly and with certainty that Paul had been in Malta just as much as they believe that Peter has been in Rome'. Quintin d'Autun dedicates some paragraphs to St Paul's crypt at Rabat, reputed to have been the saint's lodging during his three month stay on the island.

Traditions concerning the crypt were retold by other writers, like the Sicilian Tommaso Fazello who in 1558 repeated the story and other traditions already referred to by Quintin D' Autun. The Apostolic Visitor Mgr. Dusina relied on these traditions in the compilation of his report in 1575.

The discovery of Luca de Armenia's poem entitled 'Ad Patriam' has made possible a better understanding of ethnic consciousness among the Maltese élite even before the siege of 1565. De Armenia starts by recalling that Christianity has been practised by the Maltese since the times of Christ, indirectly referring to the Pauline tradition. In other words the Maltese had been Christians long before the advent of the Order of St John. He further states that the Maltese have always been loyal subjects to their rulers, recalling the homage owed to feudal overlords, as widely practised in medieval times, when temporal and spiritual power were often fused.

By the early seventeenth century the cult of St Paul was further boosted, partly thanks to the presence of the Spanish hermit Juan Beneguas who revived the veneration for St Paul's crypt, and partly due to the propaganda campaign organized by the Society of Jesus particularly after the foundation of the Jesuit College in 1592. The Jesuits promoted studies on the Pauline cult where the Apostle's role as protector of the Maltese was particularly stressed.

In the mid-seventeenth century, the publication of G.F. Abela's *Della descrittione di Malta* (1647), one of the first books ever printed in Malta, was a major achievement which determined the subsequent course of Maltese historiography and ethnic awareness. But Abela was highly influenced by the works of the Maltese Jesuit Gerolamo Manduca (1574-1643). Amongst other things Manduca dwells on St Paul's shipwreck in Malta and his subsequent stay in the Rabat grotto. In order to explain the continuity of the Pauline tradition, Manduca claims that from the times of St Paul, there was never a time when the Maltese had renounced the Faith, even in Muslim times. These early writers of Maltese history elaborate on sets of mythical motifs tending to adjust history to a preconceived model that has as its origin the culture of the ruling élite with its dominant Christian faith.

Other saints, particularly Saints Publius and Agatha, were venerated as co-patrons of the Maltese diocese. There is evidence however that the feast of St Agatha was celebrated long before the implementation of Tridentine regulations. The Apostolic Visitor Dusina, who was in Malta between 1574-1575 learnt that riotous merry-making took place in the precincts of St Agatha's church in Rabat on the eve of the saint's feast. He therefore ordered that the gates of the church had in future to be closed one hour after sunset in order to avoid this abuse.

The cult of saints became particularly strong among the masses of the population, especially from the last quarter of the sixteenth century onwards, since the Catholic Reformation Church firmly restated the usefulness of invoking saints. Devotion to the Virgin Mary increased in intensity while some new saints emerged, together with well-documented popular hero saints like Vincent de Paule who exemplified compassion for the poor, orphans and prisoners; Charles Borromeo, Cardinal-Archbishop of Milan who stood for personal asceticism and service to the poor; Ignatius Loyola, Francis Xavier and Philip Neri were all assimilated in local cults. By the eighteenth century, the patrons of various parish churches were venerated at the parochial level, thus becoming symbols of their respective parishes. Meanwhile the veneration towards the patron saint of the island, St Paul, grew so strong that by 1700 the Council of the Maltese municipality issued edicts with such invocations as 'In the name of God, and the Glorious Apostle St Paul, our Protector'.

The importance of the cult of saints is nowhere better evoked than in the village feasts. In the sixteenth century the Maltese village feast was a small affair. It was often organized thanks to the generosity of a well-to-do local benefactor. The feast generally took the shape of distribution of food and money to the village poor. By the late seventeenth century, several larger villages started to include a procession with the statue of the patron saint. However the popularity of feasts was boosted up in the eighteenth century. This was a time when Malta had achieved a certain economic stability and the Turkish menace had become something of the past. The ruling Order of St John was organising popular festivities under all sorts of pretexts – the election of a new Grand Master; the accession of a new Pope; the yearly feast of St John the Baptist (the Order's patron saint); the occurrence of a centenary such as that of the siege of 1565; the birth of a son of some royal household in Europe connected with the Order. Such occasions gave rise to street decorations, illuminations, fire-works and other merry-making.

The insular Maltese Church was naturally affected by the presence of the Knights Hospitallers. Malta entered into the main currents of the Counter-Reformation with the advent of the Jesuits, the introduction of the Inquisition, and the arrival of the Apostolic Visitor Dusina in 1574, whose report revealed numerous irregularities in matters of discipline and ritual in Malta's ecclesiastical life. The Church, reformed along Tridentine lines, managed to win greater influence over the population, particularly after 1580.

Thanks to the strengthening of the Inquisition, the Church was able to establish complete hegemony over Maltese society, a state of affairs barely disturbed in the centuries that followed. Intense religious activity embodied popular attachment to myths and memories, as enshrined in symbols and religious values, that came to symbolize the communal self-sacrifice of the Maltese. As a result, apostates or relapsers, were seen as nothing short of traitors to the ethnic cause and its survival.

Religion played such an important role in the Maltese lifestyle that the free practice of the Catholic faith was a prerequisite for the acceptance of British suzerainty. Thus under British rule, other Christian churches and religions were tolerated but no temporal power could be permitted to interfere in the spiritual or temporal matters of the diocese of Malta. Even so, in the early nineteenth century, the British did their best to introduce the Protestant faith among the people although they soon learned to respect the position of the local church hierarchy.

Soon they adopted a general policy not to interfere in religious matters, as the local church might become a powerful opponent of the British government. Thus the position of the Church of Malta became much stronger under British colonial rule since the main concern of the British authorities was the preservation of the Island-Fortress. The Church became firmly embedded in the parochial and national life of the island, and continued to provide the Maltese with a basic element of identity until the attainment of independence in 1964.

Religion continues to play a vital role in post-independence Malta. It emerges as the source of important rituals for Maltese society providing rites of passage such as baptisms, confirmations, marriages and burials. The established Church had served as a point of reference to the Maltese furnishing them with a *raison d'être*. It further helped to create a homogeneity and a list of unwritten rules by which the community could abide.

The dominant position of the Church led to a situation where the Maltese maintained a cool relationship with the British (Protestants), mixing very little until the 1930s. The islanders continued to depend directly on the local priests, making the Church the centre of village life, and the parish priest its first citizen. On their part the British authorities, whose main concern was to keep matters under control in their island-fortress, respected the position of the church hierarchy and they made it a point not to interfere in church matters. Thus under the British Protestant government the Catholic ritual was given predominance in important state functions; religious instruction, according to the Catholic principles, was imparted in all Maltese schools; and canon law was indiscriminately applied to all Maltese with respect to marriage. Consequently civil marriage and legal divorce did not exist. One may say that the local church hierarchy and the British government managed to develop a *modus vivendi* thanks to which the Church enjoyed a privileged position. This does not imply that the Church was never challenged by local politicians. In 1928 the then Prime Minister of Malta, Lord Strickland, became engaged in a fierce struggle with the Maltese clergy when he sought to curtail their influence in secular matters. Likewise in 1958 the Labour Prime Minister Dom Mintoff clashed with the Church authorities when he proposed the integration of Malta with the United Kingdom simply because the Curia was not given the required assurances that the position of the Catholic Church would remain unaltered.

After the attainment of independence from the United Kingdom in 1964, the Church's dominant position was safeguarded in several clauses of the Independence Constitution which the Nationalist government (1964-1971) agreed to respect. Moreover the Labour government which rose to power in 1971 ensured that the clauses regarding the position of the Church would remain untouched.

However when Malta was proclaimed a republic in 1974 the constitution was amended. Amongst other matters canon law ceased to be effective as Maltese marriage law and a civil marriage became compulsory; teachers' training, which until then was a monopoly of the Church was abrogated; the exemption of church authorities, parishes, religious orders and institutions from income tax was abolished; and anyone – whether Catholic or not – could be buried in the Addolorata cemetery which served as the main government cemetery of Malta. A couple of years later a number of religious feasts which up to then were considered as public holidays were also abrogated and only the feast of the patron saint of each village could be celebrated – no secondary feasts were allowed. In 1978 the Faculty of Theology at the University of Malta was withdrawn, and theology was from then on taught at the Seminary of the Archbishop.

The Labour government lost the general elections of 1987 and the Nationalist Party came to power. Knowing full well that the Church continued to play an important role among the Maltese the new power-holders introduced new legislation which gave back some of the old privileges which the church used to enjoy. These included a greater say in matters regarding education; the running of church schools; the re-integration of the Faculty of Theology as part of the University of Malta; the validity of a canon law marriage for Catholics; and the restoration of a few religious feasts as public holidays. Nonetheless the mentality of the Maltese is changing drastically and the Church has a much lesser hold on the younger generations who do not remember the old colonial days of the British rule.

# 2

## Ancient and Medieval Malta

### A. *The Beginnings of Maltese History*

In Malta there is an extraordinarily strong sense of continuity such that contemporary history can only be understood in terms of the past. It is therefore pertinent at this point to discuss the general trends of Maltese history before the islands became a state under the Hospitaller Order of St John.

### (i) *Maltese Prehistory*

#### The Neolithic Period

The advent of man into the central Mediterranean was relatively late. In Sicily clear traces of human activity date back to the Upper Paleolithic. Man did not seem to have occupied the Maltese islands before the Neolithic period. Evidence of human presence dates back to the Għar Dalam phase (c. 5000-4500 BC) when it appears that a group of immigrants crossed over from Sicily, using some sort of sea-craft, and settled on the islands of Malta and Gozo. They were essentially farmers and they may had to ship over the first specimens of domestic animals and seeds from Sicily. They also brought stone tools and a type of pottery which has very close parallels with that used among the Neolithic communities of southern Sicily. This pottery, known as impressed ware, features geometric patterns impressed or incised on its surface before it was baked. Similarities have been identified mostly within the Stentinello area (in the vicinity of Syracuse). More recently closer parallels have been drawn with the pottery from Monte Kronio in the area of Agrigento.

The next two Neolithic phases are named after Skorba, a site near Mġarr (Malta) which was excavated by David Trump in the early 1960s when he served as curator of archaeology. Trump labelled the phase Grey Skorba (c. 4500-4400 BC) due to the rather dull undecorated greyish pottery which came to replace the impressed Għar Dalam ware. Eventually the same texture started to be given a bright red coating from which it began to be identified as the Red Skorba phase (c.4400-4000 BC). One notes that the style and shape of pottery produced during the Grey and Red Skorba phases was not altered so that decorations remain absent. One notices parallels in contemporary pottery produced in the Lipari islands and Sicily. These similarities provide evidence that the Neolithic farming community of Malta had close and frequent links with nearby Sicily. Further proof of frequent commercial and social links with Sicily is apparent in the total dependence of the Maltese islands on raw-materials, such as stone implements, from Sicily. Flint and lava were imported from eastern Sicily while obsidian, used to produce very sharp cutting instruments, was imported from the Lipari islands and Pantelleria. Such essential tools for prehistoric men could have been exchanged for perishable products, produced in the Maltese islands, like food and textiles.

Archaeologists are of the opinion that the Neolithic population of Malta was somewhat small and no astounding cultural achievements were registered. There is evidence that Malta's earliest inhabitants lived in natural caves, like Għar Dalam (limits of Birżebbuġa), and later they began to live in small scattered hamlets. The only site which has been properly explored is that at Skorba. The unearthed evidence consists of small oval huts built of sun-dried brick or wattle-and-daub over a low stone foundation. The same kind of construction technique was adopted for the religious shrine in the precincts of the village.

Inside the 'Skorba Shrine' were found the first signs of religious practice in Malta. These consist of small figurines which have been connected with the worship of the Mother Goddess – whose cult appears to have been recurrent among the farming Neolithic peoples of most Mediterranean, European and other prehistoric cultures in the Balkan peninsula.

| Chronology of Maltese Prehistory | | |
|---|---|---|
| *Period* | *Phase* | *Dates BC* |
| Neolithic | Ghar Dalam | 5000-4500 |
| | Grey Skorba | 4500-4400 |
| | Red Skorba | 4400-4000 |
| Copper Age (Temple Period) | Żebbuġ | 4000-3800 |
| | Mġarr | 3800-3600 |
| | Ġgantija | 3600-3000 |
| | Saflieni | 3000-2900 |
| | Tarxien | 3000-2500 |
| Bronze Age | Tarxien Cemetery | 2500-1500 |
| | Borġ-in-Nadur | 1500-725 |
| | Bahrija | 900-725 |

*The Temple Period*

The magnificent temple culture of Malta flourished for about 1,500 years (*c*.4000-2500 BC). What is obvious about this cultural development is that while contacts with the outside world, namely Sicily and its islands, together with southern Italy and beyond, were maintained, these seem to have been limited to the continued importation of raw materials for tools and ritual objects (like the green stone axe pendants). As for the rest, starting from the Ġgantija phase, the Temple farming people developed a new cultural phenomenon in total isolation from the outside world without any apparent attempt to make any changes on their cultural values. This cultural phenomenon was probably made possible thanks to an efficient, surplus-producing agrarian economy, which together with an equally efficient social, (though primitive) organization and deeply-rooted religious beliefs, may have enabled the Temple people to realize the architectural feats which can still be seen at sites like Ġgantija, Haġar Qim, Mnajdra and Tarxien.

Several theories have been proposed as to the origins and development of this civilization. The early stages of Temple culture development belong to the Żebbuġ phase, while the earliest datable temples, and the early stages of development, in their ground plan, like the kidney-shaped plan at Mġarr East can be dated to the Ġgantija phase; the trefoil plan found at Skorba and Kordin; and the five-apsed plan of Ġgantija South and Tarxien East all belong to the latter phase. The Saflieni phase refers to a short transitional phase named after the Hypogeum (underground temple/burial site) where new types of pottery decorations were found next to Ġgantija pottery shapes. The Temple culture reached its climax during the Tarxien phase not only thanks to the perfection and finesse of its pottery crafts-

The Prehistoric Temples of Mnajdra (Mġarr, Malta).

manship but also due to the relief sculptural decorations and free-standing statues.

However this may be, there is no doubt that the Temple people were an extraordinary, highly intelligent and resourceful people who were both technologically and artistically well endowed. Evidence of their advanced technology lies in the sheer size of the stone blocks used and in the perfect interlocking between them to provide a solid structure according to a preconceived architectural design.

There are other features which seem to distinguish the cultural development of the Maltese Islands in the Temple period. This was a time when Sicily was inhabited by a population which appears to have utilized copper for which reason this phase in Sicilian prehistory is called the Copper Age. So far there is no evidence that the Temple population of Malta utilized this new metal. One may attribute this phenomenon to the insularity of the Maltese islands which enabled the native population to continue developing their unique megalithic structures. However this insularity was never complete, since the importation of several kinds of hard stone from Sicily, Lipari Islands and Pantelleria was never interrupted.

Several attempts have been made to unravel the causes of the apparent sudden collapse of the Temple Culture. This could have occurred after a breakdown of the delicate social structure or it could have been caused by a natural calamity, or pestilence, or perhaps more realistically due to the total depletion of the natural resources through over-exploitation.

## The Bronze Age

The Maltese farmer peoples of Neolithic and Temple cultures must have felt safe from any possible threat from the outside since they did not bother to surround their villages with any kind of protective walls. This attitude changed with the advent of the Bronze Age people. The Bronze Age people may have inhabited the Maltese islands after an interval of a number of years. They certainly brought with them a totally different culture since, in contrast with their predecessors, they were a war-like people who made use of copper and bronze implements as well as weapons. The first evidence of this culture was found inside Tarxien temples and the phase was thus labelled Tarxien Cemetery. The Tarxien Cemetery people cremated their dead and deposited their charred remains in urns inside the ruins of the Tarxien temples. Apart from the possession of tools, the Tarxien Cemetery Culture seems culturally inferior to the previous one. As yet no settlements have been discovered for this phase and the only architectural features that can be associated with this phase are the monocellular structures, known as dolmens, which are found scattered in the Maltese islands.

On the other hand, there exists ample evidence of their successors, the Borġ in-Nadur people. These lived on flat-topped hills and ridges which were sometimes fortified with walls on the more vulnerable sites like Borġ in-Nadur (limits of Bir-żebbuġa). The Cyclopean construction technique of the Borġ in-Nadur fortification recalls similar structures built by the Myceneans.

There are signs of contacts between the Bronze Age inhabitants of the Maltese islands, Minoan Crete and Mycenean civilization in Greece especially since the latter culture came to dominate the whole of the Aegean sea by 1,500 BC and maintained contacts with eastern Sicily and southern Italy. There may be indications that there existed some sort of commercial contact between the Bronze Age inhabitants of Malta and these two civilizations. At Tarxien a dark stone bead with symbols in gold inlay was discovered. The symbols look identical to some characters of Minoan Linear script characters. Meanwhile a shard of a Mycenean cup found at Borġ in-Nadur suggests importation from the Aegean.

Further indication of contact between Bronze Age Malta and Mycenean culture comes from the literary sources: namely the possible identification of Gozo with Homer's Ogygia, the island of Calypso on which Ulysses spent seven years of his ten-year return journey, from the Trojan War, to his native Ithaca; Lycophron relates how a group of Mycenean warriors, on their return journey from Troy, settled in Malta in their wanderings around the Mediterranean as they were prevented by the gods from reaching their homelands; Ovid connects the legendary reign of a King of Malta, named Battus, with Anna, the refugee sister of Dido, Queen of Carthage who, according to legend, gave hospitality to another Trojan War hero, Aeneas, the founder of Rome. It is difficult to assess how much of these ancient myths relate to historical facts.

The Bronze Age settlements of the Maltese Islands were established on high, easily defendable and fortified, flat hills or promontories like the fortified settlements of the Thapsos and Castelluccio cultures in Sicily and the nuraghi of Sardinia. These structures seem to reflect that this was an age of insecurity in the central Mediterranean. It was a time of great political upheavals in the eastern part of the sea which witnessed, amongst others, the end of the Mycenean civilization and the start of the so-called Dark Age in Greece; the destruction of thriving cities in the Middle East, like Ugarit, and the emergence of new ethnic groups like the Philistines in Canaan (modern Israel/Palestine) and the Phoenicians (called *Poeni*, thus the term Punic, by the Romans) in Lebanon.

(ii) Phoenician and Roman Malta

The great age of Phoenician trade was between 1200 and 700 BC Being hemmed in on the coast by the mountains their only outlet for commerce was the sea. Thus they became seasoned sea-farers and traders who by the end of the ninth century BC established colonies and trading posts on Cyprus, Sardinia, east Sicily, Malta, North Africa and even Spain. The prior presence of a Phoenician colony may explain why the Greeks did not try to establish a colony in Malta.

The earliest Phoenician presence on the Maltese islands goes back to the eighth century BC. A number of rock-cut tombs containing Phoenician pottery and some Greek luxury items, dating back to this period, were found in the Rabat area of Malta and in Rabat, Gozo. This is indicative since it may imply that the

A Punic Ivory ornament from Tas-Silġ (Marsaxlokk).

two old urban centres of the Maltese islands were already taking shape by that time. This may also indicate that during this time Malta assumed some sort of strategic, or commercial importance in the struggle, between the Greeks and the Phoenicians, to dominate the central Mediterranean. Eventually the Etruscans were to join in the quest for the control of the sea-trade routes in the area. It has not been possible to trace the process by which the Phoenicians took possession of the Maltese islands. Anthony Bonanno argues that in all probability Phoenician political control was a slow and gradual process started off by simple bartering arrangements on the sea shore with the prehistoric natives. Later it may have

> developed as a modest settlement of trading agents, possibly accompanied by their families, eventually growing into a fully-fledged colony. The systematic political control of the archipelago by the Semitic newcomers probably did not take place before the sixth century BC when as a result of the loss of political autonomy of the Phoenician fatherland in the east, the western Phoenician colonies rallied under the protectorate of Carthage, the most powerful and prosperous of them, to face the threat of the common enemy, the western Greeks.

Hostilities between the Greeks and the Carthaginians were probably only suspended by the end of the fourth century BC as a result of the invasion of Greece by Alexander the Great and its integration into the dominating Hellenistic influence of the eastern and central shores of the Mediterranean. This was a time when Malta assumed the role of an important trading link between Greek-dominant southern Italy and eastern Sicily and Tripolitania. The remains at the religious sanctuary of Tas-Silġ provide evidence that the edifice was enlarged during the fourth century with Hellenistic architectural features. Greek influence may have favoured a Hellenized-Egyptian style as is reflected in the late Punic square tower enclosed inside a private garden at Żurrieq. Hellenic influence can also be seen in the style of Punic pottery manufactured in Malta, while the Greek language accompanies Punic in the bilingual candelabra (discovered in Malta in the late eighteenth century).

The break of the balance of power between Greeks and Carthaginians came at the outset of the fifth century with the gradual emergence of Rome. By 264 BC the city of Rome had, thanks to a series of forced alliances, extended its control over the whole of the Italian peninsula. The outbreak of the First Punic War was the result of a Roman attempt to dominate Sicily. During that war the Romans fought a number of sea-battles and by the end of the war in 241 BC, Rome had become a sea power. That year a naval defeat forced the Carthaginians to surrender. They had to pay a large indemnity and agreed to withdraw from Sicily. Being enemy territory Malta was raided by the Romans in 255 BC and the countryside was devastated. However the main concern for the Romans during that war was Sicily even though they managed to annex Sardinia and Corsica soon after 238 BC.

Sicily's new colonial status did not guarantee peace and the Second Punic War broke out in 218 BC. That same year the Romans occupied Malta and integrated it within the Roman province of Sicily. The island remained part of the Roman commonwealth until the early sixth century AD. During Roman rule the Maltese islands were under the jurisdiction of the governor of Sicily, as the Verrine orations by Cicero imply. Nonetheless a bronze inscription found in Rome (in the sixteenth century) clearly states that Malta had its own senate and people's assembly. Probably this statement reflects a condition which had been achieved by the first century AD when both Malta and Gozo were issuing local coinage based on Roman weight standards. In itself the minting of coins is indicative of a thriving and prosperous local economy. Yet it was also a time when, according to Cicero, Malta was regularly used as a winter base for the pirate-infested Mediterranean – a condition which was only successfully controlled by Pompey's victory over the pirates in 67 BC.

Roman Malta appears to have been a prosperous island as the thirty or so agricultural estates with farmsteads, known as villas, scattered over the Maltese countryside, seem to imply. Several of these estates must have contained reasonably large olive-groves as evinced from several stone-pressing instruments, used for the production of olive oil, which were discovered in several parts of Malta and Gozo. Local industry must have reached a good level of refinement as the remains found in the Roman town house (*domus*) outside Mdina demonstrate. The house contains features of construction dating between the first half of the first century BC to the middle of the first century AD. The structure included some floor mosaics of the highest quality, painted walls and a set of portrait marble statues of the ruling imperial family of Claudius.

The Roman administration imposed its own language for official transactions and official religion. However this Latin culture was mingled with two other cultural and artistic currents namely the Hellenistic Greek and the Punic ones which appear to have survived until the first century AD. This explains why St Paul's shipwreck in 60 AD, as recounted in the Acts of the Apostles, labels the native inhabitants of Malta as *barbaroi*, that is, non-Latin and non-Greek speakers. Inscriptions dating at least to the second century AD provide evidence that both Malta and Gozo had their own *municipium* (town council) and some individuals even managed to become Roman citizens. Nonetheless the inhabitants of the Maltese islands as a

Roman mosaic design showing an allegory of autumn.

whole do not seem to have become full Roman citizens until AD 212 when Emperor Caracalla extended Roman citizenship to all free-born men and women within the empire. This situation appears to have endured with little change until the early sixth century AD when Malta, together with Sicily and its other islands, were integrated within the East Roman, or more precisely, Byzantine empire, although for most of the fifth century AD, the central Mediterranean was dominated by both the Vandal and Ostrogoth kingdoms in North Africa and Italy respectively.

## (iii) Byzantines, Arabs and the Norman Conquest

The first reference to the presence of the Byzantines is a brief reference by Procopius, the chronicler of the Byzantine general Belisarius, who records that the general sailed from Sicily to North Africa and on the way 'touched at Gozo and Malta' in AD 533. Most probably Malta, as part of the province of Sicily, formed an integral part of the Byzantine empire by AD 535.

Sources for a detailed picture of life in Malta under the Byzantines does not exist but the very sparseness of the evidence, even by early medieval standards, suggests that the strategic and political role of Byzantine Malta was a limited one. However recent examination of archaeological material for the sixth and seventh centuries, by Alessandra Molinari and Nathaniel Cutajar, shows a remarkably high incidence of imported wares including fine tableware, oil lamps, and amphorae (large liquid containers) from North Africa, Southern Italy and the eastern Mediterranean. According to these two authors the evidence so far suggests that Byzantine activity is detectable mainly around the harbour areas at Tas-Silġ, Marsascala and Marsa in Malta and at Xlendi in Gozo as well as at the two urban settlements Mdina and the Gozo Citadel. One must add that Byzantine wares from mainland Italy for the sixth and seventh centuries is restricted to only a few urban and military centres like Rome, Naples, Otranto and Sant'Antonio di Perti in Liguria. By the eighth century even this trickle of Byzantine supplies to Italy seems to have run dry. The relatively large quantity of Byzantine ceramics may indicate that Malta, together with the larger island of Sicily, played an important role in the period between the fall of the Roman empire and the eighth century, particularly when one compares the scanty recovery of Byzantine wares throughout the western Mediterranean. The attested presence of a drungarious (naval base governor) in the seventh and eighth centuries further strengthens the view that Malta played an important role in Byzantine strategy. However the idea that the island was an important naval base needs to be re-examined further in the light of Byzantine naval strategy as a whole.

There are a number of sources for the Muslim conquest of Malta. Muslim raiders were active in the central Mediterranean from the second half of the seventh century, and because of its strategic position Malta presumably came under increasing pressure, but there is no historical record of raids on Malta before the ninth century. The fact that such a relatively small island did not fall to the Arabs until AD 871 does suggest that Malta may have had some value in the defence system of the Byzantine empire and it was consequently well defended. Indeed it is believed that at the time of the arrival of the Arabs the whole island had been Christian for centuries as the Christian tomb complexes, or catacombs, indicate.

The Byzantine chronicler Constantine Porphyrogenitus further strengthens this argument when he states that Sicily

has notable cities… some of which have been deserted, and others of which have been conquered by the Saracens…

The Maltese islands could have witnessed a similar major exodus immediately before, or after the Arab conquest. If, therefore, the duration of direct Muslim rule shrinks to about forty-two years, that is, from 1049 to the coming of Count Roger in 1091, and the Muslims could muster only 400 able-bodied men who could wage war in 1053, it all points to a fugitive Muslim community from Sicily who may have found refuge in Malta at the time when George Maniaces, a Byzantine general, was attempting to conquer the east coast of Sicily for the Byzantines starting from Messina towards Syracuse in 1038.

It has been assumed that when the Arabs conquered the island in AD 871, they laid the foundations for the formation of the modern Maltese language. However it is worth pointing out that Maltese traces its origins from the times of the Phoenicians, and continued to develop its lexicon from other tongues such as Carthaginian, Arabic, Sicilian, and other modern European languages.

Joseph Brincat's interpretation of al-Himyari's account of the Arab colonization suggests, among other things, that the island remained practically uninhabited for 180 years. However ceramics pertaining to the late tenth and the eleventh centuries have been identified at Mdina and the surrounding area, as well as the Gozo Citadel and Tas-Silġ. Fine imported wares, attributed to Sicily or North Africa, were discovered in both urban and rural settlements while the presence of Islamic wares are markedly more plentiful at Mdina. It appears that contrary to what Arab chroniclers like al-Himyari suggest, Arab Malta was fully integrated within the cultural and economic systems enjoyed in the Maghreb and Sicily under the rule of the Fatimid and Kalbid dynasties in the eleventh century. The considerable presence of both Sicilian and Tunisian wares may indicate that the Maltese islands were involved in trade which was then plying through the central Mediterranean.

Count Roger's *razzia* of 1091 permitted the Arabs to stay on so that it appears that the Maltese islands remained within the orbit of Muslim culture. It was only after the second Norman invasion and conquest of Malta in 1127 by the Count's son, King Roger II, that a Christian community became firmly established in Malta. By establishing a Latin-Christian administration Roger II had sown the seeds for eventual intermingling between Muslims, Christians and, to a lesser extent, Jews. The language of Malta's inhabitants seems to have been exposed to various extra-Arabic influences which grew into a rich medium owing to the presence of various European influences. It is evident that under Norman rule the Maltese Islands continued to receive a considerable amount of imported wares that reached both the urban and rural settlements. The major difference lies in the cutting of commercial links with the Maghreb and the development of connections with the Tyrrhenian sea particularly with the maritime city of Genoa.

*B. The Late Middle Ages.*

(i) Malta and the Kingdom of Sicily

It is probable that after the expulsion of the Muslims in 1248, the Maltese islanders continued to speak vulgar Arabic, while the soldiers and tradesmen who came from Sicily spoke Sicilian. The linguist Joseph Micallef argues that during the High Middle

# Ages six languages,

were to some extent understood in Malta. These were: North African Arabic, chiefly spoken by the lower classes, while Sicilian was probably spoken by both (lower and upper classes). Calabrian, Neapolitan, Genoese and Venetian may have been occasionally spoken by sailors landing in Malta or settling on the Island.

To this one should add Latin primarily used by the clergy during church services and for the official correspondence of both the church and the commune.

However already in the late twelfth century, before the expulsion of the Muslims, right down to the advent of the Hospitaller Order of St John, the Maltese islands, remarks Stanley Fiorini,

swung between direct dependence on the monarchy and subjection to a succession of foreign counts and magnates.

Naturally the islanders objected very strongly every time they were alienated from Palermo. Fiorini recalls a 1198 diploma by Constance – Holy Roman Empress, Queen of Sicily and mother of Frederick II – declaring that the Maltese islands would never be separated from the royal demesne. However this promise must have been broken soon after because Frederick II made a similar promise which was likewise not kept.

Each time the islands were re-annexed to the royal demesne a charter confirming the rights and privileges which the Maltese had previously enjoyed was issued. Objections to the subjection of the Maltese islands to a fief-holder probably stemmed from a desire, by the notables, for a looser control in the day-to-day running of their own affairs. The king, who most times ruled from far away Palermo and Naples, would obviously have interfered much less than a feudal lord residing in Malta.

The first mention of municipal officials sent from Palermo dates back to 1270, during the Angevin rule, when Malta is known to have had a captain and a castellan. By the end of the thirteenth century the number of castellans was increased to two and a *massarius* (controller of the royal farmsteads), who looked after the interests of the *curia* (crown lands), on the Maltese islands were added. The crown lands were grain-producing estates worked by *villani curie* (serfs) who were slowly being emancipated so that by the early 1370s not enough hands could be found to work on the lands. The *massarie* were thus replaced by fiefs that were either leased for military service or against the payment of a census. Henri Bresc points out that a *secretus* (revenue collector) was already sent from Palermo to administer the revenue of the crown in 1373. Thus in the late fourteenth century there was a change in the administration of the crown lands and the collection of revenue – a change which is also reflected in the development of the Town Councils of Malta and Gozo better known as the *Università*.

Derived from the medieval polity, the *Università* played the role of representative assembly of the Maltese which was theoretically immune from arbitrary treatment by the ruler. The situation was however only reached after the dissolution of the feudal rule of the Catalan Don Consalvo Monroy in the early fifteenth century. From then onwards, a royal charter proclaimed that the Maltese commune was to remain a demanial town (that is, ruled directly by the king and his officials at Palermo). In reality, the *Università* was dominated and controlled by an *élite* group of landowners comprising the higher clergy, the land-owning gentry, notaries and lawyers. Claims of self-rule within the island commune strengthened the sense of local corporate and communal autonomy, particularly since the local land-owners

Aerial view of the medieval town of Mdina.

had a free hand in the management of the island's administration.

The Maltese islands enjoyed a certain measure of autonomy
in their position as demanial towns of the kingdom of Sicily. In
fact both Malta and Gozo had their own *Università* or local municipal government which raised taxes, administered justice,
regulated the market, especially the grain supply, and public
health. They often fulfilled the tasks of organizing the militia
roster for the defence of the islands and the *angara* duties for
the maintenance of the town bastions. The chief officer of the
Town Council was the *Capitano della Verga* (Captain of the Rod)
popularly known as *Hakem* who was helped by four *giurati*
(jurats) elected annually to administer the smooth running of
the *Università*. Other officials included two *cattapani* (market-
price regulators), a notary, a *marrammero* (fortress-mender),
and a *Vice Portolano* (port superintendent) who was answerable
to the *Portolano* (general port superintendent) of Palermo.

Late medieval Maltese society, according to Charles Dalli,
was made up of two main strata: those with authority, and the
subordinate peasants. Authority was shared equally between
two sectors of the land-owning *élite* namely, those with legal,
political and military jurisdiction and the clerical stratum. The
latter controlled the moral behaviour of the subjected peasantry,
but they also served as the focus of social organization, combining teaching as well as counselling duties with their spiritual role.

(ii) Economic, Social and Cultural Background

From the twelfth century onwards, the strategic position of
Malta was inviting both for the Genoese looking east for their
commerce and to the Normans looking south. The Norman conquest of Malta was part of a wider plan to gain security for the
south and east coasts of Sicily, and ultimately, to control the
entire straits between Sicily and North Africa. Pantelleria and
Lampedusa were thus valuable as well although they remained
largely unpopulated and lacked Malta's excellent harbours. The
strategic position of Malta proved vital for the Normans when

they attempted to install themselves in the North African towns. On that occasion they relied on the intermediate islands, as bases for their swoops on the Barbary coast.

Malta and Gozo were praised by King Roger II's illustrious geographer al-Idrisi for their fertility and abundance of pastures. Maltese cotton travelled abroad and could be bought in Sicily and even in North Italian cities like Genoa. Pisan and North African merchants also passed through Malta. David Abulafia relates that

> in the 1180's a Pisan ship at Malta found a boat from Gafsa in Tunisia and appropriated its merchandise. The goods were sold to a certain Alberto Bulsi in Pisa, who apparently remained ignorant of their source... Pisan ambitions in this region extended as far as an attempt to conquer Syracuse.

It appears that Malta was important as a naval base for refitting and repairing vessels. But this could not be exaggerated since the lack of wood prevented the Malta harbour from featuring more than a way-station. Thus Malta's importance was geographic rather than economic, though it appears that the islanders found a ready market for their produce among those who passed by. As a cross-roads linking the west-east route from Spain to the Levant, or the north-south route from Genoa, Venice or Pisa with North Africa, Malta was obviously overshadowed by the great commercial cities of Palermo and Messina in mainland Sicily and the Tunisian ports, like Tunis itself. Things being as they were, Malta seems to have served as a stop-over between the great centres.

Above all, Malta served as a military and economic staging-post within the political sphere of Sicily although the North Italian maritime republics involved the island in their trading orbit. By the thirteenth century the city of Genoa came to play an important role and even provided the island with counts which as David Abulafia remarks enabled her

> to protect the flank of its own long-distance trade routes to the Holy Land and Egypt. It was not enough simply to establish colonies of Genoese merchants with depots and banks at the end of these routes, at Alexandria, Acre, Messina for instance; the competition between trading powers was played out at least as much along the sea routes by means of violence, as in the foreign markets by means of capital.

With their expulsion from Malta in 1248 some Muslims chose to convert to Christianity and remained on the Maltese islands to work as *servi* working for the *curia* on the *massarie* (farmsteads) of the islands until the last of them obtained complete liberty around 1372. Thus the royal farmsteads of the thirteenth century were the consequence of the recent conquest by the Normans and the formation of a vast domain of *latifundia* (royal fiefs) were, as in Sicily, devoted to the growing of cereals. These estates were essentially dependent on the existence of a labour force of *villani*. As in Sicily Malta had a feudal-type economy which both reinforced and legalized the power of a few noble families which held fiefs and local political power. At the same time the community of free Maltese peasants were dispersed in the rural habitat which enabled them to become more than ever solidly attached to their orchards and gardens. Henri Bresc suggests that cotton production may probably be related to this market gardening economy of the Maltese peasants, which thanks to the favourable climate of the Maltese islands played a leading role in the Maltese late medieval economy. Maltese ships loaded with cotton merchandise were already frequenting the port of Syracuse before 1375. Jews from Malta and Syracuse appear to have been engaged in its exportation and processing. It is evident that the production of cotton helped to develop strong links between Syracuse and Malta.

Moreover two types of linen appear to have been produced in Malta but these were woven in Syracuse and were largely employed in mattress-making. During this time the city of Syracuse practically enjoyed a monopoly over other Sicilian towns in the manufacturing of mattresses.

Godfrey Wettinger argues that Malta's exportation of mules and donkeys must have been significant in the late Middle Ages. Nonetheless it was cotton, even more than the rearing of mules and donkeys, which provided the Maltese islands with an income capable of balancing their expenditure on grain. It seems that until around the 1370s Malta produced enough grain to supply the local population. The harvest failure of 1374 compelled the Maltese to import 560 *salme* of Sicilian wheat and after

Façade of the
fifteenth cen-
tury Palazzo
Falson (Mdina).

1400 regular and massive imports of grain became necessary
– partly due to drought but also due to the ravages of Hafsid
fleets from Muslim North Africa. From 1374 grain shortages
became a permanent element in the Maltese economy.

Yet despite the Muslim Hafsid raids, and the plague, one
notices a growth in the Malta population as reflected in the frequent wine imports and the continual emigration to Sicily, where
the Maltese found skilled jobs as fishermen in the area of Palermo, as vineyard labourers, or as workmen in general.

Archaeological evidence for this period seems to suggest that
the lively commercial activity detected for the Islamic, the Norman and Swabian periods were, according to Alessandra Molinari and Nathaniel Cutajar, overtaken by

an apparently rigid autarchic economy and the abrupt end of importation of ceramics from Sicily, Italy and the Maghreb.

The mass of ceramics dating to this phase consists of local, poor quality pottery. One may deduce that under the Aragonese crown Malta was transformed into an economically-impoverished and inward-looking community. The ravages of war resulting from the Sicilian Vespers, plague visitations and the eventual Muslim North African raids may partly account for this economic inversion.

(iii) The Church, Myths and Ethnic Values

The establishment of the Latin Christian administration by King Roger II in 1127 must have proved vital for the re-introduction of Christianity in the Maltese islands. Evidence for the existence of a Christian community dates back to 1156 when the bishopric of Malta was mentioned as a suffragan of Palermo. But the earliest evidence to the Church in Malta belongs to the thirteenth century when there is reference to a church dedicated to the Assumption of the Virgin on the island of Comino and to the existence of two churches in the *castrum maris* (castle by the sea) dedicated to St Angelo. There is evidence that 'the bishop's church of St Paul' – the Cathedral at Mdina – was already standing in 1299. It appears that Christian presence became increasingly enhanced from the fourteenth century. Stanley Fiorini points out that the Bishop had no residence in Malta as late as 1366, although a Bishop's palace had been edified a few decades later. Complete lists of Cathedral dignitaries, dating from 1419 onwards, have survived. The documentary evidence available seems to imply that the diocese was firmly established and well-organized by 1400. This was a time when male religious orders began to set up friaries in the countryside surrounding Mdina (the Franciscans were already established in 1372) while two Benedictine nunneries were soon to be set up inside the city.

The importance of the advent of St Paul to Malta must have been a main focus of attention for the early fifteenth century Church authorities of Malta. An indirect insight into the widespread homage paid to St Paul can be gleaned from a study of Christian names in Malta current in the early part of the fifteenth century. An analysis of the Militia List of 1419-1420 indicates a total of 1,667 adult males in Malta, excluding Birgu, and includes some eighty Christian names of which the more popular are: Antoni (104 examples); Johanni in its various forms (94); Nicolau or Cola (94); Gullielmu (76); Thumeu (58) and Paulu (58). Although Paulu is not the most popular name, it ranks among those in common use.

Peter Serracino Inglott suggests that the lifestyle of the Maltese people's has been impressed forever by the arrival of St Paul, since throughout his lifetime every Maltese hears the story of the saint's shipwreck on the island a number of times. The influence of this event has therefore assumed prime importance for the Maltese sense of identity as a separate community. Henry Frendo concurs with this view and goes on to argue that

'collective memory' has come to incorporate St Paul's stay in Malta, after his shipwreck, irrespective of its historicity or not. In this fashion, legends take on real life, although Maltese Christianity – which may not have survived during the Muslim period – seems to have been re-introduced, perhaps in the twelfth century, when the Maltese islands were 'Latinized and Christianized... and thereafter religious fervour became increasingly strong.

The long established veneration for St Paul was being propagated actively from the late sixteenth century. The seventeenth century Maltese Vice-Chancellor of the Order of St John and 'father of Maltese historiography' Gian Francesco Abela has given more than a helping hand in the consequent development or fabrication of traditions, some of which have continued to enliven Maltese culture ever since.

The story of the Apostle's shipwreck served also as a symbolic testimony that the Maltese did not owe their religious sentiments to the presence of the haughty Order of Knights. It should rather be appreciated against the background of Malta's geographical position, on the front-line of Latin Christianity, in dangerous proximity to Islamic North Africa, and perhaps unconsciously, as a form of compensation for the persistence of its Semitic language among the native inhabitants. The latter consideration may account for Jean Quentin d'Autun's disbelief regarding the identification of Malta with the site of the shipwreck of St Paul.

Clearly, an attempt was unconsciously being made to explain the apparent contradiction between Maltese aspiration to be considered as Europeans, and the linguistic reality pointing to their Semitic past. Maltese religion must definitely have been strengthened by a propaganda campaign that, according to Anthony Luttrell, was fostered by the religious orders, who made deliberate use of a series of historical inventions. Many of these were established almost ineradicably in Gian Francesco Abela's authoritative *Della descrittione di Malta* published in 1647. In Abela's inflated account regarding Malta's attachment to Christianity since the arrival of St Paul, mythic foundations were laid for a history of Maltese Christianity. Abela claims that Malta had been converted to Christianity by the Apostle in the first century, and had since remained faithful. In this way, the essential mythic foundations for the history of Maltese Christianity are firmly established.

In the writings of the seventeenth century, St Paul's grotto became the focus of this new devotion. Thus in a Latin poem attributed to Gerolamo Manduca, the author synthesizes the salient moments of the saint's life. Of prime importance is the list of references to the various traditions linked with St Paul's stay in Malta, with such episodes about the snake which the Apostle shook back into the fire; the Gozitans who could hear his sermons while he preached from Naxxar; the Maltese who were baptized and became fervent Christians; the anointing of the first citizen of Malta, Publius, as spiritual pastor; and the saint's stay in the grotto.

Devotion to the grotto and the Pauline tradition continued to play a central role in traveller's reports. In 1582, for example, Gio. Battista Leoni referred to the great devotion of those visiting the site, especially the grotto, where according to pious traditions St Paul took shelter during his stay in Malta. Leoni also refers to the miraculous limestone used to heal snake bites. But it was thanks to a Spanish nobleman turned Jesuit from Cordoba, Juan Beneguas, that veneration for the grotto was revived in 1607. During the seventeenth century, the growing importance of the grotto was evidently becoming symbolic of ethnic consciousness among the Maltese, as well as an important landmark of the island's Christian devotion. Not without good reasons did the Cathedral Chapter of Mdina declare on 13 May 1617, that the grotto of St Paul is 'the foundation stone of the Church in Malta'.

The illustration chosen for Abela's introductory page confirms this general belief. The iconography of St Paul holding the gospel in his left hand, with a viper hanging from his raised right hand, and a lit fire beside him, has imprinted itself deeply on the minds of the Maltese ever since. Abela's image of St Paul might even have inspired the baroque sculptor Melchiorre Gafà (1636-1667), in the execution of the Apostle's statue for the Testaferrata family around 1660. The Pauline cult came to symbolize the salient social relationships of Maltese life, embodying the emotions it generated. Above all, it provided a cultural idiom, a collective representation of Maltese society. In short, the Pauline cult helped to unite the Maltese and to give them a sort of identity.

Maltese religion was

> strengthened by a propaganda campaign sustained by members of religious orders who deliberately fostered a series of historical inventions... to cultivate popular sympathy for St Paul and other saints.

St Paul, in particular was not only the most efficacious mediator with God on behalf of the islanders, but he also came to represent 'Malteseness'. The figure of the Apostle thus emerged as the major symbol of seventeenth century Malta, enshrining the hopes and aspirations of the Maltese at large.

Some events of the Norman period, commonly referred to, clearly have a basis in fact and have been passed down the generations. The Norman period seems to provide a case for a continued – often critical – commentary upon contemporary life and what has become acceptable by and large as the norm. Above all, this period evokes the origins of the Maltese as a separate ethnic community, thanks to the re-establishment of the Catholic faith, the setting up of a Maltese commune, and the survival of a Semitic dialect in a Latin Christian *entro-terra*. One might also add references to the foundation of the Cathedral as a bishop's see, emphasising the revival of Christian values. In this

Statue of St Paul by the
Maltese sculptor
Melchiorre Gafà (1636-1667)
(St Paul's Shipwreck
Collegiate, Valletta).

way, the Norman past is linked up with the national culture of Maltese patriotism, with acts of heroism and concepts about the Maltese state.

The narrative recounts historical events which are transfigured by myth, the contents of which deal with struggle, sacrifice and victory, suggesting that the narrative was more than a story told: it was a cult enacted. It did not only remind the participants of mythic events, but above all the rite was represented. According to Joseph Cassar-Pullicino,

> The Maltese Christians have to be pictured as suffering under the Arabs… before they were liberated by the Count… Such a feat can only be accomplished after a desperate resistance by the Arabs, whom the Count fighting against great odds, succeeded in defeating, after which he was met by the Maltese Christians, whom he had liberated, and was given a reception, with palms and olive branches and songs of thanks giving, such as befitted only a hero… All benefits derived from the period of Norman rule were attributed to the Count.

Many of the legends concerning Count Roger presuppose the survival of a considerable Christian segment under Muslim rule. The legend holds that Count Roger, having landed at Miġra l-Ferħa (on the west coast of Malta and not far from Mdina), was met by Maltese Christians and led in triumph to the town. In effect, in his account, Malaterra, Count Roger's chronicler, points out that the Christians who went out to meet the Count were *captivi christiani*,

whom Count Roger subsequently carried back to Sicily from where they departed to their homes.

Folk memories about the Norman rule are, however, revealing for a number of different reasons, but especially because they are contrary to the existing evidence. According to Godfrey Wettinger none of the documentation found for the island suggests any degree of hardship or servility to Arab overlords as some of the later informants vividly describe.

One must bear in mind however that a sixteenth century audience would have no difficulty in regarding Count Roger's story as true. Maltese social memory of the sixteenth century recalled that Count Roger freed the Maltese Christians who were then suffering under the Arab yoke. This theme suited official propaganda because it was a time when Malta was engaged in constant combat with the Muslims. It was of no significance that the twelfth century chroniclers, Gaufredus Malaterra and Alessandro de Telese – closer to the original invasion of 1091 – relate that the Count liberated the enslaved 'Christians', who were not necessarily inhabitants of Malta.

Above all, the medieval Church, consistently expounded its doctrines and teachings in the form of stories, while the clergy maintained a vivid interest in heroic poetry and tales of chivalry. Thus an Arab and Muslim past, based on misery and degradation, would have well suited the cultural orientation of the clergy who would then expound it to the laymen. This may also suggest how a definite separate identity was first established. The legend of Count Roger as 'liberator' readily lent itself as a myth of origin. We have no firm evidence to confirm when this might have occurred, but it was surely well entrenched by the mid-sixteenth century as Luca d'Armenia's poem, written at that time, demonstrates.

One dubious tradition that surfaces in Gian Francesco Abela concerns the place-name Għajn Klieb or (Dogs Fountain). Allegedly, it derived its name from the discovery and suppression of a supposed Muslim plot to regain control over the island, some decades after the Norman conquest. Fortunately for the Christian community, a shepherd girl overheard the Muslims at their plottings and duly informed the Christian elders. On the appointed day, the Christians lay in ambush close to a fountain on the road leading to Baħrija in the limits of Rabat. As the Muslims approached the fountain, the Christians sprang upon them crying *Għall-klieb!* (At the Dogs!) massacring a large number. The name Għajn Klieb has supposedly retained a memory of the skirmish.

Abela's 'invention of tradition' can be better appreciated, if reference is made to another feature of historiography.

It must be remembered that his aim was to dispel any doubt on the continuity of Christianity during the Muslim occupation. Not only was the advent of Count Roger interpreted as representing the end of Muslim misrule over a liberated Christian population, but Abela goes on to assign the introduction of the Gothic style in architecture to the Goths of the sixth century – a theory intended to lend support to the thesis of Christian continuity during the Muslim phase.

Though all these arguments are recognizably false, one cannot fail to appreciate Abela's preoccupation with presenting the right image of Malta's past. Abela's main aim was to interpret the past to suit a contemporary ideological need: conformity and integration into the Latin culture, as represented by the Order of St John. One cannot help but conclude that Abela undertook the task of writing the *Della descrittione*, impelled by the need to demonstrate to the Order that Maltese notables – the class to which he belonged – had the right cultural background to justify their claim to participate in the government of the island – a right which the Order was usurping.

In his *Della descrittione* Abela also refers to a widespread and implanted belief that Count Roger had raised Malta to the rank of a small 'nation', by granting the town (*città*) to the 'Maltese', claiming moreover that in 1090 (albeit 1091) he also endowed the Maltese Church. Therefore the Norman legends sought to idealize the religious character of the Maltese people. This religious character was conditioned by the position of the Maltese on the frontier of Latin Christianity but in threatening proximity to Islamic North Africa. Thus religion served as a symbolic code of communication and a focus for social organization. Above all, religion helped to mediate the needs of the Maltese community, thus ensuring both the persistence of the religious traditions and their renewal through all the vicissitudes of history.

(iv) The Political Situation of the Mediterranean

The Muslims, the Crusades and the Italian Maritime republics:

In the tenth century the Mediterranean was almost entirely a 'Muslim lake'. The trickle of trade that was carried out at this time between western Europe and the Orient was in the hands of the cities of Byzantine Italy like Bari, Amalfi, Gaeta and Salerno. Amalfi, in particular, traded indiscriminately with the Muslims of Sicily and Egypt and also with Constantinople and Antioch. Venice was already acting as the trading link between the Mediterranean cities and Europe north of the Alps. In the western Mediterranean trade was virtually at a standstill since the Muslims were in control of the Mediterranean islands and their basis at Fraxinetum (Frainet) and Montpellier in the south of France.

Their dislodgement from southern France in AD 972 weakened the Muslim position in the western Mediterranean and enabled the fleets of Pisa and Genoa to wrest control over the Ligurian and Tyrrenhian seas. Pisa and Genoa began the offensive against Muslim control of the Mediterranean in 1016 by an attack on Sardinia leading to its conquest in 1022. This was followed by a number of attacks on Muslim ports in North Africa. By the end of the century the Italian sea powers had contributed to the success of the First Crusade and had swept Muslim shipping from the Mediterranean. The Pisan and Genoese raids on Muslim shipping and ports provided capital for shipbuilding and eventually for commerce. Yet although the First Crusade opened up trading stations in the Levant it was only after the great Venetian naval victory at Ascalon in 1123 that the Italian cities came to dominate the Mediterranean sea.

However one cannot exaggerate the influence of the Latins in the Mediterranean at this point since even Islam was spreading fast. The rise of the Mameluk Turks within Islam began to menace the Latin kingdoms created after the First Crusade. Crusading activity served as a form of impetus for western expansion but when the Mameluks allied with the Mongol invaders the Latin kingdoms in the Levant crumbled. After the fall of Acre in 1291 all that remained for the Latins in the eastern Mediterranean was the Kingdom of Cyprus.

In the western and central Mediterranean, the rigourist sect of the Almohades rallied Muslim strength. Moving eastwards from Morocco, these Berbers regained by 1160 the coast from Cape Bone to Tripoli that had been lost to the Norman kings of Sicily. Profiting from the division of the Castilian empire, the Almohades momentarily unified Spanish Islam and administered a severe defeat to Castile in 1196. During the first two-thirds of the thirteenth century, however, the Muslim counter-attack came to a halt and the Christians resumed their march. In the Iberian peninsula the progress of the Almohades was slowed thanks to the activity of five, recently created, Christian military orders and frequent French crusades. By 1238 the Almohades lost the Balearic islands and Valencia to Aragon which cost Islam its command of the central parts of the western Mediterranean. By mid-century Portugal had taken Algarve, and Islam had lost Cordoba and Seville to Castile while Cadiz fell to the Christians in 1265.

*The Normans and the Suabians*

In the meantime the power of the Normans had grown enormously since the end of the eleventh century. In southern Italy, the Lombards, Byzantines and Muslims had for more than a century jostled each other until by the early eleventh century the Muslims were expelled from the mainland and only retained the island of Sicily. Apulia and Calabria were Byzantine while the rest of the south was split into more than a dozen petty duchies, counties and marches under local rulers who shifted their allegiance as occasion demanded or allowed. This anarchic situation could have lasted for an indefinite number of years were it not for the intervention of a group of Norman knights who transformed south Italian society in the High Middle Ages.

The Normans had only recently been Christianized and thus experienced the intense piety of the newly converted. Many of them participated in pilgrimages. A small band of wandering adventurers from Normandy were in Rome seeking employment as mercenaries in 1017. In 1029 one of the Norman leaders was given the county of Aversa as a reward for services to the Duke of Naples, thus making the first Norman principality in southern Italy. The prospects of such advancement attracted more Norman adventurers including several sons of Tancred d' Hauteville. Tancred had twelve sons, of whom only one could inherit his fief in western Normandy. By emigrating to southern Italy the Hauteville brothers founded a powerful state that became a kingdom in the twelfth century. One of these, Robert Guiscard, was proclaimed Duke of Calabria and Apulia in 1059. In 1061 he helped his brother Roger initiate the conquest of Sicily as a fief to be held with the title of count. By 1091 Count Roger had conquered all of Sicily and its islands. By the time of King Roger the Great (1130-1154) the kingdom of Sicily and southern Italy had become one of the richest and most powerful monarchies in Europe. Since many of King Roger's civil servants were Greeks or Arabs his government was a model of bureaucratic efficiency.

The *Regno*, as the Kingdom of Sicily was called, became the wealthiest kingdom of Western Europe, and one of the most powerful. It could even control its trading cities of Gaeta, Naples, Salerno and Bari which were reduced to a state of subjection that none of the north Italian communes would have tolerated. Trade was carried out not only with other Christian states but even with Muslim North Africa. Large quantities of Sicilian grain were sent to the coastal towns of Muslim Tunisia. The Norman kings had been able to support their authoritarian claims with overwhelming force. During the last years of Roger's reign the kingdom of Sicily was the strongest maritime power in Italy – indeed he had a navy which was second only to that of Byzantium. This factor united Genoa, Pisa and Venice against Sicily until they had, in the second half of the century, regained mastery of the central Mediterranean but during his reign King Roger was able to exercise almost complete control over the central Mediterranean. He had an army which was composed not only of Norman knights but also of Muslim mercenaries who had been serving the Norman kingdom in Italy as early as 1098. King Roger and his successors found the Muslim soldiers invaluable especially because they were immune from papal excommunication.

Enmity towards the Byzantines increased during the reign of King Roger II and this closed off the trade routes with the Levant, to the advantage of the north Italian cities, but the king felt so sure of himself as to oppose the Papacy as well whenever he felt it was necessary. Thus when Pope Innocent II dared to excommunicate him for supporting an anti-pope, Roger fought against him, defeated and captured him and even forced him to make an abject peace in 1139. In southern Italy Roger was supreme and the Papacy was unable to withstand him singlehandedly and was faced with the choice either of co-operating with him or to seek help from the empire against him.

Under these circumstances the Papacy inherited a policy of a balance of power in Italy. The 'patrimony of St Peter' – the Papal States – was roughly situated in the middle of Italy, and it managed to maintain an equilibrium between the Holy Roman Empire in the north and the Normans in the south. When the Normans were too powerful it supported the Empire, and when the Empire was too powerful it reverted to its alliance with the Normans. Thus it was papal policy to ensure that the Empire and the *Regno* were never united under the same ruler.

This state of affairs was overturned when Frederick II – son of the Hohenstaufen Emperor Henry VI (1190-1197) and Constance, heiress to the throne of Sicily – already feudal overlord of the *Regno*, was elected Emperor of the Holy Roman Empire in 1220.

The German and Italian dominions of the empire had been in a state of civil war since the death of Frederick's father, Henry VI, in 1197. In Germany the ecclesiastical and lay princes had consolidated their position, and Frederick – like his grandfather Frederick I Barbarossa before him – legalized the usurpations which he was no longer able to challenge. In Italy he was less accommodating, although he did not insist on any rights which were lost beyond recall. He realized that if his empire was ever going to be a reality, he needed first to concentrate his resources and establish a new basis of power. It was to the *regno* therefore that Frederick II, known *Stupor Mundi*, turned in his search for a basis of power. The Norman inheritance was in his opinion more important than the German. Frederick's ambitions in Italy brought him into direct conflict with the north Italian communes as well as with the Papacy, which during the twelfth century had consolidated its position in the region of Latium. The election of Innocent III saw the claims of the popes to temporal power reach new heights. Innocent sought to secure the permanent independence of the papacy by establishing a strong state in central Italy. He also insisted for special papal authority with the Holy Roman Empire and feudal overlordship of the Kingdoms of Sicily, Aragon and Hungary. Innocent III faced the same major problem of his own predecessors. He realized that without his own military forces he had to rely on others to do the fighting. This issue put his pretences for the independence of the Papacy in question.

The conflict between the Empire and the Papacy commenced during the reign of Henry VI, was resumed by Frederick II, and resulted in nearly thirty-years of war mongering ending in the destruction of Hohenstaufen power in Italy. Both sides sought the support of the north Italian cities where rival parties in the communes adopted the labels Ghibellines (supporters of the empire) or Guelf (supporters of the Papacy) to signify their loyalty. In practice however the labels did little more than give the parties additional leverage in their struggle for local domination. Frederick enjoyed some success in the Romagna region but in general his cause was not attractive for the Italian communes since his victory would have meant a curtailment of their freedom and the imposition of taxes. The Papacy, on the other hand, appeared less threatening. When he died in 1250 Frederick had few allies left in northern Italy, and the only clear result of years of fighting was widespread devastation. For a few years the cause of the Hohenstaufen was taken up by an illegitimate son of Frederick – Manfred. By then the Pope turned to Charles of Anjou, brother of the King of France, for help. Charles marched into Italy and killed Manfred at the Battle of Benevento in 1266. His reward was the Kingdom of Sicily. Nonetheless Charles lost the kingdom of Sicily in 1282 following a local uprising known as the Sicilian Vespers. Sicily was at this point captured by the Aragonese but the Angevins continued to rule the kingdom of Naples until 1435 when Alfonso V, the Magnanimous, added Naples to his Aragonese empire then at the height of its territorial expansion.

## The Kingdom of Aragon and Spanish Domination

The reign of Alfonso saw the predominance of foreign merchants in the economy of Southern Italy and Sicily. Catalans came to form a particularly important group of merchants while Genoese bankers and merchants provided anything Alfonso needed in return for special privileges in the Kingdom. Tuscan and Venetian traders were also present in the Kingdom. When Alfonso died in 1458 his Kingdom became the battle-ground of Italy. Alfonso bestowed Naples on his illegitimate son, Ferrante but leaving his other kingdoms, of Aragon and Sicily, to his brother John. In 1479 John was succeeded by Ferdinand. The constant civil strife in Castile and the prolonged revolt of the Catalans

form the background for the reign of Ferdinand of Aragon and
Isabella of Castile. The Catholic kings, as they came to be known,
established the strong monarchy on which the predominance of
sixteenth century Spain was based. The territorial expansion of
Spain in the Iberian peninsula was completed with the conquest
of the Muslim kingdom of Granada (1481-1492), the retroces-
sion of Roussillion from France in 1494 and the conquest of
southern Navarre in 1512. The Catholic kings enforced unity
within the new kingdom of Spain by crushing Catalan sepa-
ratism; by keeping the nobility in check; by giving the choice
of conversion to Christianity, or exile from Spain, to the Muslims
and Jews; and by gaining the control of the Inquisition and
transforming it into a state department. Castile devoted its
energies on the reorganization of the newly conquered areas of
the kingdom and the colonization of the New World. Meanwhile
Aragon devoted its energies to its Mediterranean and European
territories. Following the conquest of Granada, the Spanish zest
for the riconquista had over spilt onto the Mediterranean shores
of North Africa. Such was the impetus of the Spanish crusaders
that between 1500 and 1510 they had conquered Ceuta, Oran,
Sfax and Tripoli apart from establishing a protectorate over
Tunis. Nonetheless the major task of king Ferdinand was his
opposition to French designs on the Kingdom of Naples and during the subsequent Italian wars he ended up by becoming its
king.

The loss of Italian primacy was precipitated by the French
invasion of Italy in 1494. In the ensuing Franco-Spanish struggle France was defeated and thereafter, by the Treaty of Cateau-
Cambrésis of 1559 and the French Wars of Religion, effectively
excluded France from Italy, which was dominated by Spain.
Milan was ruled by a Spanish governor, while Naples, Sicily and
Sardinia by Spanish viceroys. Genoa and its colony of Corsica
were also tied economically to Spain. The central Italian states,
pressed between Spanish Milan and Spanish Naples, had limited freedom. There were Spanish naval bases in Tuscany, a
Spanish garrison in Piacenza. Venice, which sought to preserve
independence by neutrality, was nevertheless threatened by

Spanish land-power in Milan and Spanish sea-power at Brindisi. As the front line of defence against the Turks, Italy was protected, and therefore dominated by Spain. By the mid-sixteenth century the central Mediterranean was very much in the orbit of Spanish influence.

A drastic change that took place in the sixteenth century Mediterranean was the loss of primacy of the Italian maritime republics. The sea became the theatre of a power-struggle between two multi-national empires whose interests were only partly Mediterranean: the Spanish Habsburgs and the Ottoman Turks.

Malta was at this point handed over as fief to the Hospitaller Order of St John, by Charles V, the Habsburg King of Spain and Holy Roman Emperor.

# 3

## The Hospitaller Order of St John and Malta

*The Order's Early Years in Malta*

The Order of St John, officially founded in Jerusalem in 1113 to provide hospitalling service for pilgrims to the Holy Lands, soon acquired a military role, and shared fully in the crusading activities of the time. After having been pushed out of their last stronghold of Acre in 1291, followed by a temporary stay in Cyprus, the Order spent the next two hundred years (1309-1522) on the island of Rhodes.

During their stay in Rhodes, the island organized itself on almost perfect lines. Being composed of knights from different countries of Europe, its internal organization reflected this diversity in the development of langues (division by language), each centered upon an individual auberge (inn). This system ensured that knights hailing from the same country and speaking the same language lived together communally. As a body, the knights elected one of their number as Grand Master whose appointment was for life.

The capture of Rhodes by the Ottoman Turks forced the Order to spend seven years wandering in search of a temporary base in the Mediterranean from which it could stage the reconquest of Rhodes. In 1523, Charles V, Holy Roman Emperor and King of Spain, had already offered the islands of Malta, Gozo and the Spanish fortress of Tripoli in North Africa to the

Order. However, Grand Master L'Isle Adam vainly hoped for something better, and it was only in 1529 that it was decided to accept Malta and its dependencies.

Like any other medieval chivalric Order, the Hospitallers had a peculiar inner constitution, by which the higher echelons were open to any male of aristocratic origin, while less prestigious social qualifications were demanded for other grades. Its property, collected over the years, thanks to the inheritance (*spogli*) of deceased knights, was scattered all over Europe, although a considerable amount of this property was lost in the course of the Protestant Reformation. Nonetheless, the Order of St John was still relatively wealthy and powerful when it arrived in Malta, thus making it possible for the Order to prosper while spending enormous sums on the construction of a defensive system.

The first Grand Master L'Isle Adam established the Magisterial Law Courts in 1533, and by the time d'Homedes (1536-1553) was elected Grand Master, the Order was allowed to enjoy the sovereign prerogative of coining money. However the Grand Master continued to exercise very limited authority at first, and it was only with the passage of time that the Grand Master became conscious of his dual position. On the one hand, as head of the Order of St John, he was subject to the Order's statutes and was considered a *primus inter pares* by the other members of the Order. Under such circumstances, a Grand Master was expected to lead according to the advice of the Grand Council. At the same time, the Grand Master ruled Malta as feudal overlord. The Maltese became so dependent on their ruler that by the time La Valette (1558-1568) became Grand Master the area that remained free of his control was indeed very narrow. In fact, the more intensively the Grand Master dominated the local administration, the more the Maltese shifted their allegiance from their *Università* (municipal council) to the Grand Master. Moreover, the more energetically the Grand Master's sovereign rights were exercised, the more harshly were the amount of restrictions on all sorts of common customary rights enforced.

Little heed was paid to the ancient privileges and liberties of the Maltese. In exercising its functions, the *Università* continually appealed for justification of its position. It kept on reminding the Grand Master that the source of its authority was based on antiquity, custom and traditions. It was intent on limiting the encroaching demands of the Grand Masters.

By the late sixteenth century, the *Università* had become so weak and enfeebled, that it busied itself with small matters, particularly the distribution of grain, and generally played the role imposed by the reigning Grand Master's rule. Yet it remained the organ which vested the Maltese élite with oligarchic pretensions, and the institution survived as a symbol of Maltese traditions of liberty.

In order to survive and grow, the *Università* had to depend on its usefulness as instrument of the Grand Master's government. As such, the latter did not wish to get rid of the people's representatives, but expected its representatives to be cooperative and acquiescent, consenting to money grants when asked, offering constructive counsel, rather than directing their energies to criticism or obstruction. Yet in the long run, opposition was inevitable, particularly when Grand Master La Valette tried to take over uncontrolled authority to tax the *Università*. This was the most serious accusation brought forward against the Grand Master who attempted to impose burdens in the form of taxes on the people, mainly extracted from customs duties, the selling of wine, the sale and transfer of property, and on loans. This business was originally run by the *Università*, but it was appropriated by the Grand Master who in the early 1560s, managed to raise a sum of approximately 11,000 scudi annually. La Valette even arrested and later hanged a respectable Maltese doctor, Giuseppe Callus, for having written a letter of protest to the King of Spain – a letter which was intercepted by the Grand Master.

La Valette's ability to impose taxes and to make laws, without consultation or assent of his subjects, demonstrates that in the 1560s the Grand Master was already arrogating to himself powers as an acknowledged right.

In this matter Malta seems to have been in line with political developments in most other European states. For example in the Republic of Venice it is usually asserted that by the late sixteenth century, the institutional obstacles to local autarchic systems of government were being reduced to mere formalism, falling into desuetude, or disappearing altogether. The effective powers of communal assemblies in the Venetian *terraferma* (mainland) were similarly whittled down to mere petty details of local government. Real power passed into the hands of the *rettori* (rectors) who controlled both military and civil administration.

Yet the *Università* did not hesitate to bargain with the state in times of need. Hence, on the sighting of the Ottoman Armada in May 1565, the Mdina *Università* despatched Luca d'Armenia as envoy to La Valette for advice. This situation could be interpreted as an exercise of sovereign authority on the part of the Grand Master who urged the people of Mdina to do their duty as good vassals. The eventual victory over the Turks in 1565 has been described as marking,

> a new phase of the Spanish recovery, a recovery which was not achieved by accident and which was pursued diligently throughout the year 1565.

One could thus say that the Siege brought about a radical transformation to life in the island. For most people it marked the end of an old era. This break with the past manifested itself at all levels. Immediately after the Siege, increased migration to Sicily, coupled with the continual evacuation of the countryside by a peasantry attracted to city life, led to extensive rural depopulation. The widespread destruction of houses, fields, and livestock changed the villages physically. New buildings and churches in a different style were set up. Such a situation had far-reaching effects on Malta especially from the seventeenth century onwards. The lack of secular institutions at village level continued to apply until the twentieth century and induced J. Boissevain to describe the modern parish church as

> very much the symbol of a village, for it is the hub around which community life has revolved for centuries... as part of a parish it has a leader in its parish priest... the parish church... is usually located near the geographical centre of the village, which has grown up around it... The saint to whom the church is dedicated is the patron of the parish and symbol of the village...

The fact that Maltese peasants and artisans came to form the backbone of the Christian army during the Siege had the effect of transforming them completely. It seems that the shock of battle helped to create a collective solidarity through the activation of comradeship, team-work, and *esprit de corps* in a moment of crisis. Under these circumstances La Valette's position, as the hero of the Maltese, was further strengthened, so that by his death in 1568, the Grand Mastership overshadowed completely the role of the *Università*.

In spite of this, the ever-increasing supreme overlordship of the Grand Master did not pass uncontested. Confusions of jurisdiction, rivalries and government institutions abounded. The Grand Master had in fact successfully managed to tackle the *Università* of Mdina, but there was still the authority of the Bishop. Furthermore, the establishment of a separate Inquisition Tribunal in 1574, aggravated the situation. All three authorities – the Grand Master, the Bishop and the Inquisitor – looked to the Pope as their final font of authority. The Grand Master's actual power was more like an intricate mosaic of particular prerogatives, rights and powers, rather than a homogeneous, all-inclusive authority. The result was therefore a fusion of temporal and spiritual power.

In order to consolidate and extend their power, several Grand Masters had to appropriate parts of the old system of authority and risk facing furious resistance as they did so. In the act of consolidating their position further, successive Grand Masters did not sweep the stage clean, with the result that, older and outmoded institutions survived during their rule. The *Università* proved a weak institution and had already been neutralized by La Valette's time. But a similar attempt at encroaching on the powers of the Council of the Order caused a dramatic upheaval among the rank and file of the Hospitallers.

Matters came to a head during the reign of Grand Master La Cassière (1572-1582), who had attempted to impose his authority on the members of the Order by measures designed to improve the internal discipline and upgrade moral standards.

The publication of a ban on the presence of prostitutes in Valletta triggered off a storm of protest by members of the Order and serious riots followed. The Grand Master allowed a special meeting of the Council, from which he foolishly opted to absent himself. In his absence, the coalition of his enemies took the opportunity to replace him on the grounds of incompetence and senility. His place was filled by a Lieutenant, the knight Marthurino de Lescaut dit Romegas, Prior of Toulouse and a hero of the Siege of 1565. Although humiliated and put under arrest at Fort St Angelo, La Cassière prudently refused offers of assistance by various dignitaries of the Order. This he did in order to avoid bloodshed. Nonetheless, as head of a religious order, he appealed to Rome. Representations on behalf of both sides were made to the Holy See, leading to some nasty incidents in St Peter's square between rival delegations. By late September 1581, both the deposed Grand Master and Romegas had gone to plead their case in Rome. But while La Cassière was met with full honours and great pomp, Romegas was forced to ask pardon from the Grand Master, a humiliation that proved too much for the gallant Romegas who unexpectedly died the following November. Soon after, the rebellious knights were reprimanded by the Pope, but La Cassière too passed away on 21 December 1581.

The charges brought against the Grand Master in Rome indicate that it was his disposition to act without consultation that aroused most hostility, namely his very conception of political power. It was stated that 'he wanted to do things absolutely in his own way', and that 'in the end no one liked a command so absolute'.

The election of Grand Master Verdalle (1582-1595) restored harmony within the Order of St John, largely thanks to La Cassière's restraint and great gift of moderation in dealing with his antagonists during the coup. The Grand Mastership emerged strengthened from this traumatic experience and it managed to increase its prestige particularly after the conferment of the cardinalate on Verdalle in December 1587. Every Grand Master after Verdalle enjoyed the status equal in rank to that of cardinal. The state of Malta was to enter the seventeenth century with a more 'modern' executive, one vested with greater power and authority. From then on, the Grand Master could act not only as feudal overlord, but also as a Prince, along the lines of the increasingly absolute monarchies of sixteenth century Europe.

To some extent, the following century was a period of consolidation and organizing. Stable economic conditions and a general demographic increase are evidence of a growing affluent society. The role played by the Order's small but highly efficient navy, throughout the seventeenth century, is ample proof that the Maltese islands were able to exert considerable influence on the political affairs of the Mediterranean. The state of Malta, convulsed by a long string of wars against the Muslims, seemed slowly but surely to be settling down. By then the sovereignty of the King of Sicily over Malta was exercised in name only, recognized particularly as it facilitated the importation of duty-free grain from Sicily.

## Events Leading to the Siege of Malta

### Charles V and the Turkish Menace

Charles V was heir to four separate inheritances, one from each of his grandparents. From Ferdinand of Aragon he acquired Sicily, Naples, Sardinia and Aragon-Catalonia, to which he added Milan and Tunis in 1535. The legacy of Isabella the Catholic provided Castile, Granada and the West Indies to which Charles added Mexico (1519) and Peru (1543). Mary of Burgundy provided most of the Netherlands, Charles adding a number of provinces. Furthermore, on the death of his paternal grandfather Maximilian in 1519, Charles became heir to the Habsburg possessions.

The Spanish hold on strategic points on the North African coast was precarious enough surrounded as they were by Muslim inhabitants. Several bands of corsairs had emerged in the area, the most fearsome of which grew at Algiers. The Ottoman empire, which until then lacked the requisite organization and leadership structure to become a naval power, came to rely on the Barbary corsairs for these qualities. The alliance of the two was not only a logical step but also a practical solution. Thus when in 1534 Khayr al-Din, better known as Barbarossa, the Chieftain of the Barbary corsairs, accepted the suzerainty of the Sublime Porte, he was soon appointed Kapudan Pasha (Admiral). Soon after, it was possible for the Ottoman navy to become a major force in the Mediterranean. No sooner in command, the new admiral gave the Christian powers a foretaste of things to come when in a surprise attack he captured Tunis from the Spaniards.

Although Charles V took the initiative to recover Tunis in July 1535, building the nearby fortress of La Goulette, the offensive remained largely with the Muslim side. By the summer

Monument to Khayr al-Din, known as Barbarossa, in Istanbul, Turkey.

of 1537 a large Ottoman force overpowered Otranto in southern Italy and attacked the Venetian-held island of Corfu. A hastily arranged Christian alliance of Venetian and Imperial navies, with their usual allies including the Knights of St John, met an Ottoman fleet under Khayr al-Din off Prevesa in 1538. The battle of Prevesa proved a resounding debacle for the Christian navies, and although their actual losses were small, they retreated leaving the field clear for the Ottoman navy to navigate all over the Mediterranean.

The psychological effect of the Prevesa debacle was tremendous; indeed it marks the start of complete ascendancy by the Ottoman navy over the eastern Mediterranean – a position which was to remain unchallenged until the battle of Lepanto (1571). The intervening period between 1538 to 1571 represents a new phase in the struggle between the Ottoman east and the Spanish west with the latter completely on the defensive. The frontier of the giant conflict shifted to the central Mediterranean, that is, to Tripoli, La Goulette, Malta, Sicily and southern Italy, all held by Spain and its allies, the knights of St John.

A sequence of political events made matters easier for the Ottoman offensive. In October 1540 Venice concluded peace with the Sublime Porte in order to defend Venetian interests in the eastern Mediterranean. Meanwhile the French established a close understanding with the Ottomans that enabled the Ottoman fleet under Khayr al-Din to erupt into the western Mediterranean so as to operate jointly with the French against the Spaniards. The collaboration of the French rendered the European coasts of the western Mediterranean exceedingly vulnerable to the depredations of the Ottoman fleet and its corsair allies. Reggio Calabria, Nice, Elba and the Lipari islands were ransacked and burnt in the years 1543 and 1544. In these operations Torghud Reis, better known as Dragut, distinguished himself and on the death of Khayr al-Din in 1546, succeeded as Chieftain of the corsairs.

Torghud became the best known of Barbarossa's successors and was soon proclaimed Admiral of the Ottoman navy. The strategic plan Torghud had, aimed at dominating the central

Mediterranean and none of the enormous resources of the Ottoman empire were spared to achieve this main objective. Torghud's plan came near to succeeding and some of the component objectives were attained. Tripoli was liberated in 1551, Tunis and La Goulette finally freed in 1574; yet Malta and Sicily were to remain firmly in Christian hands denying ease of access to the western Mediterranean.

The Crisis of 1551

It is, at this point, vital to understand that the events were perfectly predictable and perhaps inevitable in the logic of historical circumstances. The Ottomans master-minded three major campaigns against the more exposed Christian positions in the central Mediterranean. These campaigns took place in 1551, 1560 and 1565 and the aim was to establish military hegemony over the central Mediterranean. Naturally Malta and the Order were the major objectives of the Ottoman offensive. In 1547 Torghud landed at Marsaxlokk and although the attack was driven off with only small losses to the Order and the Maltese, the skirmish was the forerunner of several similar attacks. In 1548 and 1550 there were landings in Gozo. But the attack of 1551 proved to be the worst.

The Order had some intimations of the impending attack. Thus when the galleys of the Order returned to Malta from Tripoli on 13 July 1551, they ferried women, children and invalids over to Sicily on express instructions of the Council issued a week before.

On that very same day an Ottoman armada of well over 100 vessels carrying at least 10,000 soldiers with numerous siege guns, appeared outside the port of Messina. The Admiral Sinan Pasha, flanked by Torghud and Sinan Pasha of Algiers, peremptorily demanded the immediate cessation of Mehedija – a small outpost on the north east coast of Tunisia captured by the Spaniards the year before. On the Viceroy's prompt refusal, the armada sailed to the marina of Augusta (midway between Catania and Syracuse) ransacking and burning its harbour installations.

By 18 July 1551, the armada appeared off Malta, entered, completely unhindered, the port of Marsamxett, and swiftly discharged its load of soldiers and siege-guns. Although there was a half-hearted attempt to lay siege on Birgu, the Ottoman generals soon turned their attention on Mdina where most of the Maltese peasants managed to retreat. The old town was not only crammed with refugees from the countryside, but it was also badly provisioned with grain supplies, ammunition and soldiers. The commander the knight Villegaignon tried to instil some spirit in his demoralized men and to appease the fears of the panic-striken peasants by bombarding the enemy-soldiers sacking the suburb. For a couple of days Sinan Pasha put up his headquarters in the Dominican friary allowing his soldiers to pillage and burn the deserted houses and churches. This explains why in the fifteenth century fresco-cycle in the crypt of St Agatha in Rabat, the painted figures have their eyes hacked out – a disfigurement prompted by the Muslim taboo on representing the human figure.

Within Mdina the helpless throng of people were swept by a wave of religious hysteria and a procession with the marble statue of St Agatha was held on the bastions of Mdina. It is not unlikely that the spectacle of such crowds on the walls of the old town might have inspired fear of a drawn-out siege operation among the Ottoman commanders – that being the last thing they wanted. On 20 July, a signal from St Paul's Bay announced that the fleet had been transferred there, upon which the Ottoman army promptly retreated in that direction.

The very next day a landing was made in Gozo and in no time the weak citadel of the island was invaded and bombarded. Torghud had come to know the Maltese islands intimately during his early corsairing years; it is said he had a special score to settle with the Gozitans after losing his brother in one of his corsair incursions on the islands. The Gozo citadel was in an even weaker position than Mdina, held by a tiny garrison and just one gunner, killed early in the assault. So desperate became the position that on 26 July, the governor, the knight

Aerial view of the Gozo citadel.

Galatian de Sese, asked for terms of surrender. Except for forty old and infirm inhabitants spared by the conquerors, as well as a number of intrepid individuals who scaled down the citadel walls by means of ropes, the entire population of Gozo was carried away into slavery – most of them never to return again. This greatest of Malta's calamities left the island of Gozo deserted and in later years had practically to be resettled anew by new-comers from Malta and Sicily.

This success just whetted the appetite of the Ottoman commanders who now set their eyes on a real prize, a far more memorable enterprise. On 2 August, the armada sailed for Tripoli where the governor the knight Gasper de Vailliers had at his disposal a garrison of thirty knights and over six hundred soldiers. The invaders attacked the fortress and on 8 August launched a massive offensive. By 13 August, Vailliers and his advisors decided to open negotiations knowing full well that there was no hope of a relieving force ever coming to their aid on time. The French ambassador d'Aramon, with his armada, was rendered powerless when the French governor decided to wheedle a good deal for the top echelons of the knights caught in Tripoli. It was a disgraceful affair that was later to cause an uproar. Tripoli capitulated on 14 August, after 40 years of Christian rule.

The Ottoman commanders were understandably jubilant. For them it was their greatest feat since the battle of Prevesa (1538). Torghud's gamble had fully paid off; by 1556 he had given up the admiralship of the Ottoman fleet and got installed as Beglerberg (Seigneur) of the splendid harbour-town of Algiers with the full blessing of Suleiman the Magnificent and his Diwan (council). For the Order of St John, it was morally the nadir of their existence so far. As for the Spanish and their Christian allies, their stand in the central Mediterranean, was still to face the worse of tests.

On 3 August 1551, the very next day after the Ottoman fleet had left Gozo, Grand Master d'Homedes issued an edict giving women, children *ed altre persone inutili* (and other persons who cannot take up arms) free passage to Syracuse.

A New Strategic Plan

The ignominy of these severe defeats and the acrimony of the controversy over the surrender of Tripoli did not demoralize the Order of St John. The military reverses seem to have had an invigorating effect. Instead the Council of the Order asked for and obtained the services of the engineer Pietro Prado who together with a commission of three knights, de Lastic, Bombast and Leone Strozzi, agreed to embark immediately upon the construction of two new forts – one on the very tip of Sceberras peninsula, sited in such a way as to deny entrance to both the Grand Harbour and Marsamxett, where Torghud had cheekily brought in the armada on 18 July 1551. The other fort was to be built on Isola point so as to provide the much-needed cover to the east flank of Fort St Angelo. The first came to be called St Elmo and the second St Michael. Even the defence works of Birgu and Mdina were at the same time improved under Prado's direction; particular attention was paid to the Birgu defences which the knights continued to elaborate on almost uninterruptedly right up to the Siege of 1565.

So acute were fears of renewed Ottoman attacks on Malta that the Order exerted itself to the utmost and had the new forts practically ready by March 1552. The island's labour force was duly regimented and yet it did not prove enough to meet the forced pace of the endeavour. As a result, Sicilian workmen had to be brought over to help out. When Grand Master Juan d'Homedes died in 1553, the main defences that were to meet the repeated onslaughts during the 1565 Siege were already standing – and this was less than twelve months after the humiliations suffered in the previous year.

During the brief reign of Grand Master de la Sengle, the *Isola* peninsula – at times known as Mount St Julian – began to be surrounded with walls, and a new town (Senglea or *L-Isla*) erected within it. It helped to ease congestion at Birgu and was to prove even more invaluable in providing shelter for refugees from the countryside during the siege. The Maltese were not prepared to suffer the same humiliation as that of 1551. The Sublime Porte had missed a moment of Christian tactical weakness in the central Mediterranean and a similar opportunity was never to recur again.

The Djerba Crisis – 1560

In the aftermath of the 1551 event, the overall situation of the Mediterranean continued to deteriorate. An anti-Genoese rebellion led by Sampiero de Bastelica threatened to disrupt vital Spanish communications in the western Mediterranean. The Ottoman fleet reappeared in the region in the summer of 1552, again co-ordinating operations with a French squadron, and defeating Gian Andrea Doria off the isle of Ponza, thus enabling the French and Sampiero's forces to expunge the Genoese from all their Corsican bases except Calvi.

In 1553 the Ottoman fleet reappeared with Torghud in command and managed to lay waste Pantelleria and Licata in southern Sicily before entering the western basin. In 1554 a Turkish force landed in Malta and attacked the village of Siġġiewi. In 1555 the Spanish foothold at Bourgie fell to the Algerian pirates who in 1559, managed to score an even greater success by capturing Oran, the Spanish stronghold in Morocco.

At this stage Philip II, who had just succeeded his father Charles V to the Spanish throne, was persuaded to attempt a counter-offensive in North Africa. The chosen objective, likely suggested by Grand Master Jean Parisot de la Valette, was intended to be Tripoli which needed a large scale naval effort.

Philip II had designated Juan de la Cerda, duke of Medina Celi and the current Viceroy of Sicily, to lead this offensive for which a squadron of ninety vessels (including forty-seven galleys) were assembled in the late summer of 1559 at Messina. It took until December to reach Malta and was forced to spend most of the winter in the island due to bad weather. The delays were so great that any element of surprise had evaporated. Even the decision to attack Tripoli must have been questioned. Although La Valette insisted on keeping to the original plans, the commanders decided to redirect the force against the island of Djerba. Only token resistance was offered by the Djerba islanders. Occupation was followed by the building of a fort.

News of the Spanish offensive had long been known to the Ottoman authorities who suspected Tripoli to be the objective. A strong Ottoman armada appeared off Gozo on 7 May 1560 where at least eighty-three vessels, mostly galleys, were counted. If the Order's chronicler Iacomo Bosio is to be believed, the Ottoman authorities learned details of the Djerba operations from a Gozitan padrone of a boat by the name of Mariano Santoro, son of a priest, who was later impaled by La Valette for his excessive zeal to reveal military secrets.

On 8 May, La Valette sent out a frigate to warn Medina Celi of the approach of the enemy. That same night a brigantine was despatched too, and a second frigate went out a day later with the same urgent message. Luckily the brigantine arrived at dawn of 10 May and after a brief council, Medina Celi ordered the galleys to re-embark as many men as possible and ply out off-shore.

The next morning the Ottoman fleet emerged over the horizon and immediately pounced on the Spanish fleet. During the battle that ensued the Spaniards lost twenty-eight galleys, and a number of smaller craft while several thousand men were trapped in the small fort on Djerba. Medina Celi, and the rest of the fleet, turned up in Malta and was soon safe in Sicily conducted by the galleys of the Order. By now the Ottoman commanders were practically convinced that they had attained their main strategic objective – that of dominating the central

Mediterranean. There remained only the tricky job of cleaning the Spaniards from La Goulette, and the Knights from Malta.

### 1560-1565: The Years of Tension

From 1560 Grand Master La Valette tensed every muscle to meet the Ottoman attack which he felt certain was about to be unleashed against Malta. Indeed the Ottoman armada returned to Malta and even landed parties of marauders in Gozo on 17 August of 1560. It then sailed off to Sicily, devastated Augusta and the coasts of Apulia and Abruzzi. From then on to 1565, Ottoman pressure on the central Mediterranean never eased. Life in Malta with all the tension occasioned by La Valette's feverish preparations, became increasingly difficult and perilous.

News of a rearming of the Ottoman fleet reached La Valette early in 1561. He was so sure that Malta was the target that he issued orders to evacuate all unfit people from the island while there was still time. La Valette reorganized the Maltese militia, appointing knights to take command of this local force on a parish level.

The severe defeat suffered at Djerba, without any doubt, persuaded the Spaniards to boost their naval power in the Mediterranean. Luckily the Ottomans had worries in the east and to cut expenses refrained from launching further attacks against the Christian west. Their corsair allies of the Barbary coast remained however active, particularly Torghud, who scored a big success when he managed to capture seven galleys of the Sicilian realm off the Lipari islands early in July 1561.

The Grand Master's main preoccupation was however the strategic need of building a fortress-city on mount Sceberras to counteract the vulnerability of Fort St Angelo and the defences of Birgu and Isola.

News of a new Turkish armada started to filter into the west as early as spring of 1563. By the winter of 1564-1565 there could be no further doubt that the Ottomans were determined to send an armada in the course of the coming spring. By the late autumn of 1564, La Valette knew for certain that an attack

Portrait of Grand Master
Jean Parisot de la Valette.
Oil on canvas by Antoine Favray.

on Malta was imminent. His agents in Constantinople and several Venetian merchants reported on the feverish activity in the shipyards and arsenals of the Sublime Porte. Immediately after a Sultan's council in October, preparations had begun for the spring campaign. It became known that the Ottoman armada was destined for Malta. Vessels were sent to Sicily at once in order to acquaint the Viceroy, Don Garcia de Toledo. The message was soon passed through Europe reaching the knights who were absent from Convent. By sailing boat or by weary and exhausted horsemen, the news was carried to the absentee brethren of the Order.

The Sultan assigned the command to his foremost general Mustaphà, and to Pialì, his son-in-law and Admiral of the Fleet. Both men were well known for their military exploits, and perhaps sensing the probability of friction between them, the Sultan recommended that, in their Council, they include Torghud

Reis. As matters turned out, Torghud arrived well after the Siege
had begun, consequently the only reconciling influence over
the two commanders was not present in the important initial
stages, and divisions between them were to work against them.

Meanwhile in Malta, the rhythm of preparations took a feverish pace particularly with regards to adequate provisions. There
were rumours concerning the possibility of abandoning Gozo
and Mdina, which were inadequately fortified and therefore
practically indefensible. In an unsigned letter of the time the
writer states that:

> ...As the key lies in the Bourg and Castle it is much better and safer to have
> one position well provided rather than two badly found and in manifest dan-
> ger. It is of great importance that the City should be defended if circumstances
> should permit... the women and the children, and all the persons who are use-
> less for war purposes, should be removed at once to a place of safety since this
> provision would be equally convenient whether the place is defended or aban-
> doned... the City should be placed in a state of defence with all speed, and,
> should additional men, artillery and ammunition arrive so that it could be de-
> fended... this would result not only in the preservation of your island but also
> be of great prejudice to the enemy. For if the enemy should attack the Bourg it
> would be of advantage to have a force in the City, and, conversely, if he should
> attack the City, to have one at the Bourg.

On 9 April the Viceroy of Sicily, Don Garcia de Toledo, sailed to
Malta with a fleet of twenty-seven galleys. La Valette may well
have hoped to receive reinforcements. Instead all he obtained
were promises of substantial reinforcements and troops some-
time in the future. At least Don Garcia was able to offer sound
advice: 'Restrict your Council of War to a bare minimum, and
let them all be well-tried veterans'. The Viceroy was well aware
that every man was needed to resist the enemy's main assault
so he advised La Valette against skirmishes and sorties and
went on to say: 'Above all, take care of your own person. The
death of the prince has too often been the cause of defeat'. The
Viceroy returned to Sicily with as many old and infirm Maltese
inhabitants as possible. The evacuation was still in progress
when news of the approaching Armada put a halt to further sea
movements.

## The Ottoman Siege of 1565

White Sails Covering the Horizon

The Ottoman armada arrived, in full sail, at sunset of Friday, 18 May 1565. In the memorable words of Iacomo Bosio:

> A little before sunrise, the Turkish armada could be distinctly viewed some fifteen or twenty miles from Malta beyond Marsaxlokk; it was in full sail, in such a manner that with its white and cotton canvas it was covering half the horizon towards the south.

The fleet consisted of 190 vessels including 138 galleys – without counting the contingents of corsairs from Algiers and Tripoli. According to Francesco Balbi di Correggio, a chronicler of the siege, the Ottoman fleet carried 28,000 fighting men, including an élite force of 6,300 Janissaries (one-third of the entire Janissary army) and 6,000 volunteers.

At once, the whole countryside was awake. The peasants gathered their animals and loaded their donkeys with provisions. John Taafe in his *History of the Order of St John of Jerusalem* (1852) attempts to reconstruct the scene of confusion that ensued. There was a sounding and beating to arms everywhere. A violent commotion ensued, some labouring with the utmost diligence in polishing and preparing their arms and horses and others loading their beasts of burden and themselves with their household stuff and children, to convey them to a place of security; some gathering together and heaping the crops, already cut in many parts of the country to transport it into the fortresses. The fleet first halted off Marsaxlokk but it withdrew after a short time, and it then moved on to Mġarr bay casting off its anchor. The countryfolk soon jumped to the conclusion that its first objective was Mdina. The result was a concerted move by the peasants to seek refuge in Birgu and Senglea which seemed to offer better security. The inhabitants of Mdina and those who sought shelter there were aghast at the terrible fate that seemed to stare them in the face. The Town Council despatched an envoy to La Valette – Luca d'Armenia. According to Bosio d'Armenia travelled to Birgu on the night of 18 May and presented the view of the Town Council, namely that if Mdina was to be abandoned, shelter for the people of Mdina should be provided in the town. If, on the other hand, the Grand Master felt that Mdina was to be held, then it ought to be garrisoned by a contingent of professional soldiers who were to be supplied with arms and ammunition.

The mental anguish of the fate of the old city can be felt from the intense melancholy evinced by a poem written by d'Armenia himself in the interval between the Ottoman fleet's appearance and La Valette's reply.

> *O unhappy Malta in the past fifteen centuries*
> *Christ's holy faith was always your light. Always constant in faith, grate-*
> *   ful and loyal*
> *to all kings and to your rulers.Grand Master La Valette, like the great Caesar,*
> *Jove permitting*
> *has kept you safe from the great fleet of the Orient.*
> *Now fury or anger or a heavenly sentence is against you,*
> *powerful of his fleet, he prepares a return*
> *in blood and fire.*
> *Alas we flee our native land, we leave the city by herself*
> *dispersing each one according to one's fate.*
> *Sad city, farewell, farewell for a second*
> *and third time, we are left*
> *to our tears and grief, no other city will be like you,*
> *farewell.*
>
> *Luca d'Armenia, a Maltese Patrician.*

La Valette assured d'Armenia that he was not contemplating the evacuation of Mdina and through the envoy urged the people of Mdina to do their duty as good vassals. The Grand Master promised to send to Mdina the militia regiments of Żejtun, Birkirkara, Qormi and Birmiftuħ (Gudja) – around 2,370 men – apart from the cavalry under the knight Giovanni Vagnon.

At the start of the siege, La Valette retained under his direct command some 6,100 combatants of which 3,000 were Maltese, 500 knights, 500 originally enrolled as galley soldiers, 200 Greek and Sicilian familiars of the Order, 200 Italian and 400 Spanish infantry soldiers. By sending so many men of the Maltese militia to Mdina La Valette was taking a great risk.

On the morning of Saturday 19 May, the Ottoman armada weighed anchor and set out back to Marsaxlokk. It entered in that harbour effected various landings, leading to a number of skirmishes in which a number of knights and soldiers lost their lives. La Valette thought it best to recall his men inside the fortified enclaves, while the Ottoman army set camp in the flat low-lying area of Marsa. In effect the Siege had began.

### The Attack on Fort St Elmo

Time was a crucial factor for the Turks and the Armada had almost four months at its disposal to overcome the knights of Malta, before returning to the Golden Horn as it habitually did for the winter. This explains why the Turks ignored Gozo and Mdina. The 1551 experience had taught them that they must seize St Angelo and Birgu if they were to take Malta since the Order would make a last ditch stand in fort St Angelo if the worse were to come to the worse. Only, now a new fort had sprung up on mount Sceberras. Piali and Mustaphà agreed to concentrate on St Elmo as their first target, a choice that was determined by naval considerations since the Turkish fleet was denied access to harbour at Marsamxett.

The first real encounter of the invasion took place on 21 May, after the main body of the invaders had been put ashore in the large southern harbour of Marsaxlokk. There had been skirmishes before, but La Valette's strategy demanded that he conserve his forces for the protracted siege that he had elected to fight.

After the Turks had reconnoitred Birgu and St Michael they met in council to decide which fort should be bombarded first. Mustaphà who was supported by the greater part of the council, was of the opinion that Mdina, Birgu and St Michael should be bombarded simultaneously. Mustaphà told Piali it was his opinion that he should go to Mdina with ten thousand men and ten guns to bombard it whilst he himself would bombard Birgu and St Michael. Had Mustaphà's plan been followed the island would have been lost. But Piali irritated by the superior following commanded by Mustaphà did not support the plan.

In view of the resolution of Pialì, the council decided to attack St Elmo so that after it was taken the fleet could enter Marsamxett. The council was mistaken when it hoped to overcome St Elmo in ten to twelve days, or even in less time. They concentrated their activity on the bombardment of St Elmo until 23 June.

Their second error was in their decision not to wait for Torghud Reis (Dragut), notwithstanding the fact that they had sent for him and promised to wait until his arrival. When Torghud arrived in Malta on 2 June with some 2,500 volunteers from Algiers and Tripoli, he was of the opinion that St Elmo could have been ignored but decided to collaborate and stationed his troops in St George's bay.

The Grand Master was pleased with the news. He knew only too well that whatever happened, the Ottomans could not take the island before the fall of both Birgu and Senglea. The Ottoman decision to attack St Elmo first only meant that he had gained time to improve and reinforce the defence of the two main fortresses.

The Grand Master ordered that all women, children, and old men who had taken shelter in the ditch of St Elmo should be sent to Birgu so that only some eight hundred fighting men were left in the fort. Meanwhile the Grand Master was aware that he had to strengthen the garrison at St Elmo. He sent the St Elmo garrison food supplies: biscuits, wine, cheese, lard, vegetables, oil, and vinegar while the animals brought over by the peasants served as fresh meat. He also sent gun powder, lead, rope, fireballs, and other ammunition required for defence as well as additional reinforcements. A Provençal knight, Pierre de Massuez Vercoyran, known as Colonel Mas had recently arrived from Messina with four hundred enlisted soldiers. Colonel Mas, together with half his men and another sixty-four knights volunteered to join the original garrison of St Elmo. Before they left, La Valette is said to have told Colonel Mas: 'St Elmo is the key to Malta!'

By Friday 25 May, the Turks began to transport their heavy artillery from the fleet to St Elmo. It was no light task, for the guns they had to carry were heavy and they had to cover a distance of nine miles on rough ground.

The next day the Turks started to dig their trenches on the Marsamxett side of the fort. Under the whip of the overseers, the slaves and labour battalions continued to quarry and dig, to drag up fascines and sacks of earth despite the continuous firing of the St Elmo garrison. It was a heavy task for the ground was all rock, but they worked so hard that they soon reached the counterscarp, and as they approached it from the south, they were safe as they could not be seen from St Elmo. Then they erected some triangular wooden frames, which they filled with earth, to serve as gabions for the guns with which they intended to demolish the defences of St Elmo on that side of the fort.

The Turks had raised a parapet and a battery on the promontory of Sceberras hill, one opposite the windmills of Fort St Michael and another one opposite St Angelo. When the Grand Master became aware that the Turks intended to fire on St Angelo and the galleys which plied between Birgu and St Michael, he ordered two galleys, the *San Gabriele* and the *Corona*, to be scuttled. The other two galleys, the *Capitana* and the *San Giovanni* were safe in the ditch of St Angelo.

In St Elmo the difficulty of the defenders' position was increased when it became evident that the Turks were constructing a very large platform for a huge gun on the highest point of the Sceberras hill, and it was thought that they intended to use it in a general bombardment of the fort. La Valette was quick to counteract and ordered the demolition of some small houses in St Angelo which stood opposite the platform. He ordered a battery to be mounted on the ground where the houses had stood, thinking that if he could have it ready before the Turks had completed the platform, he could hinder their men working at it. Notwithstanding the efforts of the Grand Master the Turks were ready before the besieged because the Turks had many more men. They also had many beasts of burden which the Maltese had left abandoned in the country. Moreover they had brought a large quantity of material for their batteries. This did not prevent the Grand Master from completing the work, and when it was ready he ordered four cannons to be mounted there. The latter enabled the besieged to do great harm to the Turks. Had the Christians had enough gunpowder at their disposal the Turks would have found it impossible to establish themselves so easily.

On the evening of 26 May, only two days after the bombardment of St Elmo had started, the commander of St Elmo, Luigi Broglia, sent a Spanish knight Juan de la Cerda to La Valette in St Angelo. Broglia's intention was to inform the Grand Master that owing to the weakness of the fort, St Elmo could only withstand the onslaught of the Turks if a continuous influx of reinforcements could be provided particularly since the defenders had already suffered heavy casualties.

Juan de la Cerda arrived at Birgu while La Valette was in full council surrounded by the dignitaries of the Order who were eager to hear news from St Elmo. When asked by the Grand Master to give his estimation of the position de la Cerda painted a depressing description of the garrison and the defences. He explained how the knights and soldiers were exhausted, the

Etching of the attack on Fort St Elmo during the Siege of Malta (1565), from Lucini's edition of Matteo Perez d'Aleccio published in 1631.

walls crumbling and how St Elmo was doomed to fall in a short time. After that, the Grand Master frequently sent boats to St Elmo in order to keep himself well informed of St Elmo's stand, and also to ascertain what was required for its defence.

Meanwhile in Birgu and St Michael, work went on day and night. Each captain fortified his post as was required. Some raised walls, others constructed parapets, terrepleins, shelters made of barrels filled with earth, or levelled ground on which to fight.

*The Arrival of Torghud Reis and the Fall of St Elmo's Ravelin.*

By Saturday 2 June, Torghud joined the fleet with thirteen galleys and two galeots, together with some thirty other vessels belonging to other corsairs. These ships brought some 2,500 volunteers from the Maghreb. The Turks rejoiced greatly at Torghud's arrival. Yet the corsair was greatly annoyed to find that the bombardment of St Elmo had already commenced, because his own plan coincided with that of Mustaphà, and had he been present this plan would have been carried out. Having found the attack on St Elmo already in progress, he made suggestions for its better execution based on his experience. He finally asserted:

> It is a thousand pities that the attack on St Elmo was ever begun. But, now that it has, it would be shameful to give it up.

As a master of siege warfare, Torghud knew that it was heavy fire from many points which would finally wear down St Elmo's defence. He pointed out that while the batteries on Sceberras hill were well sited, St Elmo was only being engaged from one direction – the landward side. He realized that the strength of Fort St Elmo lays in the fact that the Grand Master had been able to reinforce the garrison by sending boats over from St Angelo during the night. From now on St Elmo was to be pounded to pieces from every quarter. Finally Torghud insisted that the ravelin – the outer works of the fort – must be captured at all cost. The next day, the Turks managed to capture the ravelin.

On 5 June, the Turkish batteries against St Elmo were very active. Under Torghud's incentive they always tried to improve their fire and aimed in all directions both at the tall tower, which stood apart from the fort, and the fort itself. This was done in order to find out the weakest spots with the result that there was not a safe place in St Elmo.

It was on Sunday 10 June that the first great night attack of St Elmo took place. The previous night the Grand Master had sent more munitions to St Elmo and in addition to the usual supplies, he sent some missiles. All day long the Turks bombarded all parts of the fort until midday, when they made a reconnaissance in force which amounted to an assault. Both sides

Portrait of
Torghud Reis.
Oil on canvas at the
Maritime Museum of
Istanbul, Turkey.

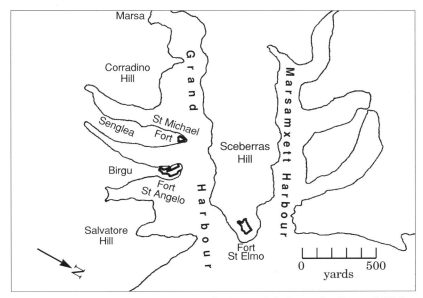

The Harbour area showing the forts and Sceberras hill, during the Siege of 1565.

fought hard for some time and many men were killed or wounded. The Turks retreated for a while and then recommenced their bombardment of St Elmo which continued well into the night. This time they made use of a large number of ladders. The advancing ranks of Janissaries threw ahead of them fire grenades similar to those thrown by the Christian defenders. It was a frightful scene. So great was the glare during this attack that Balbi di Correggio, watching from the walls of St Michael, could recall how:

> The darkness of the night was dispelled by the great quantity of fireworks which were hurled on both sides, so much so that we, who were at St Michael, could see St Elmo most clearly, and the gunners of St Angelo could see to lay their guns by the light of the enemy's fire.

The Turks attacked again at midday of the following day, Monday 11 June, and continued day and night with fury until Thursday 14 June, when the Aga of the Janissaries (the chief officer of the Janissary corps) was killed in the trenches below the fort. The defenders were continuously being assaulted and were given no rest. Furthermore the Turks sounded many false alarms so as to keep the besieged in suspense and allow them no rest for these continual alarms gave them no freedom to repair their defences but obliged them to stand to arms.

On the morning of Friday 15 June the Turks made an assault which lasted four hours after which they retired. Both sides suffered heavy losses in this attack. Another grand assault on all sides of the fort was held at dawn of the following day. It was accompanied with shouting and the beating of drums, and to the sound of Turkish musical instruments. For the besiegers it seemed as if the end of the world had come. On this occasion both sides experimented with all sorts of fire causing heavy losses on either side. On their part the Christians suffered more from their own fire than from fighting with the Turks. This was due to a wind blowing from the west. This wind drove the fire and smoke not only of the enemy but also of the beseiged into the eyes of the defenders. Needless to say this made matters worse. Furthermore the fireworks in the fort caught fire, and many men were burnt to death.

On the evening of 18 June, La Valette was only comforted by the news brought by a Lombard renegade, who told him that Torghud was dead, and that he had seen him prostrate with his brains protruding from his mouth, nostrils and ears. He added that if he lied, the Grand Master should order him to be hanged. The information was premature, for Torghud lingered on for several days but he never left his tent again. Since he was the one man able to coordinate all the military operations of the Turks – as his advice was observed by both Mustaphà and Pialì – his loss was a disaster for the Turks.

So long as the reinforcements were able to get through to and from St Angelo, the defenders were able to maintain the fort, but inevitably the Turks gained ground, and they finally encircled the entire fort. Ships from Pialì's fleet attacked from the sea, Turkish guns stood between St Elmo and the Grand Harbour, and from the high ground, sharpshooters fired into the defenders' ranks, so that it became difficult to move about behind the walls. It was only a matter of time before the last of the defenders' powder and shot was used. A message from Captain Miranda on the evening of 20 June stated that

> every new reinforcement sent into the fort is lost. It is cruelty, therefore, to send any more men to die here.

The fall of St Elmo was now imminent.

On Thursday, 21 June, the feast of Corpus Christi, the Turks bombarded from all sides without intermission and were confident that their next assault would succeed because relief had been cut off. Meanwhile the knights, who had never failed to honour the feast of Corpus Christi, went in solemn procession to the Conventual Church of St Lawrence.

On his part the Grand Master knew what the fate of St Elmo would be, and as he expected a similar attack nearer home, he pushed on with the work of the defences of Birgu and St Michael. This work was carried on feverishly by all, day and night.

The Turks spent the following day, Friday 22 June, bombarding the fort and sounding alarms indicating that they would assault the following day. At dawn the Turks advanced to make a general assault, and they attacked with great impetus and fury, making a lot of noise which was frightful to the defenders. When the Turks had retired there was not a single officer left in St Elmo. Five hundred Christians had been killed. The survivors numbered about a hundred. Most of them were wounded and had no munitions or hope of relief.

At sunrise, on Saturday 23 June, the eve of the feast of St John the Baptist, patron of the Order, the Turks began their last assault. Though with very little ammunition, the handful of defenders made a brave defence for four hours. The few Christians left, were all wounded and hemmed on all sides. Since they could no longer resist they retired to the church in the hope of making a conditional surrender but when they saw the Turks, ruthlessly, cutting off the heads of those who surrendered, they rushed to the square and fought to death. Mustaphà was in such a rage that he ordered his soldiers to take no prisoners. A few Maltese saved themselves by swimming to Birgu. Nine knights were saved because they were in the guard-house at the entrance to the ditch behind the church, and they surrendered to the Barbary corsairs. The corsairs hid them from the Janissaries and kept them for the ransom each one could pay. The rest were butchered at their posts. When the attack was over the Turks found that only sixty men had held up their advance.

There was probably little rejoicing in the ranks of the invaders, for the terrible price of St Elmo was visible to all, and the effects of the wells, poisoned on La Valette's orders, were already making themselves apparent. The base camp at Marsa was filled with sick and wounded. Mustaphà was wild with fury. He was heard to remark, 'What will the parent cost, when the child was won at such expense?' In revenge he ordered the mutilation of bodies of some of the slain and threw them into the harbour so that they would float up to the walls of St Angelo and Birgu. This was done to terrorize the Christians and to let them know what was in store for them. However at this sight, the besieged were rekindled with a great desire to avenge their dead comrades.

In order to impress upon his followers as well as the Turks that there was no question of honourable surrender, La Valette ordered all Turkish prisoners to be executed. These had their heads struck off and their bodies thrown into the sea. While Mustaphà's army was collecting the captured cannon in St Elmo, they were disturbed by the boom of cannon fired at them from St Angelo for the defenders were firing at them the heads of their Turkish prisoners.

The Battle for Birgu and Senglea

Mustaphà now decided to strike Senglea. After St Elmo it was the weakest point in the defences. Once St Michael and its suburb were overcome he could devote the entire strength of his army and Pialì's navy to win the siege. By the end of the first week of July, a large-scale attack had begun over St Michael. Some sixty to seventy guns, sited on Mount Sceberras, Gallows' Point, Mount Salvatore and the Corradino heights, opened a heavy cross fire on St Angelo, St Michael and the suburbs of

Birgu and Senglea. The heaviest fire fell on St Michael and Senglea. Seeing the palisades that had been set up, Mustaphà gave orders to break them down in advance of the attack. A party of specially-selected Turks had the task to remove this obstruction to their landing.

After the first assault on Fort St Michael the Turks came to believe that they had only to pound the defences to pieces and then use their superior numbers to gain victory in the breaches. After the Turks had failed their first attempt on seizing Fort St Michael, they held off for a fortnight having decided that the fortress required further bombardment. Pialì was now put in charge of the operations against Birgu. Mustaphà Pasha directed the attacks on Senglea and St Michael. One of the new dispositions of Mustaphà was the siting of a new large battery in Bighi. By late July the Turkish gunners started to bombard the fortified strongholds from all sides. The besieged were given no respite.

The assault came at dawn of 2 August. All Turkish batteries opened fire together. For the rest of the day, and even during the whole night, the enemy never desisted from bombarding their targets. It is said that the noise was so great that in Syracuse and Catania – the one seventy and the other one hundred miles from Malta – the inhabitants heard the sound like the distant rumble of thunder.

It was by far the heaviest bombardment that had yet taken place. Yet after six hours of continuous assault, the Christians held out. The Turks were driven back from the bastions of St Michael on five occasions. On several occasions the Turks had managed to establish themselves in a breach of the walls, only to be hurled down and counter-attacked. In the end Mustaphà reluctantly ordered his troops to withdraw. When the smoke cleared from the ramparts of Birgu and Senglea one could see that the banner of the Order was still standing. Since casualties were rather heavy Mustaphà decided to give the two fortresses another five days of continuous bombardment.

During those five days, men, women and children, worked side by side, repairing breaches, rebuilding barriers in the streets, preparing incendiaries and mending guns and weapons damaged by the bombardment. On 7 August, as the thunder of the guns ceased, the Turks attacked Birgu and Senglea simultaneously. This is how the contemporary Spanish volunteer-soldier and diarist of the Siege, Francisco Balbi di Correggio, describes the movement of troops for the assault:

> One hour before daylight, we saw that all the Turks on Cortin had commenced to move on St Michael's, and those from the fleet were being conveyed in boats from Marsamxett to Is-Salvatur... At daybreak a general assault was made on St Michael's as well as the Post of Castile, with so much shouting, beating of drums and blaring of trumpets that would have caused wonder had we not experienced it before... when they left their trenches to come to the assault we were already at our posts, the hoops alight, the pitch boiling: in fact all the materials for our defence were ready for action, and when they scaled the works they were received like men who were expected.

The assault on Birgu which at first sight had appeared to be successful, turned out to be a disaster. On this occasion La Valette was wounded in the leg, but he did not retire to rest.

Meanwhile the attack on St Michael was no less severe. Mustaphà's forces had stormed one part of the wall and managed to climb the ramparts. The Grand Master could not help but look in dismay at the Turkish advance. He was not in a position to send any of his men to their rescue. Senglea was about to fall and victory for Mustaphà seemed imminent. Suddenly the Turks heard the sound of retreat.

To the stupefaction of the Christians, after nine hours of hard combat, the Turks began to withdraw when they had thought that they could not resist any longer. For a moment the Grand Master and many of the men thought that a relief force had just arrived from Sicily. But in reality Mustaphà had just received news that a large Christian force had fallen upon the encampment in Marsa and everyone there had been massacred. Mustaphà assumed that the relief force from Sicily had managed to land and had attacked him in the rear. Alarmed at the prospect of losing his base and of having his lines of communications cut, he gave order to retreat.

The battle for the control of Malta continued its bloody course. It was now the third week of August and Malta was still holding strong. As each passing day brought the winter inevitably closer, the morale of the Turkish troops began to drop. The Turks realized that if Malta did not fall by mid-September the army would either have to withdraw or spend the winter in Malta. Mustaphà was aware that Birgu and Senglea could not hold on indefinitely due to the shortage of supplies. He was therefore in favour of spending the winter in Malta. But Pialì, who feared for the safety of the fleet, blocked the project. At the first hint of winter he would leave together with his fleet. The Turkish troops were disheartened and most were looking forward to going back to Constantinople.

Grand Master La Valette had his own preoccupations. Don Garcia de Toledo had failed to make good his promises to send assistance. In his last communication the Viceroy had declared that his troops would arrive in August. As the weeks slipped by the besieged began to fear that they would have to continue defending Malta on their own. The Christians were, on their part, in a desperate condition. Bodies of knights, men, women and children lay unburied in the streets. The wounded in the hospital would have been left to fend for themselves, had not the women of the fortified enclave taken over the duties of nurses to the sick and cooks to the garrison. The women even carried ammunition and helped repair the fortifications.

Meanwhile in Messina, more knights were arriving from their estates in central Europe. The heroic defence of Malta had aroused the admiration of all Europe. Even the Protestant Queen of England, Elizabeth I, was moved by the Siege. Meanwhile volunteers were daily arriving in Messina to join the Relief Force. On 25 August, Don Garcia with ten thousand men, embarked in twenty-eight vessels and galleys, weighed anchor and sailed for Linosa. The *Grande Soccorso* would soon reach the island.

## The *Grande Soccorso*

The fleet was unlucky enough to run into a Malta channel gale in which galley oars were shattered, sails and rigging torn away, and equipment lost. It was not until the evening of 6 September that Don Garcia's Relief Force reached the Gozo channel and came round to Mellieħa Bay. It seems that it escaped the notice of the Turkish navy so that the Relief Force could land at Għajn Tuffieħa. From there they marched under the command of Ascanio de la Corna up to Mdina. The minute his troops were ashore, Don Garcia intended to return to Messina, were a further reinforcement of 4,000 men was awaiting.

As Don Garcia's galleys left for Sicily, they made a short detour to the Harbour enclave as a sign to the defenders that relief was close at hand. Balbi recalls:

> Not long afterwards thirty five galleys went out of the Marsamxett harbour on their mizen sails and took up a position in front of the mouth of the harbour. We then knew that help was at hand and we all expected to be safe and free once more.

The joy of the garrison knew no bounds. These were the first Christian ships they had seen since the Siege had started. The Turks hastily destroyed their camps and re-embarked their troops. Many of their vessels had to be towed out of Marsamxett, and few of them were in good condition after having spent the summer moored in the scorching Maltese summer.

The Christians watched their departure with mounting elation. At the first safe moment the Spanish knight Romegas, was despatched with a small garrison to St Elmo to raise the flag of the Order over the battered ruins of the fort.

The garrison of St Elmo hastily reported to the Grand Master that the Turkish army was disembarking. The vessels were all leaving the harbour and sailing northwards, but the troops were assembling on the shore. A messenger was at once sent to Ascanio de la Corna to tell him that Mustaphà Pasha had changed his mind and was going to fight. Mustaphà hoped to march north, defeat the relief force and then, with this victory to his credit, rejoin Pialì's fleet stationed at St Paul's Bay.

La Valette knew only too well that Mustaphà's forces were larger than de la Corna's, and a Turkish victory in this battle could mean the loss of Malta. De la Corna stationed his troops at Naxxar and decided to wait on this vantage point rather than be lured to give battle in the plain.

As soon as they saw the enemy advancing, the Christians began to spur down from the ridge. The troops from Mdina and the Maltese Militia, who had been waiting on their ridge to the west, followed suit. While the main body of the Relief Force charged down to meet the enemy head on, the troops from Mdina attacked on the flank. It was a very one-sided engagement. The fresh troops under de la Corna met the disheartened Turks, and drove them back to their ships. St Paul's Bay was full of struggling soldiers and capsizing boats. Hundreds of Turks were killed in this last action and for days afterwards the rotting bodies of the victims were washed ashore in hundreds.

By the evening of 8 September, the Siege was over. The Turkish fleet put to sea with what remained of the Sultan's mighty expedition. The commanders must have trembled at the prospect of facing the wrath of the aging Suleiman after such a disaster. On his part the Viceroy, Don Garcia let them go even though many of his men would have liked to chase the enemy in the open waters.

The Memory of the Siege

The threat had passed. Outnumbered three to one, the defenders had accomplished what many had thought impossible. During the Siege nearly every family had lost at least one member who was either killed, or transported to Sicily, or at times enslaved as a direct result. The devastation of crops and livestock meant that most country people found themselves in dire straits.

The fortified walls of Birgu and Senglea, as well as the buildings inside them, had been the object of the heaviest bombardment known at the time. The villages, especially those of the populous south, particularly those nearest to Birgu, had been repeatedly pillaged, while the hamlets and their churches vandalized.

Thus among other things, the Siege wrought a traumatic break in the physical continuity of village life. Apart from the hardships that the villagers had to endure as refugees, their removal from the village brought in its wake a number of consequences. In the aftermath of this traumatic experience, social relationships assumed new state-wide dimensions.

It comes as no surprise that the siege experience exerted profound effects on the Maltese and its consequences remained imprinted in people's minds long after. A common danger had served to unite the Maltese with the Order against the forces of Islam. That is why, J. Cassar-Pullicino stresses that Maltese folk-memory does not, on the whole, show the Order in an unfriendly light.

History makes no mention of any Maltese hero having distinguished himself during the Siege, except for a few remarks by chroniclers like Balbi di Correggio. Like the ordinary soldiers of all times, their names were not considered important enough for official documents or histories. A few of them, like Luqa Briffa and Toni Bajada have survived in Maltese stories.

Honours were showered upon Grand Master La Valette by all the kingdoms of Europe. Philip II sent him a jewelled sword and poniard, the hilts of enamelled gold set with pearls and faceted diamonds. The defence of the island, the coastline of Malta, the figure and features of the Grand Master, all were celebrated in verse and histories. Incidents and details of the Siege were reproduced in many contemporary drawings, maps and broadsheets.

The period Malta spent under the Knights Hospitallers of St John is a theme constantly debated by the Maltese, focusing mostly on their incessant warfare against the Ottoman Turks and their Muslim allies in North Africa; at the centre of this interest, one invariably finds the crucial Siege of Malta of 1565. The siege experience had generated a sense of belonging and solidarity in the face of potent external enemies and dangers.

It is necessary to have a clear notion of what had occurred during this crucial moment of Maltese history. The Maltese militia force, for the most part centred on Mdina, the civilian population largely within the fortified Harbour enclave, together with the knights and foreign volunteers, found themselves all locked in one bond of solidarity against a common enemy – the Muslim Turkish invader.

But political propaganda by the state glorified the exploits of the Knights, and particularly La Valette, as the protagonists of the Siege. The aim clearly was to justify and strengthen the Order's strategic position on the island and to ensure that the loss of their own fellow people were interpreted as sacrifices to a higher cause. Patriotic resistance became identified with the religious motive and the struggle against the Muslim inevitably assumed the nature of a Holy War.

The ruling aristocratic élite – the Knights Hospitallers – employed state power to set up incorporating bureaucratic institutions under their tutelage; these even seeped down the social scale and reached out from the urban centre. Malta became a military base in the traditional confrontation with the Muslim Turks. The Hospitallers had two main aims: to invest heavily in the defence system of their base by grandiose fortifications, and at the same time to perpetuate the crusading tradition established in the Holy Land, mainly through the instrument of their action – the galley squadron – which enabled the Order to convey with speed a large troop of fighting-men, anywhere in the Mediterranean. Thus the mass of the population was tied to the state, a dependence aided by incessant warfare against a common enemy – the Muslim Infidel. Such a situation ended by producing a state culture with the active participation of the population.

A sense of solidarity became apparent among the various strata of the population who benefited from the internal stability as well as the external protection. P. Cassar, who examines the relationship between the Knights and the Maltese during the time of the Siege, argues that religion was the only ground on which both communities met on equal footing. By threatening this common faith, the Ottoman Turks strengthened the religious bond between the two entities. This situation enabled the people 'to forget their grievances... and to rally unhesitatingly around the Grand Master'.

This 'ideal' motive was still strong in the eighteenth century, when the theme of a crusade against the Muslim 'infidel', enemy of both the Maltese and the Order, could unite the people and the Order in a common aim. Agius De Soldanis gives a valuable insight of this feeling in one of the dialogues he prepared for the revised manuscript version of his *Della lingua punica* (1750), entitled *Nuova scuola della lingua punica*. It records the dialogue held between two ladies of rank, whom he describes as *puliti*, and refers to the fear of a Turkish invasion in 1760. One of the ladies is made to say:

> *Ma nistax nemmen li jiġu. Stambur wisq bghid minn Malta. Is-salib bezzieghi.*
> *Qatt ma ghamlu l-prova meta haduha maghna.*
> [I can't believe that they would come. Istanbul is too far away from Malta. The Cross scares
> them. They never won when they fought with us.]

But it is above all, the myths of war set down in epics, dramas, hymns or even children's games, coupled with contemporary accounts, which possess a long term power to shape ethnic consciousness across generations. Some age old traditions still linger on from this period. Thus for example, the celebration of carnival is ushered in by the *parata* on the morning of Carnival Saturday, an old sword-dance, which supposedly commemorates the Maltese victory over the Turks in 1565. It consists of companies of young men or boys dressed up as knights, clad in black robes with an eight pointed cross on the front, and as Turks, wearing gay coloured ribbons and tarboosh, and armed with wooden swords. Under the Order of St John, the *parata* was taken very seriously and the Maltese eagerly awaited its performance because the ruling norm was 'No *parata* no carnival'.

The deadly animosity of the Maltese for the Turks has likewise survived in children's rhymes and games. In 1948, J. Cassar-Pullicino found that in some Maltese villages children still sung the following rhyme:

| | |
|---|---|
| *Dghajsa galjotta* | A boat like a galliot |
| *Dghajsa xambekkin;* | A boat like a xebec; |
| *It-Torok kanalja* | The Turks are dogs |
| *L-Insara qaddisin.* | The Christians are saints. |

Another popular game called *Malta Tagħna* (lit. Our Malta) is practically a re-enactment of the siege. In this game, two groups of children represent the 'Turks' and the Maltese respectively. The Maltese play out the defensive role with the 'Turks' trying to dislodge them.

The survival of such games suggests that the prolonged persistence of anti-Muslim warfare mentality helped to mould a sufficient sense of common ethnicity to allow the Maltese community to absorb the effects of a political setback – that of no longer having any say in the running of the island. They came to identify with a type of dichotomy: the Turks meaning Muslims, in their majority North Africans; the Maltese meaning Christians and defenders of the faith. Therefore in order to maintain continuity, Maltese society learnt to qualify itself, and so preserve an enduring identity which memory and folk beliefs differentiated from the state. The siege came to represent a very crucial episode in a string of memories that contributed towards the creation of a Maltese identity, both in fact and in concept.

## The Transformation of Malta: 1566-1798

One could thus say that the Siege brought about a radical transformation in the life of the island. For most people it marked the end of an old era and the beginning of wider horizons. This break with the past manifested itself at all levels. Immediately after the Siege, increased migration to Sicily coupled with the continual evacuation of the countryside by a peasantry attracted to city life, led to extensive rural depopulation. The wide-spread destruction of houses, fields, livestock changed the villages physically. New buildings and churches in a different style were set up. The fact that Maltese peasants and artisans came to form the backbone of the Christian army during the Siege had the effect of transforming them completely. The shock of battle often helps to create a collective solidarity through the activation of comradeship, team-work and *esprit de corps* in a moment of crisis. But it was also in these circumstances that La Valette's position, as the hero of the Maltese, was further strengthened, so that by his death in 1568, the Grand Mastership overshadowed completely the role of the *Università*.

When in 1530 the Hospitaller Order of St John was granted the Maltese islands – originally together with Tripoli – as a fief on such generous terms that the Order turned the island into a sovereign state in all senses of the word, the 'isolation' of Malta melted into thin air. Various categories of foreigners, attracted by good work opportunities, settled in Malta, importing social, cultural and ideological components which were different from those originally predominating in the island. After 1565, with the surge of activities and the bustle engendered by the Order's presence, this traffic was directed primarily to Malta. A reversal of tendency occurred during the outbreaks of plague, especially those of 1593-1594 and that of 1676, and also during periods of grain shortages.

This business rush enabled the Order to maintain its vast construction programmes and to man its fleet. Indeed an element of adventure was offered by the *corso* (piratical activities against the Muslims) and the *caruane* (crusading sea-faring campaigns) of the Order's galleys that enjoyed a redoubtable reputation in spite of occasional reverses. Both activities involved a large number of men and attracted many non-Maltese to serve the Order at sea.

Slaves were obtained almost exclusively from corsairing activities. In 1590 slaves numbered over 3,000. Some were pressed into service on the galleys, but at least half of them were incorporated into the local economy. They were purchased by most sectors of the population, including the clergy and the relatively well-off. Male slaves appear to have been in the majority and they fetched higher prices than female slaves. Giacomo Cappello's *Descrittione di Malta – Anno 1716*, explains that there was a thriving slave market which in the writer's opinion was

> an extremely profitable business which was widely renowned throughout the Mediterranean.

Regulations to control the considerable liberty of the Muslim slaves were issued from time to time but this did not prevent the Muslim slaves to organize a conspiracy in 1749. The slaves were led by Mustaphà, the recently enslaved Pasha of Rhodes, who had been forcibly brought to Malta after a mutiny by Christian slaves on his galley in 1748. The plot was planned to take place on 29 June, feast of Saints Peter and Paul known as *L-Imnarja* (a Maltese traditional festival which is held at the Boschetto [lit. a small wood] in the vicinity of Mdina). On that day many inhabitants of Valletta, including the Grand Master and his retinue, left for Mdina where they spent the night. It was an ideal date to attempt an uprising, break into the armoury and assault the Valletta bastions. They then planned to wait for reinforcements from Tripoli. Nonetheless the plot was discovered by a Jewish neophyte, who learned about the matter during a quarrel in a Valletta coffee-shop and hastily reported the matter to the Grand Master. It is evident that the presence of a large number of slaves presented the Order with as many problems as they solved. However one may safely argue that slaves were an important asset of the labour market both in the domestic and public enterprise.

The Order came to represent a concentration of international capital which, coupled with an incredible reserve of human resource, made possible a vast programme of urbanization, successfully carried through, since the Order set foot on Malta in 1530. Even so, it is surprising to realize that all this could be achieved on an island with a population-base of merely 30,000 (1590). The creation of a new urban area around the Grand Harbour had effectively revolutionized the human geography of Malta and the life of its people. But the factor which dominated and conditioned Maltese life after the Ottoman Siege of 1565 was the emergence of Valletta as the administrative capital of the Maltese islands.

The new city upon the Sceberras heights was a long felt strategic need, perceived as early as 1524 by the Order's commissioners, and subsequently recommended by each successive engineering expert brought over by the Knights, starting with Antonio Ferramolino in 1541.

The project was scheduled to start almost immediately after the Siege and Pope Pius V loaned one of his top engineers, Francesco Laparelli, who reached Malta in late autumn 1565. Acute labour shortage caused delays in starting upon this ambitious project. The foundation stone was ceremoniously laid on 28 March 1566, with priority being given to the erection of fortifications. Nonetheless Maltese migrants in Sicily, as well as Sicilian workmen, refused to come to Malta until the summer of 1566 had advanced sufficiently to assure people that a return of the Turkish armada was no longer likely. Thereafter the work continued apace, providing Malta with a vast extension of its urbanization. By March 1571 the Order saw it safe enough to transfer its administration from Vittoriosa to Valletta.

By 1581, Valletta was reported to have two thousand houses. The writer Mgr. Visconti must have probably meant that two thousand plots had been allotted and were in various stages of construction. He adds too that the Grand Master's palace, the *auberges*, the Hospital and the Conventual Church, dedicated to St John the Baptist, were already erected. The city was also equipped with public ovens, two armouries to supply arms for 6,000 men as well as a court of justice. Mgr. Visconti states:

> in the city one can hardly find any more plots which are not occupied for construction, in such a manner that all the streets have already been laid straight, the streets outlined, and the rows of houses regulated.

The new system created a dual social structure which becomes sensible immediately after the Knights Hospitallers set foot on Malta and becomes even more apparent after the siege of 1565 and the building of Valletta. This duality did not only exist at the social level, but it also pervaded the mental and cognitive structures of Maltese society. Two different cultural blocs, strictly separated from each other, formed two opposing camps, namely, Mdina and its suburb of Rabat as the seat of the countryside; Birgu (Vittoriosa after 1565) – and later Valletta – the seat of the urbanized harbour area.

On the one side there were the typical classes of an agrarian society, consisting of landowners, a small class of notaries, clerks and priests, and a mass of peasants. These had their own 'cultural traditions', to which they were strongly attached. On the other side, there were the new town dwellers and other settlers, often in the direct employment with the Order, who were 'alien', lived in the city, were cosmopolitan in their orientation and had no 'ancient culture' of their own. Yet in the Harbour towns social distinctions prevailed, the fundamental difference based on economic affluence. The property owners and independent members of the town such as merchants, craftsmen, shopkeepers and professionals spurned those who were subservient or economically dependent by virtue of being labourers, apprentices and servants.

In reality, to speak of the Harbour area is to speak of a conglomeration of four towns: Valletta was the political and economic capital. In the upper part of the city, the Grand Master, the Grand Council and high society lived and exercised their authority. The common people lived mostly in the lower districts. On the south bank of the Grand Harbour, there were the 'Three Cities' of Vittoriosa (known as *Birgu* before 1565), Senglea (or *L-Isla*) and Cospicua (previously known as *Bormla*). Between them the four towns had a population of around 10,000, that is, approximately one-third of Malta's population in 1590. The 'Three Cities' eventually came to form part of the poorer district, together with lower Valletta with their narrow streets packed with foreigners, merchandise, sailors and Muslim slaves. The entire economy of Malta was ruled from Valletta. The political influence of the Harbour towns on the countryside, the power of the Grand Master, the highly concentrated nature of trade, all combined and contributed to the vast development of the Harbour area. This growth imposed an order on the area it dominated, and established a wealth of administrative and trading connections. As well as being a very busy area, handling practically all Malta's foreign trade, the Harbour zone had by the early seventeenth century developed into a cultural centre. Strictly speaking, the Harbour towns could not prosper without the protection of the Order of St John.

The creation of a new urban area around the Grand Harbour had effectively revolutionized the human geography of Malta and the life of its people. But the factor which dominated and conditioned Maltese life after 1565 was the emergence of Valletta as the administrative capital of the Maltese islands. Urban theory recognizes cities to be, not merely dense concentrations of people, but above all, concentrations of people doing different things, where the urban character derives more from that variety of activity than it does from sheer numbers.

The Harbour towns were multifunctional and together they performed roles that were essential for the whole society. Thus the more technically efficient the Harbour towns became, the more potentially dependent did the countryside become. The virtual monopoly of Valletta, over importation of all commodity items and exports including that of cotton (the major cash crop), enabled the new capital, from very early on, to control all the production and redistribution within the Maltese islands: it was, above all, the central sorting station. Whether bound inland or abroad, everything had to filter past the Valletta harbour.

One may compare the role played by the Order of St John to that pursued by the Teutonic knights in fourteenth century Prussia. In both instances, there existed close ties between an Order of celibate knights and the burghers whose relationship was not based on subordination of the latter to the former, but rather established in the recognition of common interests. Both Orders encouraged the inhabitants to participate in the running of the state. Furthermore Teutonic Prussia and Hospitaller Malta saw an increase in population not only in the new towns but throughout their territories. Besides individual village communities were combined to form larger, economically more efficient, agricultural units. Finally the respective position of Valletta and Danzig is worth considering. The two cities were essentially dominant ports, with complete control over a hinterland of peasants. Like Danzig, Valletta exploited and moulded the countryside to her own ends.

The Harbour town dwellers were well aware of the influence of the government upon their daily existence. The intensification of traffic and trade, the new technical possibilities of administration, and the economic development of the Harbour area, are part of the picture of the systematization of authority and the strengthening of the Grand Master's political role.

The heavy influx into the new urban areas of foreigners and people from the countryside, starting from the sixteenth century onwards, altered the ethnic character of the population of Malta. Even if the newcomers did not bring a distinctive culture of their own, as the case seems to be, their physical preponderance managed to transform the distinctiveness of the Maltese lifestyle. One may rebut that cultural patterns, exclusively attached to urban dwellers, may be grouped together and defined as urban culture. After all, what is essential here are not the internal contrasts of urban culture, but its different character from peasant mentality.

It was common for the early modern middle classes to mingle with the ordinary folk on account of the ever-growing demographic pressures. Thus, both wealthy Maltese and the Knights often occupied sumptuous buildings, while the workers were housed wherever space was available. The ground floor of these imposing edifices usually contained a stable, stores and a workshop with an entry from the street – sometimes the displays of the workshop extended into the street itself.

Very often a number of families had to share the same dwelling in order to be able to pay the rent. Matrimonial contracts indirectly refer to the shortage of space within the Harbour towns. Thus, whereas it was normal for peasants to own a normal house, maybe consisting of some rooms at ground floor level, it was common for poor artisans to live in one-room cellars, whose only means of light and air was the street door. The mezzanines, constructed above them, were likewise small and ill-ventilated. Except for the houses of the rich, tenements in the harbour area were economically planned. Such an atmosphere made family life difficult, and therefore most of the socialization processes took place not in the family, but at public levels. The working-class family enjoyed no privacy. Urban culture did not just renew or transform earlier cultural practices, but organized them according to fundamentally new principles based on a 'market economy'. Obviously city life, independently of class attachments, ethnic identity and other traditional prejudices, was looked upon by the indigenous population as 'alien', right from the very beginning of the Order's rule.

The immense surge of activities generated both by the foundation of Valletta and by the Order's presence, with its manifold interests, made the island one of the busiest centres of the Mediterranean. It served to create a heterogeneous atmosphere

Fountain on the line of the aqueduct at Floriana built by Grand Master Wignacourt (1601-1622), to supply Valletta with fresh water.

that impressed itself on the character of Valletta and helped to enrich the country especially in the more creative activities. The Order of St John had thus managed to establish a ruling system which seeped down the social scale and gave character to the Harbour area.

But these dominant cultural patterns failed to infiltrate the entire structure of peasant society. Philip Skippon, writing in 1664, could visibly distinguish city dwellers from villagers. He sums up the situation by noting that while most city dwellers spoke Italian well, the natives of the countryside spoke a kind of Arabic.

In practice, however, the 'Great Tradition' did influence village life as the latter went on to absorb and adopt elements of city life in such a way as to make it its own. The heterogeneous character of Valletta helped enrich the island-state, especially in the more creative activities. The architectural boom spilled from the new city into the surrounding countryside and by the early seventeenth century, the parish churches of larger villages like Birkirkara, as well as, smaller ones like Balzan, Lija, and Attard, could boast of a parish church that was built on a magnificent scale. After the disastrous earthquake of 1693, the old medieval town of Mdina itself was largely rebuilt in the baroque style. Thus one could say that urban culture possessed such a great integrating force that it quickly achieved hegemony. It was able to create a mode of behaviour and a way of life by and large acceptable to the whole society.

The cultural magnetism of the city was underlined by its political centrality. Functioning as an administrative capital, Valletta broadcasted the fashions and values of the Grand Master's court.

> Ideas and styles, fashions, manners, and habits, artists, architects, and Belgian tapestries, were all imported from 'trading Europe', and paid for by the Order's accumulating capital',

says V. Mallia-Milanes. The city attracted litigants to its Law Courts, and then passed on the government's proclamations to the rest of the island.

In the economic field, the city became the harbinger of modernity with markets which 'were as much a meeting place for social intercourse as they were for business transactions'. Artistic and cultural influence, information, and news were thus disseminated to the country. Valletta, like any other early modern European capital, was the power house of cultural exchange. Together with the other towns of the Harbour area, it monopolized the economic and administrative resources of the new state.

*Maltese Attitudes to the Order*

In his history of the Knight Hospitallers of St John, Bosio recalls how Grand Master L'Isle Adam was received at the doors of Mdina,

> by bearded Maltese, some of them extremely old, mounted on donkeys, armed with swords, daggers and azagaghi or axes, and dressed in bullet-resistant, arrow-proof lengths of quilted cotton.

The attire of the Maltese notables appeared sufficiently exotic to the sixteenth-century Italian chronicler to suggest that the islanders were somehow detached from the current sumptuous European styles. Indeed, the Hospitallers themselves were rather reluctantly received by the notables who considered the enfeoffment of the Maltese islands as an infringement of their own traditional rights and privileges. Perhaps, more worrying still might well have been the realization that the days in which they played out their dominating role over the island were numbered.

Nonetheless since the days of La Valette, there ran a general discontent among the Maltese population which was frequently spearheaded by the secular clergy. The unpublished *relazione*, attributed to Don Filippo Borg, is the earliest treatise to attempt an interesting interpretation of the people's attitude towards the government of the Order and the role of the Maltese élite during the first part of the seventeenth century. Borg – who became parish priest of Birkirkara in 1594, and on various occasions acted as Vicar-General for the Maltese diocese – wrote his *relazione* in the 1630s and has been described as our main source on the popular attitude of the Maltese as distinct from that of their ruling classes to the coming of the Order in 1530 and to its rule over them during subsequent years.

Borg relates how the Maltese were happy with the Order's rule during the first decades of the Knights' stay in Malta, but then goes on to add that the general situation began to degenerate, so that the Maltese of his time were both unhappy and resentful.

In 1677, Mgr. Negrone, Apostolic Visitor in Malta, observed that the Maltese, who 'lived amongst themselves in extreme disunity and divided into factions', found a point of consensus only in their common hostility 'to the Knights and the Religion'. As the eighteenth century wore on, popular disturbances became frequent 'beginning to assume a more articulate manifestation'; so much so that a contemporary chronicler, writing in 1776, was able to identify six different uprisings in the period between 1760 and 1775.

It has been argued that the rule of Grand Master Pinto de Fonseca (1741-1773) was marked by long periods of economic setbacks. Amongst other measures, he tried to control hunting by promulgating strict laws due to the allegedly severe shortage of game. Possibly these hunting laws were enforced to allow the Grand Master more space for pursuing his own passion for hunting. At the same time, the peasants continued to complain of the island's excessive wildlife, implying that they were being deprived of their main source of meat supply. The agitation, which had culminated during the last years of Pinto's rule, subsided with the news of the election of the new Grand Master, Ximenes de Texada (1773-1775).

Ximenes had frequently given assurances to the people that upon his election, he would reform the administration and reduce the cost of living. But Pinto's grandiose aspirations had depleted the treasury, and Ximenes found he was unable to fulfil his promises. As a remedy for food shortages, the new Grand Master introduced a new economic policy, which prohibited the hunting of wild rabbits for some time, in order to allow them to breed so as to ensure an abundance of cheap meat. This very measure irritated most of all the peasants who feared that their crops would be ravaged by the rodents. Worst of all, Ximenes triggered off an incident with the Bishop of Malta, Mgr. Pellerano (1770-1780), who had expressed alarm about the harm done to his estates by the great number of rabbits, while the Grand Master insisted that the clergy should abide by the law. The long standing friction between the Order of St John and the Bishop can best be judged by the fact that this relatively trivial dispute was only solved through the intervention of the Holy See.

A number of discontented priests, led by Don Gaetano Mannarino, grasped the opening afforded by the troubles that this squabble had generated to attempt an open insurrection. On 9 September 1775, whilst the Order's navy was away raiding Algiers, the rebels – comprising a small group of priests and a few supporting clerics and laymen – surprised the small garrison of Fort St Elmo and occupied the stronghold. They immediately lowered the Order's flag and hoisted the red and white colours of the Maltese *Università*, symbol of a free Maltese state. The conspirators had probably anticipated a popular uprising, which would have been difficult to suppress without the help of the navy, but in this they were disappointed. Consequently the rebellion was quickly suppressed and several ring leaders executed, or given long jail sentences.

The Dutchman Dierkens, who visited Malta a mere three years before the Rising of the Priests, offers us a brief but significant insight into the attitude of the Maltese towards the Knights. He noticed that there was 'a strong undercurrent of hostility among the Maltese towards members of the Order'. R. Cavaliero considers the rising of 1775 as symptomatic of the growing general discontent among practically all sectors of Maltese society, particularly directed against the autocratic rule of the Grand Master. The atmosphere had become so tense, that at one point the Knights did not dare move out of Valletta, while peasants on errands in the city dreaded the idea of having to spend a night there. This situation is confirmed by Dierkens who comments that

> the people are so irritated and so unhappy about the knights' proud behaviour that between themselves they [would] shout 'Watch out – a knight', [just] like Christians in Turkey [would] cry out 'Watch out – a Turk'. ...it is very obvious, that in case of attack, the knights will be the only ones to defend the city.

Matters got worse during the final years of the Order's rule, so that in 1796 the Venetian representative in Malta, Antonio Miari, feared the imminent outbreak of a serious revolution as he was quick to report to his accredited authorities. Miari's fears were not without basis, for in January 1797, a new plot was discovered and the ring leaders were either condemned to death or exiled. Amongst the plotters was M.A. Vassalli, the young intellectual with strong nationalist, pro-French, and revolutionary feelings, and a severe critic of the Order's government. Vassalli, who had just published his Maltese/Italian/Latin dictionary entitled *Ktyb yl klym* the previous year, was condemned to death although the sentence was commuted to life imprisonment.

On their part, the French had long been nurturing hopes of occupying the island. The opportunity presented itself on 9 June 1798. On that fateful day, General Napoleon Bonaparte stopped off Malta, on his way to Egypt, and demanded entry into the Grand Harbour to enable his ships to take water. When the request was refused, French troops were put ashore. Resistance was so weak that by 11 June, Grand Master von Hompesch (1797-1798) asked for an armistice. The terms offered by Napoleon in the capitulation led to the expulsion of the Order from Malta, so that the island became a possession of the French republic.

*The Order's Foreign Policy and the Powers of the Central Mediterranean: 1530-1798*

The definite intention manifested by the Order after 1565 to entrench itself on the island, served to change Malta into a minor Mediterranean power. But the general political situation of the Mediterranean saw several dramatic events before a kind of equilibrium was established in the 1580s. Its political role further increased in importance during the course of the seventeenth century when the peculiar development of Mediterranean politics permitted the Order to string repeatedly the Sublime Porte without the latter being able to react suitably, although all this was to follow after 1581 when it had become clear to everyone that both the Ottoman and the Spanish empires had somehow lost their interest in the Mediterranean region.

In the new political map of the Mediterranean, the smaller powers thus came to play a more meaningful and significant role in the affairs of the region. This development took place in the vacuum left by the gradual decay of Ottoman authority and the near disappearance of Spanish interest in the Mediterranean. It was destined to last almost a century, when greater French involvement inevitably attracted British competition. When the British fleet occupied Gibraltar in 1704, a big naval power was again present in the Mediterranean, and it was the turn of the smaller powers to fade.

But the intervening century gave the lesser states a chance and a breathing space which they quickly exploited. Among them the Knights of Malta were to play a political role far above the geographical limitations of their base, using their small and disciplined navy as an effective instrument. As the Order dug itself deeper in Malta, it developed with increasing energy and zest its dreaded fleet. In the deployment of its galley-fleet the Order was following a logical anti-Ottoman policy that the events of the seventeenth century were largely to justify. As other lesser states came round to the same point of view, the Order was able to increase its prestige, making its weight felt by hitting its giant foe where it hurt most – in its trading interest. It proved so effective that by about 1670, the Sublime Porte was wondering and asking 'Is France as powerful as Malta?'

However odd that might seem to us, the Ottoman dignitaries had every reason to express surprise; they were reacting from a series of catastrophic shocks culminating in the War of Candia

(1645-1669). How can one measure the relative weight exerted on Mediterranean affairs by the Order during the late sixteenth and seventeenth centuries? If one is to judge by the naval effort that the minor states of the region were able to mount, it would appear that the Order compares favourably with such powers as the Papal States, the Duchy of Tuscany, the Republic of Genoa and the Kingdoms of both Naples and Sicily. Thus during the War of Candia the Order participated in most annual campaigns with six or seven galleys. The Papal States never exceeded five galleys, the Grand Duchy of Tuscany five, Naples at times contributed five galleys but most times only four, while Sicily fitted and sent solely four galleys in 1667.

Thus if we are to apply the above criteria, then it is legitimate to conclude that at least on the plane of action the Order was not exactly a negligible power in the Mediterranean milieu of the seventeenth century. One can even understand the healthy respect the Sublime Porte entertained for the Order right to the end. While the Order was not able to bring large forces into play, it more than compensated by the reckless indefatigability of its effort, making its Muslim enemies treat it with circumspection, while her ambiguous allies, like the Venetians, were forced to court its assistance.

By the late seventeenth century the Ottoman Turks ceased to be a real threat in the Mediterranean. The Treaty of Karlowitz signed on 21 February, 1699 brought to an end the general hostilities between Christians and Muslims. One can claim that the Treaty of Karlowitz concluded a phase of Mediterranean history – which had commenced in the 1580s – when the lesser powers had a military and political say on their own affairs. In the seventeenth century Spain was challenged by France but the effective changes were dynastic not territorial. The outbreak of the Spanish War of Succession (1701-1713) marked a new era during which all the major powers entrenched themselves permanently in the Mediterranean so that all the small powers lost the effectiveness of their autonomy.

The actual provisions of the Treaty of Karlowitz proved disastrous for the Ottoman empire, who had to surrender Morea and parts of the Dalmatian coast to the Venetians. Both the Austrians and the newly arisen Russia of Peter the Great were also able to make considerable in-roads into the European part of the Ottoman empire, which, for a time, appeared on the brink of dissolution.

Yet history was about to prove more considerate to Ottoman imperial existence, for the rivalry of the big powers, now firmly entrenched in the Mediterranean scene, ensured that either one of the big rivals – France or Britain – would exercise its whole-hearted influence to prevent precisely that dissolution from taking place.

Almost immediately, the expansion of the Habsburg empire into the Balkans aroused French envy. Thus after the next round of wars, the Sublime Porte was able to recoup most of its losses at the Peace of Passarowitz (1718), most of all at the expense of Venice who lost the majority of its 1699 gains. The cutting down in size of the Venetian republic was symptomatic of the new age dominated by the big powers. The seventeenth century interregnum of the lesser states simply melted away, supplanted by a new reality in which the super powers of the time – France, Britain, Austria and Russia – in order to extend their influence, played on the chessboard of Europe that now came to incorporate the Mediterranean region too. The lesser states lost their faculty of initiative and, like the government of the Order on tiny Malta, were reduced to client-states or emasculated as neutrals by the Treaty of Utrecht (1713).

The French

The French were drawn by Cardinal Mazarin's designs into a more active Mediterranean policy, starting with the intervention of 1664 against Gigeri and followed in 1668 by their participation in the War of Candia. During the revolution of Messina (1674) the Sicilian rebels refused entrance to Spanish troops and sought help from France which was then at war with Spain. Well aware of the strategic importance of Sicily, Louis XIV sent Admiral Duquesne to intervene by defeating a combined Spanish-Dutch fleet under the brilliant Ruyter. Another attack on

Algiers itself followed in 1682-1683. Behind this accretion of interest in Mediterranean affairs there were also plans for substantial French expansion in the region propounded by the philosopher Leibnitz who, 125 years ahead of Bonaparte, instigated Louis XIV to occupy Egypt.

The British

The Order's presence in Malta, in a way, appeared to secure a safe base for the French if the need for it was ever to be felt – as Bonaparte recalled in his own good time. But no sooner did French interest in the Mediterranean become clear, than the British took steps to counteract it. In 1620 Captain Mansell sailed the British navy into the Mediterranean to settle scores with the pirates in Algiers. Cromwell's navy under Blake entered the Mediterranean repeatedly, first in 1650 in pursuit of Prince Rupert and the Dutch, and again in 1652, 1653 and 1654. On the latter occasion Blake operated against the French fleet, under the Duke of Guise, who had designs on Naples. In 1655 Blake entered the Mediterranean to chastise the Algerian corsairs. Blake burned nine galleys at Porto Farina (near Tunis) bombarded Tunis and coerced the Bey of Algiers. The British navy returned once more to the Mediterranean to undertake action against Spain in 1656-1658, while in 1694 Admiral Russell conducted another campaign against the French. From 1662 to 1683 the British held Tangier thus guarding the entrance to the Mediterranean. This was the beginning of British naval intervention in the Mediterranean which culminated in the capture and retention of the rock of Gibraltar – whose strategic importance was earlier discovered by Blake – by Admiral Rooke in 1704. This event gave the British a solid footing in the Mediterranean, presaging the course of events to come, and encompassing the destiny of Malta as well.

The Russians

At this juncture too Russian interest in the Mediterranean was awakened, and this also impinged on Maltese events. In July 1696, Peter the Great, Czar of all the Russias, had occupied the town of Azov on the Black Sea from the Tartar tributaries of the Ottoman empire. He then proceeded to build a naval base at Taganrog. Whether to ask technical advice from his new arsenal, or as a kind of sounding the long-term possibility of an alliance against the common enmity against the Ottoman Turks, the Czar sent a delegation to Malta headed by his cousin Michael Boris Petrovitch Svemevetieff, Lieutenant of Wiatska, who was ceremoniously received by Grand Master Perellos y Roccaful in May 1698 and to whom was conferred the Cross of Honour.

But Russia's Mediterranean hopes received a temporary setback. The energetic Czar's designs were baulked after his debacle at Pruth in 1711, forcing him to come to terms with the Sublime Porte, which meant the handing back of Azov. Still the experience proved a useful one for the Russians: they discovered an easy way to reach the Mediterranean, a policy which Catherine II (the Great) and most of her successors were to pursue with determination.

The Order's Last Days

Thus by the early eighteenth century, the big powers had already installed themselves in the Mediterranean, or were well on the way to reach its shores. The era of the autonomous lesser states had thus fizzled into nothing. On its part the Order of St John continued to keep the North African corsairs in check. However the Order's function gradually became less important in the eyes of the western European powers. The Order's role gradually became outmoded and it became exceedingly difficult to develop new functions or to maintain their position in relation to other European powers.

The Order was highly dependent upon outside agencies. It had to worry about the reaction of the Vatican to its actions, France was a protector, who provided the largest contingent of knights, and had to be respected. Relations with Spain could not be flaunted since it controlled Sicily on which Malta depended for its food supplies. However the Order's fate depended primarily on France which was the Order's greatest source of revenue. The financial problems of the eighteenth century received a great blow during the French revolution when the Order – an aristocratic and religious body – received less and less sympathetic hearing. By 1792 the Order ceased to be an economically viable organization. Yet the magnificent system of fortifications built by the Knights and its geographical position in the central Mediterranean induced the major European powers to take an interest in Malta.

The French soon realized that if they wished to retain a hold on Malta their only option was to conquer it from the Knights. Many French knights were in league with France when, on 9 June 1798, Napoleon on his way to Egypt stopped at Malta. The following day French troops were put ashore. As resistance crumbled Grand Master von Hompesch asked for an armistice on 11 June and then sent representatives to discuss the capitulation of the Order. The terms offered by Napoleon were harsh: the Order would give up the islands and all its property therein; the Grand Master was given the promise of a pension; the French knights would receive pensions and be allowed to remain in Malta or return to France; members of the Order were to retain their private property in Malta; and the Maltese were promised their freedom of religious practice and other privileges.

Within a few days the Grand Master and his followers had been bundled out of Malta. The party was allowed to take a few movable possessions including the relic of St John the Baptist's arm and the icon of Our Lady of Philerimos. The Order found temporary shelter under Czar Paul I of Russia who was later proclaimed Grand Master by a group of knights. The Order, greatly altered in form and function exists to this day, maintaining a headquarters in Rome, together with hospitals and representatives in many parts of the world.

# 4

## The Emergence of the National Question: 1798-1880

*The French 'Week-End' and the Advent of the British*

The French had long been nurturing their intention of occupying the island. The opportunity presented itself on 9 June, 1798. On that fateful day, General Napoleon Bonaparte stopped at Malta, on his way to Egypt, and demanded entry into the Grand Harbour to enable his ships to take on water. When the request was refused, French troops were put ashore. Resistance was so weak that by 11 June, Grand Master von Hompesch (1797-1798) asked for an armistice. The terms offered by Napoleon in the capitulation led to the expulsion of the Order from Malta and the island became a possession of the French republic. The surrender of the Order of St John to France on 12 June 1798 brought to an end a system and method of government which had lasted for 268 years. Napoleon spent only six days in Malta but during his short stay he dictated a large number of instructions to transform the running of the government of Malta and bring it in line with French republican ideals.

Yet, less than three months later, the Maltese rose against French republican rule. The reasons for the very short period of French effective rule of the island are usually attributed to the lack of a sound financial basis for the administration. The financial situation of the French was such that it necessitated looting from the conquered land. A large part of the Order's wealth was removed to sustain French armies elsewhere. The Maltese administration, which was placed under the leadership of General Vaubois, was short of funds and had to resort to expedients which kindled unrest. Among other things, the French refused to pay the debts of the Order; new taxes were introduced; the payment of pensions to civil servants was stopped; and leases on government land were altered to suit the administration; the French invasion also disrupted trade; Maltese soldiers were sent to fight the French campaign in Egypt; and new laws to restrict the influence of the Church were enforced. Roderick Cavaliero sums up the situation thus:

> the grievances of the Maltese were many... But it was the cynical spoliation of
> the Churches that supplied the naked flame to the touch paper passions of a
> devout and Catholic people.

The depredation of their churches embittered the Maltese further against French rule and the continued spoliation of churches served to unite the Maltese as no other issue could. Rumours of the French disaster at Aboukir Bay towards the end of August, coupled with a decision by the French to strip the ecclesiastical establishments of Mdina, served to further kindle Maltese re-

Napoleon Bonaparte disembarking from his flagship *L'Orient* at the Valletta Wharf on 12 June 1798.

sentment. On 2nd September, the Maltese of the old town and the surrounding countryside, rioted and massacred the French garrison. The latter were soon chased out of every town and village in Malta so that by 4 September they were confined to the Harbour area. A military organization emerged very quickly under the leadership of Canon Francesco Saverio Caruana, Notary Emmanuele Vitale, and the businessman Vincenzo Borg.

Thus, in September 1798, the Maltese rediscovered their unity in a popular uprising against the French. Courageous and successful against militarily superior odds, they had for the first time an inkling of what nationhood could entail. The Church was the only influential organization in Malta, and it was the ill-advised direct assault against ecclesiastical property that had stirred the 'natives' against French rule. The Maltese transformed the old *Università* into a National Assembly and, realizing that by themselves it would be impossible to oust the French from their fortified position, immediately sent out an emissary, Luigi Briffa, to seek help from King Ferdinand IV of the Two Sicilies, nominally still the suzerain of the Maltese islands. The King of Sicily was in fact recognized as lawful sovereign of the Maltese islands, thanks to the old Spanish connection, as stipulated in the deed of fief granted by the Habsburg Emperor Charles V in 1530. Luigi Briffa sailed to Naples and hailed his Sicilian Majesty as the 'father' of the Maltese and Sicily as their 'ancient mother and provider'. Briffa explained that the Maltese wanted the direct intervention of the King of the Two Sicilies to help them free themselves from the French whom he described as enemies of the Catholic Church and of public peace.

Meanwhile on 15 December 1798 General Vaubois, whom Napoleon had left in command at Valletta, evacuated the four fortified cities still under French control, throwing out all Maltese residents who could not support themselves. These had until then depended for provisions on the limited food supplies available to the beleaguered French behind the bastions. The directive added to the insurgents' ranks the famished urban lower classes, and since no practical assistance was forthcoming from the King in Naples the Maltese Assembly, representing now all the towns and villages, petitioned His Sicilian Majesty to allow it to seek the intervention of the British fleet since the choice before Malta was 'either to die of starvation or to surrender arms'.

King Ferdinand intervened with Lord Nelson, Commander of the British fleet, then using Sicily as its base. The improving fortunes of the British fleet in the Mediterranean enabled Nelson to despatch a Portuguese squadron to Malta, and within a short time a small detachment of British vessels under Captain Alexander Ball arrived in Malta. By February 1799 the increasingly desperate insurgents even asked that Malta should be run by the English captain who had become acquainted with the woes of the Maltese. Shortly afterwards the Neapolitan Minister of War conceded to this request. Captain Ball was thus able to manoeuvre himself into overall leadership of the Maltese insurgents.

Following a British naval blockade, and with all food-supplies completely depleted, the French position became very difficult. In July 1800 Vaubois sent word to Paris of their imminent surrender unless aid was soon forthcoming. On 4 September of that year, Vaubois, after consulting his senior officers in a Council of War, opened negotiations for capitulation with Major-General Pigot. To draft the terms there appeared General Vaubois and Admiral Villeneuve for France, and Major-General Graham and Commodore Martin for Great Britain.

In his eagerness to finalize matters Pigot completely ignored Captain Ball – as the representative of His Sicilian Majesty – not to mention the Maltese, who had suffered untold misery for two interminable years of fighting during which thousands of Maltese had lost their lives. The Capitulation was signed on the 5 September 1800 by Vaubois and Villeneuve as representatives of the French government and Pigot and Martin for the British. The terms allowed the French to be conveyed to France on British vessels as prisoners of war with full military honours even though they had to leave their arms behind them in Malta.

Meanwhile it was not at all clear whether Britain intended to keep Malta. Neither was it clear what price was placed upon it in the wider context of the ongoing Napoleonic Wars. The Maltese Congress was not at all pleased when it got wind of the prospect that, in the interests of a European peace, Malta could be returned to the Order of St John. At first the Maltese representatives simply requested that in such an event all fortifications should remain firmly under British control. However as the prospect of Malta being returned to the Order of St John seemed more probable the Maltese petitioned to His Britannic Majesty questioning his right to dispense of Malta as if he were the rightful ruler.

On 18 May 1802, Article 10 of the Treaty of Amiens proclaimed that Malta was to be returned to the Order of St John. However the Article, published as a proclamation in Malta by the British Civil Commissioner Charles Cameron, further stated that Malta would be an independent state, but under the guarantee of Great Britain, France, Austria, Spain, Russia, and Prussia, and as such it would be obliged to observe neutrality. There were also plans to develop a Maltese Langue. Plans were also made to set up local armed forces half of which had to consist of Maltese troops. Moreover, a Sicilian garrison was also envisaged.

Nonetheless the Maltese leaders were not pleased with such an arrangement. In a remonstrance to Lord Hobart in London dated 1 March 1802, a delegation of six Maltese personalities demanded that Malta and Gozo should remain independent under the mutual guarantee of Great Britain and France on the grounds that they were not conquered territory. The Maltese delegation offered two options: they suggested that Malta be returned under the sovreignity of the Kingdom of the Two Sicilies, as stipulated in the Charter of Charles V in 1530; or granted independence under the protection of Great Britain or the great powers.

Shortly after the return of the Maltese delegation from London in June 1802 the *Dichiarazione dei Diritti degli abitanti di Malta e Gozo* (Declaration of the Rights of the inhabitants of Malta and Gozo) was drawn up. This declaration of rights was, without any doubt, influenced by both its American and French precedents. The declaration clearly presumed that the King of Britain would reign, not rule, over the Maltese. It also asserted that freedom rested on the rule of law. The Maltese were evidently powerless and it was

> to English emissaries and lawyers [like William Elton and John Richards] that the Maltese [were] obliged to have recourse in order to seek to represent their case… in London… Their requests [were] almost always the same or very similar in one petition after another

remarks Henry Frendo. Frendo also comments on the instructions sent to Richards in a document of 25 February 1806 in which Alexander Ball's rule is described as a form of

> 'unlimited despotism', a situation in which 'nobody dared speak his mind freely, or send to England signed petitions'.

Furthermore the instructions stated that it was necessary to have the means of protesting against the government without fear of victimization, that the judgements given by the courts be not influenced or controlled by the governor, and that the governor would not have the right to remove judges whenever he liked. Torture should be abolished. No person, especially employees, should be forced to sign documents under threat of imprisonment or dismissal. There should be means of ensuring that the mail be not tampered with by the regime. Last but not least, no Maltese or Englishmen should be exiled from Malta, least of all to the Barbary states.

Nothing came out of the Treaty of Amiens due to the changing international conditions. The Napoleonic Wars were resumed and the British continued to run the administration of Malta. However the manner in which this was carried out went contrary to the aspirations and expectations of the Maltese. The Maltese expected His Britannic Majesty to act as protector rather than as sovereign of Malta hence the Maltese continued to insist on the retention of their independence since the Maltese islands had been delivered from the French but not conquered.

Clearly the Maltese had no illusions about the ready application of British liberty to subject peoples of the Empire. Alexander Ball, Malta's saviour from French despotism and 'true friend of the Maltese' was himself a worse despot. Ball died in October

1809 and a few months later the Maltese sent an Appeal to London via Richards in which they complained about the imposition of a system of government without their consensus. Another petition of 10 July 1811, addressed directly to the British sovereign, so irritated the new Civil Commissioner Sir Hildebrand Oakes (1810-1813) that it induced him to issue an insulting proclamation and sack the leading Maltese representatives (who had signed the petition) from their government positions. These gentlemen included Sir Paolo Parisio, who after hosting Bonaparte at his house in Valletta, sided with the Maltese insurgents and even lodged a British regiment in the grounds of his residence at Naxxar. Another Maltese petitioner was Vincenzo Borg known as 'Brared'. It was he who had organized the insurgents of Birkirkara and who had previously been persecuted by Ball.

In 1812 a Commission of Inquiry was sent from Britain. This Inquiry was sent because Malta had been

> valued formerly only for its military importance [but] has now a further claim on the attention of His Majesty's Government as one of the most flourishing of our commercial positions.

The Commissioners were instructed to examine everything but military matters and were to make recommendations on the manner by which civil government ought to be run. They were also instructed to suggest how the Maltese could be granted some form of civil liberty as far as this did not threaten military stability. The Commissioners advised caution on any alterations to the system since the Maltese 'habits, customs, religion and education, are in direct opposition to our own'. For this reason although they believed that the legal system needed to be totally re-organized they suggested few alterations to it and continued to be based on the code drawn up during the rule of Grand Master De Rohan. They did however recommend that the judges be paid a salary rather than be given a fee according to the duration of the cases they heard. This practice had given the judiciary a vested interest in prolonging cases indefinitely in order to increase the fee due to them.

The Commissioners also commented on the economy and the finances of the island. They suggested that Malta was not in a position to develop its agricultural produce and suggested the colonization of Pantelleria, Lampedusa and Linosa to increase Malta's food supplies. The idea was however abandoned even though a private enterprise colonization of Lampedusa was undertaken by a small group of Maltese in 1800. Among the new sources of revenue recommended by the Commission, was a one per cent duty on all imports, together with taxes on foreign residents and wine shops. However their approach to the question of taxation was limited for fear of upsetting certain sections of Maltese society.

The Commissioners also discussed the role of the diocese of Malta and particularly its Curia with its ecclesiastical law courts and special privileges. They believed that no alterations to practices in this area should be carried out area since it would anger the Catholic clergy – the most influential class among the mass of the Maltese – and alienate them from the British. The Commission then went on to discuss the need of a *Consiglio Popolare* or *Università* the functions of which had been greatly curtailed by the Order of St John. The Commission – like most nineteenth-century British administrators of Malta – was convinced that the local politicians were not capable of enjoying any kind of political power and of holding offices concerned with finance. On the other hand, the ordinary folk were not interested in politics and simply wanted a sound administration, prosperity and peace. On the basis of this judgement, remarks Godfrey Pirotta, the Maltese were denied their long cherished *Consiglio Popolare* and Maltese public servants were removed and remained excluded from departmental headships. The Commissioners concluded that a *Consiglio Popolare* might very well be set up of fanatics whose main aim would be to stir the population against His Majesty's government. The Commission thus suggested that the prevailing division of Malta's administration into civil and military should in the future be held under one administrator who would serve as governor and commander-in-chief of the Armed Forces. The governor could then be advised, if he so wished, by a council composed of Maltese residents.

The Commissioners' Report was influenced by the changing political circumstances of the period in question. Malta had by then become an important base for the Royal Navy and the British could not afford to have the running of the base upset by local political activity. The report of the Commissioners was scrutinized in London and it was decided to create a new position of Civil Commissioner and Commander-in-Chief for Malta. The man chosen for this new position was Sir Thomas Maitland (1813-1824). Maitland had already build a reputation as the successful administrator of Ceylon. Maitland arrived in Malta in 1813 as Britain's first Governor to Malta. At that time a plague epidemic was afflicting the island. His strict quarantine measures helped to contain the outbreak and by 1814 it was possible to remove all restrictions of movement.

Maitland then set about transforming and re-organizing the administrative set-up. His ruthless methods earned him many critics. Not only was the *Consiglio Popolare*, (meant to serve as a council) never established, but the old *Università* – which continued to run the grain trade – was abolished and so was the committee of *giurati* (jurats). He even abolished the Sanitary Board. Furthermore the state archives, including the privileges and charters of the Maltese, were sequestered. The Law Courts were greatly reformed to suit British needs, although Maitland set up a system of justice and abolished torture, while the scope of ecclesiastical courts was restricted to matters that concerned the Church and its teachings. Notaries and lawyers were from then on expected to learn English before they could qualify and all petitions and government contracts had to be presented in English. The Maltese were replaced by Englishmen in almost every decision-making government position. But perhaps his most odious measure was the introduction of a heavy duty on wheat, as a source of revenue. One must bear in mind that most of the wheat consumed still largely had to be imported. One may conclude that in the first few years of his despotic rule Maitland took all necessary steps to transform Malta into a Crown Colony.

Malta was given to Britain as a possession by the Treaty of Paris in 1814, a measure that was ratified in June 1815 at the Congress of Vienna and confirmed in Paris in November 1815. The Maltese had absolutely no say in this matter. From then on Malta was to be run by Governors and Lieutenant-Governors, almost invariably military men, who ruled the Maltese islands as despots. This state of affairs had already been pointed out to the 1812 Commission by the highly educated ecclesiastic Onorato Bres. Bres declared that Malta was being run as a military dictatorship even though the Maltese expected and deserved the right to govern themselves. But Bres's declaration fell on deaf ears, while Maitland, referred to as 'King Tom' by the Maltese, set the seal on a method of government adapted by future British Governors and Lieutenant-Governors of Malta.

*Attempts at Political Representation in a Crown Colony*

Maitland remained governor of Malta until his death in 1824. He was not just the governor of Malta but in addition he was Lord Commissioner of the Ionian Islands and was also responsible for the British consuls of the North African coast. He even had to oversee British interests in the Mediterranean, including Gibraltar.

Thanks to its geographical position in the middle of the Mediterranean, Malta had been transformed into the focal point of interest in the area. Even so, Maitland rarely resided in Malta, and in the latter part of his governorship he was more involved with the administration of the Ionian Islands. Finally under Maitland no advisory council of any sort was ever constituted.

In 1821 the Maltese protested to the House of Commons against Maitland's despotic rule. They claimed that the people of Malta had been ill-treated and deceived by the British and that they were better-off under the Order of St John when the islands witnessed increasing prosperity, whereas under British rule, many were facing starvation. The petitioners complained that the repressive measures imposed by Maitland had reduced many Maltese to a state of destitution. They demanded a return to the old system including the additional formation of a National Assembly which would have power to authorize the imposition of any new laws or the introduction of new taxes. They particularly complained about the abolition of the grain monopoly. The picture of Malta as described in the 1821 remonstrance is one of misery and widespread discontent. Unfortunately the petition was deemed to be too long and it was sent back to Malta to be shortened and modified. Perhaps this was one typically British way of delaying tactics!

By the early 1820s the two main claims of the Maltese were representative institutions, including free elections to send deputies to a local assembly; and the abolition of censorship, hence a free press to enable information and debate about public affairs. On his death in 1824, Maitland was succeeded by the Marquess of Hastings, an incomparably amiable man, who unfortunately left most of the administration in the hands of his deputy, Chief Secretary Sir Frederick Hankey (1824-1837), who was in turn a power-monger so that it was difficult for the Maltese to put in a word. However in 1824 Sir John Richardson, was asked to report on the administration of justice and local laws and he advocated the establishment of a Legislative Council. Unfortunately the Richardson proposal was turned down. Hastings died in office in 1827 and was replaced by Sir Frederick Ponsonby as Lieutenant Governor (1827-1836). Ponsonby introduced the jury system for grave crimes and there was a general improvement in the administration of justice. Yet Ponsonby's rule was weak, and like Hastings before him, allowed power to be wielded by his subordinates.

Meanwhile changing political circumstances in Europe and the rest of the Empire ensured that the Maltese would not be ignored indefinitely. The 1830s witnessed a change in the political climate of Britain and Europe. In France the Bourbons, restored to the throne of France in 1815, were overthrown and a constitutional monarchy under Louis Philippe was set up;

the Italian and German states envisaged various outbursts against despotic rulers. The rebels, acting in the spirit of the French revolution, demanded liberal constitutions and the unification of the various states into one nation. In Britain the Tories, who had been in power since the start of the Napoleonic Wars, and had only just come under the premiership of the Duke of Wellington, were defeated in the general elections of 1830. The newly-elected Liberal party, under Lord Grey, enabled the passing of the Great Reform Bill of 1832.

In Malta the 1830s were important because they were to see the formation of a Maltese liberal movement known as the Comitato Generale Maltese which spearheaded the agitation for political rights that led to the Royal Commission of 1836 and its far-reaching recommendations. The Comitato Generale was set up in 1830 when a number of meetings, under the chairmanship of Camillo Sceberras, were held to prepare a new petition. On 28 June 1832, after many consultations, the Comitato finalized its petition. It was drawn in Italian with an accompanying English translation, and was made ready to be despatched to the King and Parliament in London. In their petition the Comitato explained that they wanted back the *Università* and the appointment of *giurati* (jurats) to administer the grain trade. They also wanted a municipal corps, a free press, public instruction, and a code of laws. They also deplored the high duty rates on basic commodities, as well as the bad state of the agricultural and educational systems. There was also reference to the low salaries of public officials. It appears that Lieutenant-General George Brown, who was acting governor in Ponsonby's absence, asked the petitioners to modify their claims. Among the Maltese there were those who were prepared to modify the wording of the petition before it would be sent to London and those who were not ready to accept any talk of modification. The latter group included Sceberras himself, Giorgio Mitrovich, Dr Arcangelo Pullicino and Dr Isidoro Spiteri. Another petition, also written in Italian, was presented by the Sceberras group on 18 July of that year. Two petitions were thus forwarded to Governor Ponsonby with a few days between them. One was signed by 506 persons including Sceberras and Mitrovich, while the other had 135 signatories. Both petitions were sent to the Secretary of State in two dispatches dated 20 and 22 July. Although both petitions insisted on the formation of a National Council, they differed on the qualitative and quantitative nature of the council.

In his covering memorandum Ponsonby justified the way Malta was being administered and argued that the lack of prosperity in Malta was due to the high density of the population – in relation to local resources – and the stagnant commercial activity. The governor was against the proposal of a freely-elected council of Maltese as these would create a lot of difficulties for the good administration of the Crown Colony. Both the Governor and the Secretary of State were fully conscious that some kind of council was necessary but in the correspondence exchanged between them from 1833 to 1835 they agreed on a council in which the Maltese would be in a minority. This would prevent fears, earlier expressed by Ponsonby, whereby the wishes of the Maltese would be at odds with those of British colonial interests.

On 1 April 1835, King William IV issued instructions for a Constitution for Malta. It was essentially a non-elective seven-member council to advise and assist in the running of the administration. Four members were to be selected ex officio, namely the Chief Justice, the Bishop of Malta, the Chief Secretary to the Government, and the Senior Military Officer. There was also a provision for a non-voting clerk of the Council. The unofficial members of the Council were selected by the Governor: namely two from among the Maltese landed proprietors and merchants and a leading British-born merchant who had been resident for at least two years in Malta. Members of the council were to be titled 'Honourable' and were meant to hold office for two years. Among the issues put forward in the 1835 Constitution one finds that the Chief Justice was only to attend sessions when legal matters were raised, while the Governor or his deputy had had to attend all sessions. Council meetings had to be convened by the Governor, with a quorum of two members in addition to the Governor himself or his representative. Members enjoyed freedom of debate and vote in all affairs of public interest but the Governor could suspend any member for a just cause. On his part the Governor was to consult the council only on occasions of importance or difficulty. In case of urgency he could dispense with the advice of the Council, but any action taken had to be discussed in the meeting following the action. The Governor, as head of the Council, could act against the Council's advice but had to explain his reasons to the Secretary of State and full reasons had to be registered in the Council Minutes Register. In urgent cases the Governor could also legislate but in normal conditions he was obliged to consult the other members of the Council.

The creation of the Council of Government was announced in a proclamation dated 1 May. But even before the proclamation was issued, Bishop Francesco Saverio Caruana objected to being placed third in the order of precedence. A notification of 22 June placed him second after the Governor, or his delegate. The Bishop then objected to the wording of the oath of office which each member had to take as this oath included allegiance to the Church of England. The Bishop never sat on the Council. Likewise the Chief Justice, Stoddard soon resigned since he demanded seniority over the Senior Military Officer. The Maltese merchants chosen were Baron Giuseppe Maria De Piro and Agostino Portelli and the British merchant was a man named Aspinall. It goes without saying that the two most powerful men on the Council were the Officer Administering the Government, George Cardew, and the Chief Secretary, Frederick Hankey. It was obvious that the Governor, through his officials, continued to do as he pleased after 1835. Without any doubt, the British imperial policy saw Malta only as a military base.

The Council of Government of 1835 was thus little more than an advisory council. Henry Frendo insists that 'it is misleading to class the constitution of 1835 as some 'major' development'.

It was

considered an insult, a rebuff, by the Maltese, especially by the Comitato Generale, whose efforts were directed towards a Consiglio Popolare having at least 30 and at best 100 members in it, with the right to decide on matters of public policy.

Nonetheless it may be considered a step in the right direction.

Meanwhile Giorgio Mitrovich, a self-employed businessman and leading member of the Comitato Generale, was in London writing letters, and meeting British MPs. It was during his stay in London that Mitrovich published two pamphlets tracing historical justifications for the claims of the Maltese to self-rule entitled: 'Claims of the Maltese founded upon Principles of Justice'. An attempt to have an Italian translation of this pamphlet published in Malta was blocked by the local government which then owned the only licensed printing press in Malta. The pamphlet was published in Italian as *'Indirizzo ai Maltesi da parte del loro amico Giorgio Mitrovich attulamente in Londra'* in London. The fact that Mitrovich could freely publish his pamphlet in London but not in Malta served to give greater credibility to his claims. While in London Mitrovich was in touch with several liberals including Daniel O'Connell. On 8 September 1835 Mitrovich even wrote to the new Secretary of State for War and Colonies Charles Grant, known as Lord Glenelg (1835-1839), in which he appealed for the establishment of a National Council with a number of elected members. Thanks to a public relations campaign in the British parliament and the British press Mitrovich was able to push his claims.

In a letter of 27 October 1835, Mitrovich was asked to present proofs of his allegations in his 'Claims of the Maltese founded upon Principles of Justice'. On that same day Lord Glenelg wrote to the Acting Governor Cardew to report on Mitrovich's accusations in order to be able to decide whether to present them to a Parliamentary Commission or to send a Royal Commission to investigate matters. Mitrovich's efforts and meetings in London helped to instil some courage in the hearts of the Maltese after thirty years of seemingly useless efforts. There were some who thought that Mitrovich was overdoing it and was even accused of having taken upon himself responsibilities without having consulted anyone. He was even suspected of double-dealing when it was learned that a new Royal Commission of Inquiry was about to visit Malta. Meanwhile Camillo Sceberras refused to discuss matters with Acting Governor Cardew since Mitrovich, was at the time, negotiating with the Colonial Secretary. This refusal, based on a dignified political stand, was seemingly misunderstood by some of the Maltese leaders. Meanwhile Sceberras formed a committee known as the Comitato di Petizione, which included Dr Arcangelo Pullicino and Giovanni Battista Vella, to prepare a petition in which they demanded, among other things, a modern code of laws, a free press, an independent health board, a free port, general primary education, and a reform of technical education with special attention devoted to the new technological and scientific advances of the time. The Comitato di Petizione wanted action not another enquiry. So they were very annoyed when they learned that Mitrovich accepted Lord Glenelg's proposal of holding a new inquiry. The Sceberras petition, (containing 2,359 signatures) – together with three other petitions from Malta – was presented to the House of Commons on 7 June 1836 by William Ewart, a liberal MP from Liverpool, who had assisted Mitrovich both financially and politically while he was in London. Before he left London for Malta on 1 September 1836, Mitrovich wrote several other publications including *The Cause of the People of Malta*, *Ai Maltesi miei cari compatriotti*, *Lettera al Popolo Maltese sulla Stampa*, and *Raccomandazioni ai Maltesi*.

Meanwhile Sceberras had formed a Comitato Generale Maltese which was divided into districts covering all of Malta's territory. Members from all walks of life were represented as each district sent two representatives. The Comitato Generale thus served as a form of Consiglio Popolare. It even had an inner circle consisting of twenty members.

The Commission of Inquiry arrived in October 1836 consisting of John Austin, Professor of Jurisprudence at the University of London; George Cornwall Lewis, a lawyer and former liberal minister; and Thomas Tod who was to serve as secretary. The commissioners had to look at the civil administration of

Malta as a whole. The report of this Commission – particularly their recommendation in favour of a free press and the elective principle in the selection of a Council of Government – was perhaps the most noteworthy development during the first fifty years of British rule.

Although there were attempts to introduce forms of British Protestantism among the Maltese, it proved by and large a fruitless exercise. On the other hand, the British administrators, appreciating the strategic significance of the Maltese islands in the imperial defence system, realized that in order to retain the confidence of the people, they had to concede to their freedom of religious practice. Thus, protection of the Catholic Church in Malta and co-operation with its hierarchy formed the basis upon which the British modelled church-state relations. This assumption was made clear in the recommendations of the Royal Commission of 1836. Assuming that all children were Catholics, the Commissioners suggested that religious instruction in schools should be exclusively left in the hands of the clergy. For this reason, parish priests were allowed access to schools at any time during the day, and it was stipulated that they could supervize catechism lessons.

Until then the press was rigorously controlled, and although newspapers started to be published in 1838 the press ordinance was only consented to in March 1839 when Ordinance IV stipulated that

> no printed writing shall be subjected or liable to the censorship which is now exercized in these Islands by Her Majesty's Government therein.

However the press remained under surveillance, while requests for the setting up of new printing presses being often refused. Permission was only granted to some religious institutions and to Protestant Bible societies who published bibles for distribution in various parts of the Mediterranean. Some attempts were made by these societies to distribute, among the Maltese, Protestant editions of the Bible in Italian and Maltese. But the local Catholic clergy energetically fought this kind of Protestant infiltration by banning their reading among Catholics.

The Bishop of Malta was thus a strong opponent of the freedom of the press and wrote formally to the Governor against it.

This was a matter upon which the Church had been bitterly opposed to, since it feared that the Catholic religion would be 'ridiculed' by the large number of highly anti-clerical Italian refugees residing in Malta and by Protestant propaganda. The Bishop even warned of 'the incalculable damage' which was being caused by the presence of the Italian nationalists 'in this small island whose language they speak'. This explains why the King of Naples also feared the freedom of the press in Malta. He was afraid that Italian liberals and nationalists would utilize this freedom from their base in Malta. But, in spite of the vigorous representations by the Bishop and the King of Naples, strongly backed by the Vatican, freedom of the press was granted in 1839.

One may conclude that freedom of the press was conceded after repeated requests by the Maltese. However such improvements as were made in the latter part of the 1830s were possible due to the changing conditions in Europe and Britain itself. The reactionary post-Congress of Vienna governments, previously opposed to the diffusion of the printed word, had somewhat mitigated their conservative approach after the liberal revolutions of 1830. In reality, concerns over the liberalization of the press were not totally unfounded, particularly since the highly-active Italian exiles in Malta were determined to make full use of this facility. Besides, Maltese liberals could co-ordinate their hitherto isolated efforts on a much wider scale, resulting in a profusion of printed literature. Consequently many newspapers were published in Italian, in English, and in Maltese – 180 in all between 1838 and 1870. In the long run, journalism was to prove enormously effective in arousing popular interest in political matters and also in providing intellectuals adequate means of communication.

*The Italian Refugees and the 1849 Constitution*

Between 1839 and 1848, following the concession of the freedom of the press, many Italian liberals sought refuge in Malta, a good number of whom took up journalism as an occupation. Their publications evidently helped to propagate many new ideas on topics like freedom and education. In the early 1840s – when over 800 arrived from various parts of Italy – there were so many Italian refugees that the British authorities of Malta became concerned not least because they were sure that the Italians would exert influence on their Maltese friends. The Sceberras family befriended many of these Italian refugees and Emilio, son of Camillo Sceberras, was a keen supporter of the ideas of Giuseppe Mazzini. Other refugees included Ruggero Settimo, Nicola Fabrizi, T. Zauli Sajani, and Francesco Crispi – who was later elected Prime Minister of a united Italian kingdom. However the British were also concerned with economic matters. Malta was a small island without any resources and with a fragile infrastructure that was already over-burdened in order to service British imperial interests.

The twenty years following the granting of freedom of the press were a relatively calm period in Maltese history, which witnessed a transient economic prosperity resulting from the Crimean War between 1853-1856. Various effective and progressive measures were undertaken by the ruling governors, especially during the rule of Richard More O'Ferrall (1847-1851) who besides being the first Civil Governor of Malta was an Irish Catholic by birth.

The Comitato Generale Maltese and the Comitato di Petizione, later set up by Sceberras, were both disbanded by late 1840 but many Maltese were of the opinion that Malta needed some sort of a National Council. In 1841, Sceberras attempted to form a new Comitato di Petizione. By 1849 he had managed to forward a petition signed by 919 persons through the local administration asking for a legislative council. Thanks to this petition together with the multitude of published articles and pamphlets the Secretary of State became conscious of a need for some drastic changes in the running of the Island Fortress.

The carnival riots of February 1846, which erupted as a result of the Governor's decision to ban merry-making on Sunday, brought these problems into the open. The local liberals and Italian refugees saw an opportunity to protest against the rough treatment of those who had protested and claimed the need for the setting up of a council in which the locals would play an important role. A memorial was sent to the Secretary of State, Earl Grey (1846-1852), in which the Maltese representatives – including Dr Nicola Zammit, Dr F. Grungo, Giuseppe Montebello Pulis, Dr Paolo Bonavia, Revd S. Schembri and Dr Raffaele Bonnici – condemned the handling of the Carnival riots by the British administration of Malta. Representations on behalf of the Maltese were made at the House of Commons by two friends of Giorgio Mitrovich, Mr Ewart and Mr Hume. Nonetheless on 16 July 1846 Lord Grey informed the Governor of Malta Sir Patrick Stuart (1843-1846) that the Council should not be changed. The situation became so difficult for Governor Stuart that he resigned the following year.

The appointment of the Catholic Irishman Richard More O' Ferrall as Civil Governor, was meant to calm the troubled waters. The Maltese had long demanded a civil, instead of a military administrator, a decision which, for strategic reasons, had

The Main Guard and the Grand Masters' palace in a drawing of 1822. The Palace was at the time seat of the British Governor.

been strongly opposed by the Duke of Wellington in the 1820s. The Maltese were now very pleased that they had a fellow-Catholic as Governor. They took heart and prepared another petition in which they asked for a National Assembly of twenty-one members.

Between 1848 and 1860, the Italian political situation turned Malta into a hot-bed of political exiles and refugees, creating many problems to the local British administration. In April 1848 Earl Grey had instructed Governor More O'Ferrall

> not to permit the landing in Malta of persons who may seek to refuge here from political motives, in any of the countries bordering on the Mediterranean, provided such persons are in a situation to comply with the law of the Island.

In 1849 alone, sixty-two refugees were refused permission to enter Malta. The Governor's frequent refusals to permit refugees to enter Malta exposed him to a great deal of criticism.

The situation became more precarious since the Chief Secretary, Mr Henry Lushington (1847-1855) was – unlike his predecessor Hector Greig (1837-1847) – a liberal, who sympathized with the Italian Risorgimento. It so happened that in 1864 Giuseppe Garibaldi, who had chased the Bourbons out of the Kingdom of the Two Sicilies thus uniting them with the Kingdom of Italy, spent two days in Malta on his way to London. On this occasion some hailed him as 'the defender of liberty' but the Bourbon refugees who had been exiled from their kingdom were naturally hostile to him. Garibaldi, who had been excommunicated by the Catholic Church for his activities was thus labelled 'the enemy of the Church and its Vicar'. It was a time when prounification of Italy refugees were returning home while antiunification refugees, notably from the Bourbon kingdom of the Two Sicilies, were finding refuge in Malta. Followers of the unification movement had conceived the view that Malta should be part of the new Italian Kingdom. At the same time the newly-arrived anti-unification refugees considered everything connected with the British as directed against the Catholic Church. Naturally it was a time when Italian influence was taking hold over the Maltese who began to insist on more freedom and local autonomy.

On his part the Governor was quite sensitive to the aspirations of the Maltese and in 1848 he sent various dispatches to
the Secretary of State on the need to introduce constitutional
reforms. In a confidential report dated April 1848 he even suggested to add a number of Maltese members to the Council as
had been constituted in 1835. More O'Ferrall put forward several names of potential members whom he believed would be
more trustful and tolerant of the British administration. Still
neither the Governor nor the Secretary of State were ready to
allow the number of unofficial members to exceed that of the
official ones. Nonetheless on 11 May 1849 a Letters Patent for
a partly elected council was issued.

Perhaps the most important point feature in 1849 was the
introduction of the elective principle. It was a time of turmoil all
over Europe. After the defeat of Napoleon in 1815, the victori-
ous powers were hostile to nationalist aspirations, which they
considered to be associated with liberalism and therefore a threat
to constituted authority. At the Congress of Vienna the powers
had adopted the principle of 'legitimacy' as a basis for redraw-
ing the map of Europe. Prince Metternich, the Chancellor of
Austria, believed that any concessions to nationalism would be
fatal and he resisted them on all fronts until 1848. During this
period only Greece and Belgium (1830) obtained independence.
Elsewhere national risings failed.

But in 1848 the constitutional monarchy of Louis Philippe in
France was replaced by a republic under the presidency of Louis
Napoleon, nephew of the great Napoleon Bonaparte. In Germany
the liberals within the various German states had not only managed to obtain a constitution, from their erstwhile autocratic
rulers, but they even managed to temporarily create a federal
parliament at Frankfurt. However perhaps more significant
then, was the end of the rule of Prince Metternich in the Austrian Empire. It was Metternich who had managed to restore
the traditional rulers to their power in 1815. Although during
the period of restoration there had been some unrest it was not
until 1848 that nationalist movements began to re-emerge in
Italy, Germany and the Austrian empire.

The 1849 Constitution gave Malta a council of eighteen members: the Governor, ten official members and eight elected ones. Of the ten official members five were Maltese: the Collector of Land Revenue, the Crown Advocate, the Quarantine Superintendent, the Charities Surveyor and the Cashier of the Treasury. The form of the Council was altered slightly and considerably enlarged in the 1849 constitution. Although the Council had a built-in official majority the Maltese were at least being allowed to take part in the debates leading to the formulation of public policy. Technically there was a Maltese majority but this could only make sense if the official members could vote freely. The 1849 Constitution is chiefly important because of the introduction of the elective principle. It was the first time that the Maltese were allowed to vote for their representatives in the Council. Thus any male over 21 who possessed land or property of an annual value of 100 scudi (equivalent to £8.32) or who occupied a dwelling valued at 50 scudi annually, or was a partner in a business firm that had the necessary qualifications, could vote. It is evident that the emphasis was on property and commercial interest rather than on academic qualifications. But the British – who had been called 'a country of shop-keepers' by Napoleon – considered entrepreneurship as an indication of initiative and ability. Few were therefore eligible to vote but at least one could speak of an election in which public debate and the prospect of some measure of responsibility and power were established. In all 3,767 people (of whom 281 were Gozitans) were eligible to vote. Those elected for Malta were: Michelangelo Scerri (610 votes); Dr Arcangelo Pullicino (489 votes); Giovanni Battista Vella (424 votes); Giuseppe Pulis Montebello (714 votes); Canon Dr Filippo Amato (620 votes); Mgr. Leopoldo Fiteni (514 votes); Mgr. Dr Anetto Casolani (617 votes). Dr Adriano Dingli (116 votes) was elected for Gozo.

Bishop Mgr. Annetto Casolani and Dr Adriano Dingli were considered to be pro-government. Two of the elected members – Canon Dr Filippo Amato and Giovanni Battista Vella – had contested the election on behalf of Il Circolo Maltese headed by Dr Giovanni Carlo Grech Delicata. Giovanni Battista Vella, together with Dr Arcangelo Pullicino, had originally been members of the Comitato Generale Maltese, while Giuseppe Pulis Montebello had been an active member of the revived Popular Committee which was formed after the disintegration of the Consiglio Popolare Maltese.

Both Camillo Sceberras (34 votes) and Giorgio Mitrovich (26 votes) fared badly in these elections. Had these two been elected to the Council they would have had an excellent chance of fighting for more rights for the Maltese. As it turned out the members were mere puppets in the hands of the Governor. About sixteen per cent of the electorate did not turn up to cast their vote and such abstensionism may have had a marked effect on the outcome of the election.

During this period a most significant change was carried out by Grech Delicata who transformed Il Circolo Maltese into a political organization called Associazione Patriottica Maltese. The new political formation published its statute and a political programme in the first issue of its organ *L'Avvenire* in December 1849.

### British Colonial Policy and the Imposition of English: 1858-1880

The period 1832 to 1858, remarks Godfrey Pirotta, may be considered as a 'period of liberal colonial development for Malta'. A new, partly elected, Council of Government was set up. There was the introduction of the freedom of the press while Maltese civil servants were re-admitted to executive offices in the public service. But when Sir Gaspard Le Marchant (1858-1864) took over from Sir William Reid (1851-1858) as civil governor late in April 1858 things took a different turn. Le Marchant abandoned the separation between civil and military responsibilities.

The 1849 Constitution enabled the Governor to act over the Council's head if he deemed it necessary. But it was only during the governorship of Le Marchant that the official members of government were obliged to vote as a bloc. In the late 1860s and 1870s this method became a *sine qua non* hence leading to the development of a government and an opposition on the local scene. Thus there were members of the Council who had to support the government and another group of members who were, strictly speaking, free to vote as they liked but who generally chose to vote in opposition. The opposition group which emerged in the 1860s, was known as the Four Lawyers. These four lawyers: Ruggiero Sciortino, Francesco Torreggiani, Filippo Pullicino and Pasquale Mifsud closely monitored and, whenever necessary, opposed the military flair that predominated Malta's administrative policy. Their popularity among eligible voters is indicated by the fact that they were all elected to the Council in the 1865 elections while those who took a pro-government stand lost ground. The Four Lawyers pioneered a petition in 1864 – signed by 4,464 persons – to reform the constitution and appoint a Civil Governor. This move was largely the direct result of Le Marchant's habit of forcing all official members to vote in line with him against the elected members thereby reducing the latter to a permanent minority.

By the middle of the 1870s until the introduction of the 1921 Constitution a shift of policy by Britain towards Malta was to become clearly apparent. It was a time when Anglo-Maltese relations deteriorated rapidly reaching a situation of crisis in the early 1900s. The immediate cause for this crisis appeared to be the language question which largely centred around British efforts, especially after 1880, to replace Italian with English as the dominant language of Malta and the resistance offered by the Maltese élites against this policy.

It is true that the Secretary of State, Lord Bathurst (1812-1827) had in 1813 instructed Maitland to establish public schools where children could be taught reading and writing in English. However the Royal Commission of 1836 had shown that this instruction was disregarded by Maitland and his successors who were afraid to upset the Catholic Church which tended to regard the inability to communicate in English as an effective obstacle curbing the attempts, by Protestant Evangelical groups, to spread Protestantism in Malta. Furthermore the Commissioners of 1836 concluded that Italian was 'far more useful to a Maltese than any other language, excepting his native tongue'. They had thus recommended that Italian should remain the language of instruction at school while English was taught as a secondary option. The situation only changed slightly in the late 1850s when a system of competitive examinations for clerkships made English and Italian a requisite for joining the civil service. This clause had encouraged many Maltese, particularly the urbanites, to learn English since the language opened prospects of employment not only with the civil service but even at the dockyard and with the armed forces.

The real cause of conflict between the British and the Maltese was however based on the changing status of Britain as a world power. In the 1840s and 1850s Britain was acknowledged as the world's naval and economic power. It was a time when the British proudly considered the world to be in need of Britain. There was even a tendency to consider the empire as an obstacle to British interests rather than as an advantage. Godfrey Pirotta concludes that

> although no government minister subscribed to this view, it was this frame of mind which, among other things, had helped to forge concessions to fortress Malta.

Since threats to British supremacy appeared remote, Britain could afford to be generous with Malta. The situation changed drastically in the 1860s when British naval and economic supremacy were being challenged by other powers, especially France and Prussia. Britain's sense of security began to seek ways of reasserting its military interests in Malta. Until 1880, it hoped to achieve this without antagonizing Malta's upper and middle classes. Unfortunately governors who ruled Malta from 1858 to 1878, with the exception of Sir Henry Storks (1864-1867), tended to make frequent use of the official majority – the use of the official majority did not in itself violate the constitution – in matters which involved no imperial interests and thus managed to alienate the Maltese. Storks was more cautious since he adopted the earlier policies of More O'Ferrall and William Reid to either postpone or shelve matters where consensus was not arrived at.

In the earlier years the Secretary of State for Colonies sided with the Maltese, and governors were warned not to abuse of their powers. In 1864 the Secretary of State, Viscount Edward Cardwell (1864-1866) went so far as to rule that finances budgeted could not be used against the wishes of the majority of elected members, other than in exceptional circumstances. In 1873 Earl Kimberley (1880-1882) went so far as to publicly censor Governor Sir Charles van Straubenzee (1872-1878) for departing from this rule. Furthermore the Secretary of State for Colonies was not convinced that it had taken the right step when it re-introduced a military form of government. Indeed until the early 1870s the option for a return of civil governors was left open.

The problem arose when the Maltese political élite began to press for a new constitution which would give them greater control over local affairs. It was a period when the international situation was rapidly changing and British domination was increasingly being challenged by the other great European powers. Developments in the Mediterranean further urged a change in the British stand over Malta. It was a time when France was expanding her empire in North Africa. It was also a time when a multitude of Maltese labouring poor chose North Africa as a place for migration. Furthermore the opening of the Suez Canal by the French in 1869 had revolutionized the world's trade routes. Britain soon valued the canal as a shorter route, through the Red Sea, to its rich Indian empire and was soon disputing the control of the Suez Canal with France. At the same time Italy had just been united under the House of Savoy and the new kingdom of Italy, like France, had developed an expansionist policy in the Mediterranean. Thus the British Secretary of State for Colonies feared France as Maltese migration to the newly-acquired French colonies could lead to an extension of French influence on the Maltese lower classes. At the same time the newly-established Italian kingdom was also considered a threat to Britain as it could inspire an irredentist view among the Maltese upper and middle classes that could instigate an Italian claim on Malta. In short from the

1860s onwards British administrators in Malta feared that Maltese loyalty to Britain may not survive the test given the existing choice of powerful masters. Therefore the only reasonable policy seemed to be to launch a campaign to Anglicize Malta and to make the Maltese population completely dependent on Britain.

Britain thus reviewed its policy for Malta. It was believed that the limited autonomy which had been enjoyed by the islanders since the 1849 constitution had to be curtailed. Cardwell's rule of 1864 was modified and re-interpreted. The option of installing civil governors was put aside and it was decided that the authority of governors was to be publicly supported at all times. For the first time a real effort was made to integrate Malta more fully into the British empire and to make Maltese interests coincide more closely with those of Britain and the rest of the empire. Thus every attempt was made to start off an Anglicization campaign among all strata of Maltese society and from every aspect whether social, cultural, economical, or even political. It was envisaged that such a policy could only be effective if there was a wider diffusion of the English language among all classes of Maltese society. It was hoped that thanks to a good knowledge of English the Maltese would have better opportunities to migrate to other parts of the empire. This would in turn consolidate the loyalty of future generations of Maltese for whom English, rather than Italian, would become the language of education, culture, commerce and government.

Thus it was only in the 1870s that official efforts at Anglicizing the Maltese were introduced. No less than three royal commissions were sent to investigate the local situation in the 1870s: one by Rowsell, director of navy contracts; another one by Keenan, Commissioner of the National Education Board of Ireland; and another by Julyan, an elderly crown agent for the colonies.

Francis N. Rowsell was appointed Commissioner in 1877. Rowsell found out that one major source of government expenditure was its large civil establishment. This was no news to the Secretary of State for Colonies since earlier commissioners, governors and administrators had pointed it out. Rowsell however suggested a new salary scale and a system of promotions which would help inculcate a sense of loyalty among civil servants. He wished to reduce public expenditure and suggested the abolition of the Land Revenue Department, the Treasury and the Printing Office which would enable the Malta government to save £3,000. Rowsell even suggested abolishing or at least greatly reducing the grain tax, imposed by Maitland, and introduce taxation measures instead.

Rowsell found out that in 1876 the Charitable Institutions had cost the colony £27,000. He considered this sum to be excessive as it cost the government nearly £80 a day. His major complaint was that there was

no poor-house... nor any general organization for the relief of the poor and the suppression of mendacity.

It was such type of statements that led Godfrey Pirotta to state

that nearly eighty years of British rule had not been sufficient to establish in Malta British concepts of charity.

Rowsell even wanted to increase the fees for the Lyceum and the University although in effect he wanted to abolish the local University since whoever wanted to study at a tertiary level could go abroad. However Rowsell's immediate focus was on the taxation system and particularly the grain tax which he proposed to reduce by a half. The loss of revenue could be recovered by new taxes on alcoholic drinks, licences, education fees, tonnage dues and store rent on bonded goods. These proposals led to an uproar in Valletta on 15 May 1878 against Rowsell and Sigismondo Savona, Rowsell's most prominent Maltese supporter. During the following years every attempt to push the tax reform through Council was blocked by the elected members.

Two very important enquiries were held in 1878 under a new governor Sir Arthur Borton (1878-1884). The first of these was conducted by Penrose Julyan concerning the running of the civil establishments of Malta. Julyan, had already prepared a similar report on the Mauritius. He concurred with Rowsell on a number of points. He praised the work of civil servants, but like Rowsell before him, criticized the administrative set-up and thought that it needed to be reduced, although salaries should increase. He recommended the formation of the office of Receiver General, the suppression of the treasury, and the re-amalgamation of a Land Revenue and Public Works Department. He further insisted that rents from government property should be collected properly on a regular basis. He even found 'too much charity' in Malta as the sick were entitled to free hospital treatment. He therefore suggested that the Medical Police should be placed under the Charitable Institutions and renamed District Medical Officers.

For Julyan the public service appeared to be the best vehicle by which the study of English could be promoted. He found that it was a standard practice, among civil servants, to keep books and prepare documents in Italian. Julyan even discovered that clerks were in the habit of conversing in Maltese and Italian while at work and this tended to encourage those proficient in English to forget all they knew. He therefore recommended that English should become the sole language of administration. Julyan even strongly recommended that English should become the official language of Malta and proposed that it should be the only language of the Council of Government. He even suggested that in the Law Courts there should be a gradual change from Italian to English. Having made his recommendations Julyan declared that he was against the idea that Italian be 'in any way forcibly restrained' among the educated Maltese nor that the Maltese language should be eradicated.

Penrose Julyan had been instructed not to inquire into the educational system of Malta as this had been assigned to another commissioner, Patrick Keenan. Keenan submitted his report in June 1879. In his report it is evident that he wanted to transform the education system stating that the two most useful languages for the Maltese were Arabic and English. Therefore the language of the schools should be English taught through Maltese, while the study of Italian should become an extra option in the higher classes of primary education. He proposed a similar reform in the Lyceum where all teaching should be carried out in English. Keenan even suggested the use of English in all the faculties at the University with the exception of theology. He proposed that Maltese school teachers had to improve their knowledge of English, and made special emphasis on pronunciation or else they would be sacked or forced to retire. Finally he suggested that the Education Department was to consist of the General Council of the University with control over the University, the Lyceum and the Primary Schools.

The reports of the three commissioners may be considered as a clear attempt to make Malta an Anglophile society. One thing is certain. The three commissioners were, at the time, considered to be hostile and contemptuous of Maltese social and cultural values.

This new British policy developed a great dispute over the Language of High Culture at a time when throughout Europe the recognition of language amounted to a recognition of national identity. In Malta the role of Maltese remained limited until the late nineteenth century, on account of its Semitic base which forced it to function solely as a local dialect. Indeed it only attained the function of a literary language when Malta began to culturally detach itself from Italy, and British imperial policy used it as a wedge to oust Italian. Until that stage was reached, Maltese held the same status as that of Italian dialects, while Italian itself froze into an official language on the same lines as Latin – useful for lyric, poetry and high culture, but unavailable to the majority of a society, still illiterate and economically backward. This is not surprising at all for even in Italy, Tullio de Mauro, himself an Italian linguist, remarked that in 1861, not more than two or three per cent of Italy's population could understand the 'official' language. The overwhelming majority of the Italians continued to employ regional dialects, some of which were distantly related to Italian in form, grammar, accent and vocabulary.

In Malta, the situation was not much different. Miège reports that in 1834, sixty-nine per cent of the population were illiterate and only twenty-two per cent could read and write in

Italian, the language of the élite culture. Throughout the British rule, Malta's geographical proximity to Sicily continued to make itself felt. So much so, that the earliest Maltese migrants to the United States of America were regarded as Italians – Sicily being considered as a sort of extension of the Italian peninsula. Ever since the sixteenth century Italian had established itself as the only language of culture in Malta. The earliest known document in Italian dates back to 1409. A basic conflict to be resolved in Malta, was therefore of a linguistic nature. Here was a European island whose native speech was of Semitic origin, whereas its culture was Latin. Well into the nineteenth century it was still credible to state that

> for a Maltese to be educated, and for him to know Italian, was one and the same thing; for countless generations, Italian had been the language of town and gown, of court and cloister.

Thus while medieval Malta remained culturally Sicilian, Malta of the Knights imbibed Italian and French cultural tastes. The presence of a large number of non-Maltese in the Harbour area induced the locals to adopt Italian as *lingua franca* and this helped transform Malta into an area *au courant* with happenings in the major cities of Europe. The forceful imposition of English after 1880 led to the development of the language question – a theme which was to dominate Maltese politics for the following sixty years. This inevitable twist of fate acted as a stimulus for the Maltese to come to terms with themselves, by helping them to become mature when outlining their rights and expectations as an ethnic community.

## Church and State Relations

The British did not try to impose themselves on the strongly influential Catholic Church which had been most conspicuously present in Maltese life since the late Middle Ages. Rather its presence became heavier and pervasive throughout the rule of the British thanks to the détente between the British colonial rulers and the Church hierarchy. The Church was able to flourish in the nineteenth century so that the number of parishes, collegiate chapters, churches and homes of religious orders continued to increase. The Church was not only strong it even became more than ever firmly embedded in the parochial and national life of the island. It had a monopoly in higher education and charity and was able to expand in organization.

In accepting British protection the Church did not forfeit any privilege and the Declaration of Rights of 15 June 1802 affirmed that the British Sovereign was to uphold and protect the rights and religion of the Maltese. While other religions were to be tolerated no other sovereign should be permitted to interfere either in the spiritual nor in the temporal privileges of the Maltese. In reality the British never fully agreed with the articles of this declaration but they never officially opposed them. Thus the British administration was largely co-operative with the Church authorities. The Royal Commission of 1812 concluded that the time was not yet ripe to abolish the special privileges enjoyed by the Church hierarchy. Indeed, according to Hilda Lee it was a feature of British policy, to grant religious liberty wherever necessary. Religious liberty had been granted to Canada in 1774, Martinique and Santo Domingo in 1794, while the Cape of Good Hope and other colonies began to enjoy these liberties in 1815.

In spite of the general courtesy with which the British comported themselves towards the Church, some prerogatives of the Catholic Church were subsequently abolished. Among these privileges was the right to ecclesiastical asylum, which was abolished in 1828. Another 1828 law limited the jurisdiction of the ecclesiastical courts to purely spiritual matters. The British colonial administrators were sometimes thus required to touch upon the domain of the Church. A more important issue was that of landed property. In the early nineteenth century the Church owned one-third of all immovable property of the Maltese islands. At the same time while the landed proprietors had to pay taxes on their landholdings, the Church was exempted from such impositions. One must point out that this property was not owned by the Bishop's curia but by different units that belonged to the Church such as the Cathedral Chapter, the religious orders and the various parishes. Nonetheless the British administration must have realized that too much immovable property was exempted from tax and this was hampering a fair taxation system on the land. The Mortmain Law of 1822 was enacted to limit the Church's right to hold property. From then onwards the Church, or other pious or religious institution, could not acquire immovable property, except under the condition that it should be sold or disposed of within a year otherwise it would *ipso facto* be forfeited to the government.

On the whole, however, the British government did not only respect the liberty of the Church; it even protected the Catholic Church in Malta from proselytism. To strengthen this view Joseph Bezzina argues that a Biblical Society founded in 1814 was forbidden to designate itself 'The Biblical Society of Malta' even though a few years later the 'American Missionary Society' and the 'Society of English Independents', were permitted to operate a printing press at a time when there was no freedom of the press. Nonetheless the Papal Secretary of State was assured that Britain intended

> to protect the Roman Catholic religion against the attempts of any society or class of persons, provided the forms and practices constantly observed in the British Dominions were not violated.

Thus when the Advisory Council of Government was set up in 1835 the Bishop of Malta was to be one of the official members. It was only after consultation with the Vatican that he resigned his position. The Royal Commission of 1836 thought that the clergy had largely lost influence and interest in politics. But this was not so, for out of eight elected members for the 1849 Constitution, three were Church prelates: Canon Filippo Amato, the titular Bishop Annetto Casolani, and Mgr. Leopoldo Fiteni. However the stand taken during the debates on the Penal Code by the three ecclesiastics elected in 1849, and the approbation of their conduct by the Curia, convinced the Governor that politics could serve as a stepping-stone for advancement in the Church.

During the debates on the Penal Code, Mgr. Casolani had insisted that an amendment should provide for heavier punishments for offences against the Catholic Church which he called '*religione dominante*' (dominant religion). For him the other religions were simply protected and tolerated. This induced an outcry from the Anglican Bishop of Gibraltar, resident in Malta, and an outcry from the British community in Malta so that the Secretary of State for Colonies rejected the amendment, on the assumption that there should be equal punishment for offences against both the Protestant and the Catholic churches. It was also decided that from then on Church-State issues, previously discussed confidentially between the Maltese Curia and the Colonial administration, could become public and put the erstwhile cordial relations in jeopardy. It was only in 1854 that a decree was agreed upon whereby a new criminal code was enacted. In this code the section on offences against religion was removed entirely. In 1857 the Secretary of State for Colonies, foreseeing possible episcopal interference on the way priests voted, decided to exclude any clergy from becoming members in the Council of Government. This rule was only changed in 1869 when the elected members of the Council moved a petition to readmit the clergy. In 1870 the matter was submitted to a referendum and the great majority of voters voted in favour. Consequently the rules were changed once more. However from then on no more than two ecclesiastics could become members of the Council.

In actual fact the Catholic Church remained *de facto* the dominant church. Thus it was only in 1844 that the Anglican Church opened a place of worship in Malta. The Archbishop of Malta was accorded military honours. Similar honours were later bestowed on the Anglican Bishop of Malta and Gibraltar even though his See had been established in 1842.

Unlike the French, the British had managed to win over the confidence of the masses largely by paying every respect to the religion of the Maltese. This enabled the British to succeed where the Order of St John, and later the French, had failed. However such tactics did not stop the British from dismantling all ecclesiastical immunities and abolishing the Ecclesiastical Courts.

The abolition of the Ecclesiastical Courts gave rise to many clandestine marriages. It was only after a formal request by the Curia that the British administration enacted legislation to restrain similar marriages in 1831.

The British co-operated with the Church in education, which had been 'exclusively in the hands of the Catholic clergy' since the time of the knights. In 1845 a group of Jesuits were given tacit permission to open the St Paul Boarding School. In 1859 rumours of radical changes at the University and the Lyceum induced the Governor to assure the Archbishop that he would be consulted before any changes would be introduced. In 1864 Gozo managed to split off from the diocese of Malta and became a See in its own right. The Gozitans had been requesting an independent diocese since 1798.

The dominant position of the Catholic Church particularly annoyed Protestant clergymen, who visited Malta in the late nineteenth century, since they knew fully well that they could not proselytize among Malta's British subjects. One such pastor, the Revd H. Seddall, was so disapproving of this that he wrote in 1870:

> Religious fervour is one of the leading features in the character of the Maltese people, and it discovers itself... in the building of churches and chapels; the erection of images at the corners of the streets, to be devoutly worshipped by the populace.

He further commented on the poor education of the Maltese clergy, and how 'they look with suspicion on everything that is stamped with the religion of England'. Seddall pointed out that the religion of the Maltese was directed to the senses rather than to prayer. Hence,

> it takes the gross form in which we find it in Italy, Spain, in South America, in all the countries completely under the ecclesiastical domination of Rome.

Malta, a British colony on the Sicilian coast, used Italian as its official language. To make matters worse it was a British possession where the Roman Catholic religion held sway and this irritated Protestant pastors and missionaries, Anglican residents and other non-conformists who were keen to debunk the Catholic faith with its idolatry of statues of patron saints, and ecclesiastical hierarchies. It was seen as intolerable that Malta, while a British colony, had been left for so long to its own devices. From the 1870s the nature of colonial government gradually changed from the 'relatively stable easy-going routine' Henry Frendo points out 'into a business-like, intrusive, more authoritarian rule'. The conflict between military needs and civil rights became the central issue of Maltese politics. Indeed it was a clash of cultures in which every effort was made to root out all those aspects of Maltese culture which could interfere with Britain's imperial policy – except of course for the Catholic religion.

On their part the Maltese could indeed have benefited from the wealth of advanced British technology and healthy financial resources. Unfortunately however Malta ended up becoming a mere pawn in the hands of the British.

# 5

## The British Fortress-Colony

*Colonial Rule, Constitutional Development and Self-Government*

### Constitutional Development and the Formation of Political Parties

In 1813, Malta became a Crown Colony and was ruled autocratically by a Governor. Not before 1835, did Malta receive its first semblance of a constitution, one that made provision for an Advisory Council to the Governor. The Council consisted of seven members and the Lieutenant Governor. The Maltese were represented by three members, one of whom was to be the Bishop of Malta. Nonetheless, the Council was only an advisory body and the Governor retained overall responsibility. After 1835, the political campaigning of the Maltese liberals led to the eventual granting of a partly-elected Legislative Council in 1849. Thus half a century after the occupation of Malta, the British introduced the elective principle in the island's constitution, providing for a Council of eighteen members: the Governor, nine official members and eight elected ones. Although this constitution still enabled the Governor to act independently of the Council, members were allowed to participate in debates concerning policy.

However the Maltese members still felt that they should have had a real measure of control over the internal affairs of the island. Soon the 1849 Constitution ceased to serve any useful purpose, and a more intrusive authoritarian stance was adopted under Governor Sir Gaspard Le Marchant (1858-1864). This British official used to intervene to bring a debate unceremoniously to a close, whenever one of the elected members got up to oppose a measure introduced by the Governor. By 1881 an executive council consisting of the Commanding Officer of the Regular Forces stationed in Malta, the Chief Secretary of the Government, and the Crown Advocate, was established by Letters Patent to advise and assist the Governor in the running of the colony. In the exercise of power the Governor was required to consult this Council but since he alone was entitled to submit questions to this council he could act in opposition to its advice. Nonetheless he had to report his reasons to the Secretary of State for Colonies.

The turning point of the British occupation of Malta came with the opening of the Suez Canal, with the unifications of Italy and Germany, and subsequently by the expansionist policies of the great-powers in the Mediterranean. All these factors together with the fact that Malta was growing in strategic importance, as a station linking Britain to her most important colony, India, induced the colonial government to change from a relatively stable, easygoing affair into an intrusive and authoritarian rule – a condition which heightened, indeed provoked, the clash between Anglicization and *Italianità*. Under this new set of circumstances, the study of English was privileged, while an anti-Italian bias marked routine government administration. In the long run, Italian unification itself proved detrimental both to those Maltese who sympathized with the Italian culture, and to the fate of the Italian language in Malta. Maltese political leaders found themselves divided into two camps, engaged in a conflict between civil rights and military needs.

Until the late 1870s political parties were essentially fluid groupings, crystallizing around prominent politicians rather than ideologies. The perquisites of power were essential if politicians were to have any chance of satisfying the insatiable demands of their voters-cum-clients. Given the rudimentary development of the economy, the state assumed a disproportionate importance as a source of employment. In the never-ending competition for political power, and hence access to patronage, politicians were forever willing to form kaleidoscopic and shifting coalitions. Elections were fiercely and frequently roughly contested. The foundations were thus laid for that political polarity that was to mark Maltese politics ever since.

In the 1880s a group of Maltese who were keen on introducing the reforms wanted by the British came into being. These Anglophile reformists were mainly identified with Sigismondo Savona (1837-1908), a former sergeant-major and schoolmaster, who was later appointed Director of Education and Rector of the University of Malta. Savona knew from his teaching experience how the use of Maltese could facilitate instruction, and thus help motivate people to learn. Savona and his Reform Party came to believe that Malta needed to be Anglicized for the sake of those who depended for their livelihood on the British, or those workers seeking employment in the government service, the Armed Forces, and the dockyard. Savona's Reform Party included the Crown Advocate, as well as some members of the clergy and the Maltese nobility. To help broadcast his ideology, Savona began to publish the newspaper *Public Opinion* but he was supported and even defended in the emergent Anglophile press such as *Il Risorgimento* owned by the newspaper owner and businessman from Cospicua, F.S. de Cesare (1836-1905).

The political unrest instigated by the reforms suggested by Sir Penrose G. Julyan, Francis Rowsell and Patrick Keenan in the administrative, fiscal and educational fields led to the formation of the Partito Anti-Riformista (Anti-Reform Party) which opposed these reforms and was soon renamed Partito Nazionale (National Party). This party came to consider the utilitarian disposition of Savona and the Riformisti (Reform Party) as opportunistic and self-negating.

By contrast, the Nationalists opposed plans for integration with Britain, advocating instead greater autonomy. To the

Nationalists, imperialism meant thinking of Britain in Malta, rather than of Malta in Britain. The party based its arguments on the assumption that the Maltese were being treated not as a people, but merely as native inhabitants of a colonial fortress. The party was founded in 1880 to fight Anglicization with the weapon of *italianità*, and to demand a new constitutional order, in line with the ideas of Fortunato Mizzi (1844-1905), the party's founder.

The son of a Gozitan magistrate, Mizzi had married an Italian resident in Malta. Mizzi viewed Malta as an Italian-like island in a Latin Mediterranean context. He held that the English language was a necessity for Malta, being under British rule, but he strongly argued in favour of Italian as a *lingua franca* for Malta's relations with other Mediterranean countries.

The Mizzi party considered the British military administrators incompetent and not in the least bit interested in the Maltese whose economy was strongly tied to imperial interests and was unable to generate new sources of wealth. Furthermore they argued that in Malta, the British had found a society which was culturally and geographically European. Thus they felt no compulsion to 'civilize' the people in a colonialist sense, since they found a community, relatively sophisticated, represented by a political élite, in possession of values similar to those in any other south European community of the time.

In the course of the nineteenth century, ethnic groups in Europe, were awakening to a new sense of identity, giving expression to their nationalism through the natural outlet of linguistic studies. Maltese national feelings had been precisely generated in this field in accordance with the nineteenth century romantic vision. It included a cultural evaluation of Malta's ancient identity, founded upon Christian values, a series of heroic events, the moral and physical virtues of the Maltese, and above all, the Maltese language as the most distinctive feature of the community. However they wanted the Church to be independent from the state and they were critical of the tendency of the Church hierarchy to ally itself closely to the colonial government.

The party, under the leadership of Fortunato Mizzi (1844-1905), soon became a movement which by 1885 began to publish its own newspaper called *Malta*, had a national club in Valletta, a party secretary and according to police reports had 'the capacity to muster crowds of up to 30,000 in the capital's main streets with bands playing and banners flying', so we are told by Henry Frendo. The new political party began to make its presence felt in the Council where its representatives insisted on internal self-government. They made boycotts, resigned from office and had re-elections.

Exasperated by the military intransigence of governor General Sir J.A. Lintorn Simmons (1884-1888) they deliberately elected imbeciles and scoundrels to the Council with the object – as Earl Kimberley, the Secretary of State for Colonies remarked in 1882 – 'of bringing the Council of Government under contempt'. On 19 December 1882 Governor Sir Arthur Borton dissolved the Council after the resignation of some of its members.

There were many attempts to pull the carpet from under the feet of Mizzi and his supporters. For example the idea of laying more emphasis on property rather than education was promulgated. This was done because it was believed that the Reform Party was supported by the well-to-do while the Anti-Riformisti mainly received support from educated persons. All male British subjects over the age of twenty-one, who either paid rent of at least £6 annually or who had an income of at least £6 from immovable property were eligible to vote. As for candidates, anyone who had at least £100 worth of immovable property for at least one year before the election was eligible. Alternatively one could have a rent of immovable property worth at least £10 per annum or had to pay £40 per annum for lodgings as long as they had not received any charitable relief during the five years prior to their candidature. The Letters Patent of March 1883, which introduced such changes thus extended the franchise to many illiterate persons, while a number of prospective candidates coming from the professional classes did not qualify and were barred from contesting the elections for the Council of Government. The number of registered voters was thus increased from 2,400 to 10,637 in 1883. It was evident that the extension of the franchise was an attempt to try to change the elected members of the Council so that new, more pro-British, members could be elected.

Another important reform was carried out later that month. The Earl of Derby, Secretary of State for the Colonies, was of the opinion that in any geographically-strategic crown colony the Executive Council should be comprised of a larger number of the chief officers of government. Thus in addition to the ex-officio members specified in the 1881 instructions, the Governor could, from then on, appoint other public officers as members of the Executive Council. The Auditor General, the Collector of Customs and the Director of Education were thus appointed as members. Nonetheless the Secretary of State thought that during discussions over matters of local interest, which involved no increase in expenditure, the number of elected and official members had to be equal and the Governor had to cast his vote in line with the unofficial members if these voted unanimously for or against a particular motion. To ensure the smooth running of the Council, Lord Derby issued further instructions on 2 June 1884 suggesting the creation of the offices of Lieutenant-Governor and that of Chief Secretary to the Governor. From then on the Governor could dedicate himself mostly to Council matters. Although these measures were intended to improve the overall running of the Council of Government, discord continued to reign supreme so that episodes, wherein the elected members of the Council used to resign and getting re-elected, were frequent.

Discord between the government and the elected members of the Council reached a nadir level by 1885. The frequent holding of elections, followed by resignations, led to a situation where even scoundrels and men of dubious character were proposed and elected as members of the Council. Not only was the work of the Council rendered difficult but the administration itself was often ridiculed. In short the elected members were making everything possible to convince the Colonial authorities of the urgent need for constitutional changes.

Several members of the Maltese political class came forward with proposals for constitutional changes between 1885 and 1886. But the most comprehensive were those put forward by Fortunato Mizzi and Gerald Strickland. The two politicians had a meeting with the Secretary of State in January 1887. In their proposal they asked for the formation of a 30-strong Legislative Assembly of whom only eight were to be nominated members. They further suggested that the Executive Council should consist of an equal number of official and responsible ministers all of whom had to be chosen by the Governor. They even proposed that a two-thirds majority was necessary in order to defeat the responsible element of the government. Finally they insisted that the Governor should be a civilian.

It was evident that the proposals put forward by Mizzi and Strickland were meant to lead to the introduction of responsible government which the Secretary of State for Colonies thought was incompatible with the British policy for Malta it being a strategically-placed Island Fortress. The government soon became convinced of the necessity for a new constitution. Following the resignation of the elected members of the Council, with the exception of Fortunato Mizzi and Gerald Strickland, Governor Lintorn Simmons dissolved the Council.

The new representative system was introduced in the 1887 constitution. For the first time the people's representatives could decide on votes of public money and other financial and local matters. The Governor was to propose the money to be voted in the Council. Power to implement any decisions through legislation rested in the hands of the British administration. It was suggested that the elected members should be allowed to participate in the preparation of the Estimates of Revenue and Expenditure and on all other measures regarding finance and administrative matters that were introduced by the Council of Government.

The new Council of Government was set up, by Letters Patent dated 12 December 1887, for a maximum of three years. It was to consist of the Governor, who acted as Chairman of the Council or in his absence, by the Chief Secretary, and twenty members. There were six official members namely: the Chief Secretary to the Government; the Crown Advocate; and four others holding public office who also served as members of the Executive Council, appointed by the Governor. In the new Executive Council the Commander-in-Chief of the Armed Forces in Malta, the Chief Secretary of the Government, and the Crown Advocate retained their place together with four public officers. However the Executive Council was now to have at least three other salaried elected unofficial members who were to be paid £300 per annum.

Ten of the unofficial members were elected by popular franchise – nine in Malta and one in Gozo – and the remaining four members were to represent the clergy, the nobility and land-owning classes, the University graduates and the merchants. To be eligible to stand for election a candidate had to be registered as a voter and was to possess, either in his name or that of his wife, immovable property in Malta valued at least at £100 for at least one calendar year prior to the election, or was paying a rent of £10 per annum on immovable property in Malta, or was paying £40 annually for board and lodging or £10 annually for lodgings only. Holders of office under the Crown or with the government of Malta were ineligible and so were bankrupt persons, the insane, criminals or those who had received public charitable relief during the previous five years. It was also stipulated that no more than two ecclesiastics could be elected at any one time. With regards to the clergy however, an amendment to the 1887 Constitution was made where, by Letters Patent in December 1898, ecclesiastics were barred from becoming members of the Council of Government.

All in all the 1887 Constitution enabled the Maltese to elect representatives that would be in a majority in the legislature. The Council also had the power to legislate on most matters concerning Malta's internal affairs, and had 'for the first time a specific power of deciding questions of finance'. The British Crown retained full power to intervene, but these powers were only to be used in exceptional circumstances.

The opposition to a representative government, led by Sigismondo Savona, was by then rather weak although its main spokesman at the time, F. de Cesare, continued to publish his newspaper *Il Risorgimento* regularly. Following the publication of a Report by a new Royal Commission of 1888 Malta was divided into nine single-member electoral districts. The 1888 elections resulted in a resounding victory for the Partito Nazionale of Fortunato Mizzi which won all fourteen seats reserved for the elected members. Mizzi's party now had to ensure that the new constitution would function.

However the 1887 Constitution, also known as the Knutsford Constitution – after the Secretary of State for the Colonies Sir Henry Holland, later Viscount Knutsford (1887-1892) – turned out to be short-lived. The division of legislative and executive control, led to an inevitable conflict between the elected representatives and the Executive Council. The elected members had been given power without responsibility and since they had no responsibility the Executive Council was not responsible to them. In 1889 Mizzi resigned from the Executive Council of Government and the Reform Party of Savona went on the offensive attacking the new constitution and demanding self-government. That same year Gerald Strickland, was appointed Chief Secretary to the Government.

Both Mizzi and Savona were offended by the attitude and pretensions of Lintorn Simmons whose actions induced the two erstwhile opponents to join forces. Perhaps the most important note of discord in this phase was the appointment of the Bishop of Gozo, Mgr. Pietro Pace, as Bishop of Malta. Pace had ousted the popular Bishop Buhagiar thanks to his well-known sympathies for the British administration as expressed by Lintorn Simmons. At this point Governor Lintorn Simmons hoped that with Pace at the helm of the Maltese diocese there were hopes for improved relations with the Vatican. This would in turn facilitate the strengthening of the bond between Britain and Malta 'by the spread of the English language, and by the dissemination of English ideas' among the Maltese. Thus Lintorn Simmons intended to promote assimilation and loyalty through linguistic and ecclesiastical pressures. By July 1890 Bishop Pace had excommunicated the Nationalist organ, *Malta*, which had long described Pace as a 'sycophant and careerist'. Mizzi quickly changed the name of his paper to *Gazzetta di Malta* and continued his campaign against Pace and Governor Lintorn Simmons. Fortunato Mizzi was at this point petitioning the Vatican for the transfer of Bishop Pace to Gozo. Unfortunately for Mizzi when Pace denied the allegations which Mizzi had made against him, the Vatican believed Pace. On the other hand, Savona, who had just been appointed leader of the Partito Unionista – which was the newly-formed party made up of the followers of Savona and Mizzi – won the elections of 1891 and 1892 and began petitioning London for Strickland's removal as Chief Secretary.

The political parties believed that they, rather than the Governor, should have the prerogative to select members to sit on the Executive Council. Letters Patent issued in August 1891 removed the requirement that at least three of the elected members of the Council of Government had to be members of the Executive Council. It also proposed that if eight or more members voted against an ordinance, vote, or resolution on public revenue, it should not be carried. All business in the Council was to be carried by a majority vote of the members present, excluding the Governor or his delegate. It was hoped that such measures would prevent obstructions to the smooth running of government by the elected members. But these constitutional amendments, as well as the proposed customs tariffs produced great unrest among the Maltese.

In 1893 the Partito Unionista split up once again into the Reform Party led by Savona and the Partito Nazionale led by Fortunato Mizzi. That year the Council was changed so that it consisted of twenty-two members namely: the Governor as President, a deputy president, fourteen elected members and six ex-officio members. Sir Adrian Dingli was appointed deputy president and was to hold his position until his retirement in 1895. In 1895 Savona formed a new party, the Partito Popolare which included Mgr. Ignazio Panzavecchia. Savona clamoured for changes in the constitution which led to a direct clash with Strickland. The new party began to publish a newspaper written in the Italian language but Savona soon started to identify the Maltese language with Maltese national revival.

The new party received a popular boost on its stand over the question of mixed marriages. In Malta the validity of marriages, even as a legal contract, was based on Canon Law as enacted in the Council of Trent in 1564. In 1889 an agreement had been reached, between Governor Lintorn Simmons and the Vatican representative, Cardinal Mariano Rampolla, in which it was affirmed that a marriage between two Catholics or between a Catholic and a non-Catholic partner was only valid if celebrated according to the Tridentine rite. All other marriages remained subject to Civil Law. However the Colonial Office decided to settle the issue by a specific legislation that was binding to all areas of the British empire. Thus in 1892 the Foreign Marriage Act declared all mixed marriages as valid.

In Malta the Act was considered as a violation of the former agreement and an open defiance to papal authority. No dramatic consequences took place until 1896 when Governor General Sir Arthur Fremantle (1893-1899) informed the Archbishop had he had to introduce the Act into the local legislation. The question of mixed marriages thus came to a head. Savona's party made a big political issue out of the question. The effective use of mass meetings and newspaper articles managed to stir up public opinion to such an extent that the British decided to drop the matter.

By 1898 matters had turned sour for Savona and disgruntled, he resigned from the Council of Government. This resignation coincided with Mizzi's return to politics. Mizzi was in fact elected in the 1898 elections as head of the Partito Nazionale.

But 1898 is best remembered for the suspicious incident which took place in the law courts. On 25 February, Colonel J.L. Hewson, of the Army Pay Department, was a witness at a magisterial court inquiry connected with a charge of embezzlement involving one of his employees. Hewson refused to sign a transcript of his evidence since it was in Italian, a language that he did not understand. The magistrate assured Hewson that the transcript was accurate but decided to give Hewson time to reconsider his position. At this point Hewson agreed to sign the evidence but at the same time registered a protest in English for having to sign a transcript written in Italian. The magistrate therefore condemned Hewson to three days detention for contempt of Court.

Hewson was never detained in a prison cell – he was merely made to stay in the office of the superintendent of police, until a short while later he obtained a pardon from Governor Fremantle. The incident however did not go unnoticed by the Secretary of State for Colonies Joseph Chamberlain (1895-1903) who soon suggested to the Governor that English should be made an optional language of the Law Courts. The Governor agreed and in December of that year, he stipulated that when a British non-Maltese subject was taken to court, both the proceedings and the verdict were to be carried out in English. The imposition of this new rule led to protests by the elected members of the Council of Government while Chamberlain expressed his satisfaction. Chamberlain then expected the Governor to pass another Order-in-Council by which English was to substitute Italian in all legal proceedings after a period of fifteen years. According to this new order, Summons and Court Orders were to be served both in Italian and in English while the latter language could be used in all judicial practices involving non-Maltese subjects in Malta.

Chamberlain's arrogance was felt to have exceeded the limits and the elected members of the Council of Government felt they could no longer swallow their pride. In May 1899 Fortunato Mizzi, accompanied by another elected member of the

Council of Government, Salvatore Cachia Zammit, left for London on behalf of the elected members of the Council and the Chamber of Advocates. They not only demanded responsible government but they even presented a petition for an elected Legislative Council, a responsible Executive Council, a Civil Governor, and an elected agent-general to represent the interests of the Malta Council of Government in London. Among other things they insisted that Italian should remain the language of the Law Courts.

When Chamberlain met the Maltese delegates he deplored the attitude of the Maltese population which, he said, had shown scant interest in elections and the running of the administration. Chamberlain even warned the Maltese delegates that if the Council were to be impeded in its work, it would have to resort to governing by Orders-in-Council. Chamberlain considered the 1887 Constitution a progressive one for an important fortress colony as Malta was.

When they discussed the Language Question Chamberlain informed them that he had been stunned by the Hewson case. Mizzi and Cachia Zammit continued to hold that Italian should not be substituted by English in the educational system as had already occurred in the Law Courts. They even suggested that the Council ought to consist solely of elected members, since the official ones had no popular backing. The courageous affront of the Maltese delegates does not seem to have left much effect on Chamberlain. During his visit to Malta in November 1900 Chamberlain rebuked Mizzi for agitating the people against the local administration – evidence that he had remained steadfast in his views.

Chamberlain only changed his position in 1902 when, due to the mounting political tensions, he relinquished his language substitution proclamation of 1899 although he retained the free-choice policy of the language used. This free-choice policy meant, in practice, that English was eventually to substitute Italian since English was much more useful for anyone aspiring to join the civil service, or the Armed Forces, or even to merely

exercise a liberal profession. The refusal to agree with the education votes and the principle of free choice in the Language
Question led to the revocation of the 1887 Constitution and the
proclamation of a new more autocratic one in 1903.

*Gerald Strickland, Enrico Mizzi and the Changing Scene of the Early*
*    twentieth Century*

Lord Gerald Strickland (1861-1940), the son of an English naval
captain and a Maltese lady of aristocratic antecedents, had
studied law at Cambridge. At twenty-seven, he was elected to
the first Council of Government under the 1887 Constitution,
and immediately afterwards promoted to Chief Secretary, the
highest local civil post after that of Governor. As Chief Secretary, Strickland saw Malta as a link in the imperial network,
arguing that the closer Malta was to Britain, the more she stood
to gain. Strickland's method of government was inspired partly
by his desire to make the Maltese 'as English as possible'. Strickland was in power as Chief Secretary in Malta from 1889 to
1902 when he was appointed governor of the Leeward Islands
and was later appointed governor of Tasmania, Western Australia and New South Wales. Between 1927 and 1932 he was
also elected Prime Minister of Malta. In 1924 he was elected a
member of the House of Commons in London and later became
a member of the House of Lords until his death in 1940. In the
1920s Strickland established the 'most modern printing press'
Malta had ever seen so far.

    As Chief Secretary for Malta he managed to wield great
power, partly thanks to the fact that successive Governors only
actually administered Malta for brief periods. It was thus
possible for him to introduce some great public works projects
which Henry Frendo states, 'fired the imagination of his constituency and which Malta for one reason or another needed'.
The projects included a breakwater at the Valletta harbour,
which was partly built with imported workers; he conceived the
need for a new general hospital; he wanted to construct quays
to protect shipping at Mġarr, Gozo. During his rule as Prime

Minister he wanted to introduce airport facilities and realized the need for transshipment facilities. Even his wife, Lady Strickland, backed this innovative approach to Malta's infrastructure. She was responsible for the development of the Phoenicia Hotel, this being Malta's first modern tourist facility, and the endowment of St Edward's College, as a public school (on the tradition of the English public school) intended for Maltese pupils.

The pro-British party thus came to regard the Italian language as a great obstacle, arguing that the language of Malta was Semitic rather than Italian. Taking up where Savona had left, Strickland stressed the need to instruct the Maltese in native Maltese and in English, pointing out that both languages were necessary for the amelioration of working-class conditions. Strickland went so far as to maintain that the Maltese were ethnically closer to the English, than to Latins or even Semites. In his zeal to prove the Aryan ancestry of the Maltese, Strickland attempted to develop a new theory of descent. He postulated that the Maltese were descended from the Phoenicians, allegedly distinct kinsmen to the British. In this quaint way, he sought to legitimize his anti-Nationalist policy, as well as uniting these two strands of descent in his own person as an avatar of the past and a man of the future.

Obviously, Strickland's theory of blood-kinship was overstretched. Even so, the 'Arabization' of Maltese was strongly opposed by all sectors of Maltese society. It was then a common assumption that Arabic heritage was synonymous with Muslim civilization, a culture that had no place in any prototype of Christian Europe. Even Savona's party, while holding rightly that Maltese was derived from Arabic, maintained that the Maltese people were Phoenician in origin. Thus the author of a pro-government *Xirka Xemia* (Semitic Society) pamphlet in 1885 affirmed that if you scratched a Maltese you found a Phoenician. Hence Strickland was given full encouragement to propagate Phoenician ancestry for the Maltese. In so doing, Strickland was perpetuating a belief originally mooted by the French Chaplain of the Order of St John, Jean Quintin d'Autun in his *Insulae Melitae descriptio* (1536), and further propagated by Canon Agius de Soldanis and Count Ciantar in the eighteenth century.

Maltese public opinion had thus crystallized around two major political blocs. A reform group supported the British, considering Malta's membership of the British empire as a unique opportunity for the creation of a different economy, for the enhancement of local business, and a higher standard of living. On the other hand, the Anti-Riformisti (later Nationalist party) postulated that ideally the Maltese should control internal affairs, especially public expenditure, and cultivate Malta's ancient heritage which was Catholic by religion and Italian by culture. These provided sufficient reasons to have representative government revoked in 1903, and the 1887 Constitution replaced by another which returned to the principle of an official majority.

It seems incorrect to view the Language Question as a struggle in which a privileged group of Maltese society attempted to maintain its position. It appears that the principal motive behind the Language Question was defensive – that is the retention of those recognized cultural traits that historically distinguished Malta. It is important though to recognize Henry Frendo's assertion that the pro-British and pro-Italian factions seem to have conceived the term 'nation' differently from each other. According to Frendo the pro-British, primarily led by Sigismondo Savona, pointed to the message 'to the Maltese nation' by the Maltese linguist Mikiel Anton Vassalli, who regarded native speakers of Maltese as true nationals (*veri nazionali*). On the other hand, the Nationalists led by Fortunato, and later Enrico Mizzi, referred to the proclamation 'to the Maltese nation' made by the Civil Commissioner Sir Charles Cameron in 1801 wherein the Maltese had been promised 'full protection, and the enjoyment of all dearest rights'.

In short the Language Question focused on the conflict between two great linguistic traditions within the narrow context of a small island. Oliver Friggieri asserts that traits of this conflict can also be identified in the literary field. The influence of Italian novelists served to help the Maltese novelist assimilate and adopt the typical narrative pattern of the historical novel and to apply it to the local situation. Friggieri concludes that the Italian Romantic heritage was instrumental in enabling the Maltese writers to find for themselves the appropriate methods of narration and forms of expression they badly needed to project their own anti-colonial sentiments.

The pre-war period saw the emergence of Dr Enrico Mizzi (1885-1950) son of the elder Fortunato Mizzi and his Neapolitan wife of noble origins. His mother was the daughter of the erstwhile General Consul of the Kingdom of the Two Sicilies in Malta and man of letters Giuseppe Folliero de Luna (1813-1894). Mizzi read Law at the University of Urbino (Italy) and for him Italy was more than it had ever been to his father. For Enrico, Malta was 'the furthermost fringe of Italy' (*l'ultimo lembo d'Italia*) and the Maltese were by natural attachment linked to the 'great mother Italy' (*gran madre Italia*). Mizzi argued that the 'soul of a people' which had been moulded over the centuries could not be transformed instantly. In an article which he wrote in 1912 in the *Rassegna Contemporanea* – the monthly magazine published in Rome – Enrico Mizzi went so far as to propose a federation between Malta and Italy. Mizzi wrote:

> Centuries of tradition are not cancelled. A mother language is not abandoned for another, like a change of clothes...

To Enrico Mizzi, Italy was the fountain of culture, and above all, the spiritual mother of the Maltese at large.

According to Henry Frendo, Mizzi's proposal for a federation was influenced by the changing international situation. Italy had just occupied Libya. The arms race was in full swing and since Germany was building a strong navy it was vital for the British navy to concentrate her activities nearer at home. Indeed Britain had negotiated a naval policy with France whereby the burden of defence could be shared between the two powers: Britain could thus concentrate in the North Sea and France in the Mediterranean. However Mizzi held that Britain could not rely on the French navy, should a war erupt, since France had interests in the Mediterranean to protect.

He argued that 'in case of a German invasion, France would
need soldiers not ships, but Britain's army was relatively small'.
In this context Mizzi wrote that Britain would do well to consider that, 'sooner or later, the natural mistress of the Mediterranean must necessarily be Italy' since only the Italian navy
would always be in the Mediterranean. Britain thus badly
needed Italy's friendship, and this fact, Mizzi opined, was not
greatly appreciated by the British. He stated that if Malta went
to Italy, Britain would enjoy the position of 'most favoured
nation' and gain the alliance of Italy, which Mizzi considered
to be a strong Mediterranean power. Finally he believed that
if Britain would free herself from 'direct, political, territorial
dominion' of territories like Malta, Cyprus and Gibraltar she
would 'retain the advantage' of a Great Power.

A Maltese soldier,
wearing the British
uniform (right), shaking
hands with an Italian
soldier friend (left) during
World War One.

Henry Frendo explains that Enrico Mizzi's 'disposition towards Italy' was similar to 'Strickland's disposition towards Britain'. However since Malta was ruled by Britain, Mizzi had to suffer for his ideas while Strickland was promoted. This explains why in 1917 – during the Great War – he was court-martialled for alleged sedition, his house was searched and his study ransacked by security officers. Mizzi had previously made a speech in the Council of Government, where he had inveighed against 'the proverbial English hypocrisy'. The charge of sedition was intended to make life difficult for Mizzi. He found some support in his colleagues within the ranks of the Nationalist Party who in protest at this court martial reaffirmed their refusal to sit in Council or to co-operate with the Colonial Government.

*The Socio-Economic Crisis at the Turn of the Twentieth Century and the Sette Giugno Riots of 1919*

But the younger Mizzi was not the only one who spoke clearly against British Colonial interests. Emanuele Dimech (1860-1921), a former convict who had transformed himself into a populist journalist and teacher of foreign languages, wrote an article in 1913 in which he declared that Britain should 'leave us', and that Malta should be independent from all other powers. According to Henry Frendo, the economic hardship and political discontent of 1911 induced Dimech to found 'a politically-minded workers' benefit society'. Dimech had just returned from a long stay in Genoa, Italy and revived the paper *Il-Bandiera tal-Maltin* which he had originally published between 1898 to 1905. Frendo claims that Dimech 'was possibly the first public figure determined to express his desire for total independence from Britain'.

Emanuele Dimech was expelled from Malta shortly after the outbreak of the First World War in September 1914, by Governor General Sir Leslie Rundle (1909-1915). Dimech was interned in a prisoner of war camp in Egypt where he died in 1921 – three years after the end of the war. When, in 1921, Lord Allenby, the British High Commissioner in Cairo, insisted on Dimech's repatriation, Governor Field-Marshal Viscount Plumer (1919-1924) wrote back saying that 'Dimech is regarded as a dangerous enemy of the Roman Catholic Church'. Lord Plumer considered Dimech to be 'a clever and dangerous criminal', since his presence was considered a danger to the state. Dimech was said to have made attempts 'to tamper with the loyalty of the employees of His Majesty's Dockyard' amongst whom he propagated 'Socialist and revolutionary principles' and his readmittance to Malta was thus undesirable.

A new Council of Government was set up after the publication of a Letters Patent dated 3 June 1903. It was to be chaired by the Governor and was to include the Lieutenant Governor, the Chief Secretary to the Government and seventeen other members, nine of whom were official members, including the Crown Advocate and eight other public officers. The rest of the members were to be elected from the nine electoral districts. Judges could be summoned to the Council, if required, for the discussion of any law. The Executive Council lost its elected members and the Governor, or his representative had no casting vote.

In effect the 1903 Council was considered to be a backward step since it reverted to the official majority principle of the 1849 Constitution. J.J. Cremona emphasizes the fact that

the elected members of the Council referred to it as 'one of the narrowest and most oppressive oligarchies that ever mocked the form of free government' and protested against it by systematic abstentionism.

There was a general outcry and strong reaction against the new constitution by the political parties. No less than seven elections were held between August 1903 and April 1904. The first six were only contested by Mizzi and members of his Partito Nazionale and these resigned immediately after making declaring that they could only uphold self-government for Malta. After April 1904 the Partito Nazionale refused to contest any more elections unless they were contested by other parties. Due to the crisis of the Council of Government the administration was run on the advice of the Executive Council and whenever legal matters arose the Legislative Council was consulted for advice. Meanwhile on 23 January 1905, the Associazione Politica Maltese was formed with, as its main aim, that of rallying popular support and question the legitimacy of the government. Fortunato Mizzi was appointed President but on his death on 18 May 1905, Francesco Azzopardi, took over the leadership of the Associazione Politica Maltese which had come to represent the interests of the Partito Nazionale. In May 1907 the elected members of the Council of Government resigned as a sign of no confidence in the colonial government.

Yet, unlike Mizzi, Francesco Azzopardi favoured cooperation with the administration and he argued that, once elected, a member of the Council had to abide by the rules of the Council rather than resign. His views were shared by other elected members like Dr (later Sir) Filippo Sceberras and Dr (later Sir) Arturo Mercieca. Because of his views, Azzopardi was forced to relinquish the editorship of the influential Mizzi newspaper, *Malta*, to Fortunato's son, Dr Giuseppe Mizzi, who had just returned from Rome's Pontifical University where he had read law. In turn Azzopardi began to publish *L'Avvenire*.

In reality two opposing poles had been created within the Partito Nazionale as early as 1901: the abstentionist group led by Dr Giuseppe Mizzi and Dr Andrea Pullicino and the anti-abstention faction led by Francesco Azzopardi. Following Azzopardi's retirement from politics – he was to make a successful political comeback in 1915 – the Partito Nazionale and the Partito Popolare joined forces as a new party called Comitato Patriottico which was formed in 1911 under the leadership of Mgr. Ignazio Panzavecchia. This new political party followed a rigid abstentionist policy between 1911 and 1914. It was a time of economic depression, unemployment and a lowering of the standard of living.

During the First World War, Malta served as a hospital for wounded soldiers, a dockyard for the British navy, a prison camp for prisoners-of-war, and a home for refugees from Egypt

and other Middle Eastern Countries. Maltese soldiers joined
the British Military on missions to various destinations like
those of Salonica and Gallipoli. During the war the cost of living soared to unprecedented heights and the prices of bread,
sugar, and meat were those mostly affected. Despite the government's strict control of prices and the subsidization of flour
to millers, a black market economy reigned supreme.

The illiberal 1903 constitution prevailed until the end of the
First World War in 1918. Political dissension and heated debates
over the Language Question played a secondary role in the
minds of the masses of the population during the early decades
of the twentieth century. Thus it was the grave financial and
economic condition, rather than language, which dominated
Maltese politics. In the period between 1898-1906 Malta saw
the greatest boom ever to be experienced under British rule.
It was a time of great public works like the implementation of
the drainage scheme, the transition from stone aqueducts to
iron pipes for water distribution, the introduction of a railway
line between Valletta and Mdina, and works connected with
the introduction of electricity. These works were being carried
out on the instigation of Strickland in his role of Secretary to
the Government, and new excise duties had been proposed to
cover the expenses. The elected members of the Council began
to suspect that such projects as those for water, sewage and
electricity were being introduced for the benefit of the British
forces and for this reason opposed Strickland's proposals as well
as the introduction of new taxes. Most of Strickland's projects
were sanctioned by means of Orders-in-Council without consulting the elected members. Thus agitation increased.

The newly formed Comitato Nazionale, presided over by Dr
Filippo Sceberras, expressed its wish that the expenses should
be borne by the Imperial Government and, in its opposition
to the proposed taxes, organized two mass meetings at Ta'
Braxia on 5 May and 11 August 1901. That same year further
works included the drainage system which from the harbour
towns was extended to the country districts, the building of
new elementary schools, the introduction of water works, the

building of new hospitals and roads. All this reached a total expenditure of £380,500. Shortly afterwards the construction of a breakwater at the mouth of the Grand Harbour and a new drydock, this time paid for by the Admiralty, were also began. The War Office had also partly contributed towards the cost of some of the works, particularly the installation of the new drainage system, the breakwater, and the new roads, since it was deemed that these works could effect 'naval and military interests'. Indeed, as Frendo remarks, the British Armed Forces were spending an estimated £2,000,000 annually in Malta.

By 1906 the works were ready. Unemployment rose and wages were lowered to such an extent that panic set in and many wanted to emigrate. The government bill for charities rose to £68,000 by 1909 while the revenue plunged. In 1906 the Malta government recorded a deficit of £14,330; in 1907 of £17,592; in 1909 of £24,842, and in 1910 of £26,246. The boom was thus followed by one of the worst depressions that the Maltese were ever to suffer. Godfrey Pirotta argues that

> between 1906 and 1911 a series of successive annual deficits… the cost of a number of extraordinary works, and a sharp decline in government revenue, rapidly drove Malta towards bankruptcy.

In British Malta economic boom was always followed by depression. The major reason for this was that Malta had a client economy servicing the needs of the fortress-colony. Hence a sharp increase in imperial spending, due to public works connected with the maintenance of the fortress, or by the military regiments or naval warships stationed in Malta, usually gave rise to a situation of relative economic prosperity. During the boom periods prices of commodities and rents increased but when the works ceased or for some reason British military or naval presence was reduced crisis normally followed. Unemployment rose sharply during these periods followed by a sharp decrease in wages while rents and prices took time to fall proportionally.

By 1911 the Government reserve fund had been practically exhausted and the local authorities had nothing to fall back on. In November of that year a Royal Commission, consisting of Sir Francis Mowatt, Sir Mackenzie Chalmers, and Russell Rea, arrived in Malta to inquire into the financial system, judicial procedures and the general economic condition of Malta. In the report which they submitted on 22 April 1912, they concluded that military and naval considerations had given rise to a system of public works on a scale that was far more extensive and costly than would have been justified 'if the government had been administered solely in the interests of the Maltese'. The Commission made some valuable suggestions on the development of agriculture and the irrigation system and on economizing on public expenditure. They proposed that Malta should either discontinue her payment of the military contribution or else the British should start paying Malta rent for those sites occupied by the military for reasons other than fortifications. They even suggested an increase in the imperial contribution towards the construction and maintenance of public works which, directly or indirectly, affected the Armed Forces.

Among other things, the Commission also advocated compulsory elementary education, a reduction on the grain tax and the imposition of higher duties on imported tobacco, alcoholic drinks and sugar besides the introduction of a duty on imported articles, a house tax and the succession duty. They also recommended that the government should encourage emigration outside the Mediterranean to places like the United States while tourism to Malta should be encouraged. Finally they suggested various changes in the judicial establishments such as recommending that oral proceedings in the inferior courts should be conducted in Maltese and that in the superior court if a Maltese was on trial, then the person should have the right to have his case tried in Maltese. In the case of an English-speaking person proceedings were to be in English.

In the first decade of the twentieth century, Anglo-German rivalry shifted attention to defence requirements in the North Sea, and this detracted from Malta's naval importance. Arthur Clare concludes that between 1906 and 1914, the problem of how to solve the unemployment problem was a constant source of worry to the British administration. Increased expenditure on public works had only a limited temporary effect. It was during this period that large numbers of Maltese began to leave the Islands in search of a better future abroad. Indeed this crisis in the shortage of work, was to have a terrible impact on the rapidly expanding population of Malta. It was made worse by the rapid inflation which accompanied the Great War of 1914-1918. At first, the First World War brought an economic revival which helped neutralize the situation for a few years. But this reprieve was short-lived.

It was soon followed by grave food shortages, spiralling prices, and mass unemployment. Immediately afterwards the Maltese political leaders, seeing that their strong verbal protest were serving no use, convoked a National Assembly to petition for home rule. The Assembly met under Sir Filippo Sceberras. Tension due to the political and a grave economic situation reached a peak on 7 June 1919, better known as *Sette Giugno*, when rioting broke out in Valletta, leading to a bloody confrontation with armed forces.

On that fatal day, a 'National Assembly' was set up to draft a new self-government constitution. The meeting was held at the premises of the Giovine Malta in Valletta when crowds, gathered in support of the Assembly and in anger at the general

British troops retreating into the Valletta Law Courts after having fired on the Maltese crowd on 7 June 1919.

situation. The British troops were called in to restore order and fired into the crowds, armed at best with sticks and stones. Rioting broke out and the situation got out of hand so that there was much looting, pelting and manhandling, yet all those who died were Maltese. Three Maltese men were shot dead on 7 June, while another was bayoneted on the following day. Two more died later from injuries and several dozens were wounded, while no casualties were reported on the British forces' side. The *Sette Giugno*, with its tragic associations, has since become a symbolic date in the genesis of Maltese nationalism.

The final outcome of this crisis was the granting of a modified form of responsible government to Malta in 1921. It seems that the Imperial Government became convinced that no improvement in the finances of the island could be expected unless some form of responsible government was introduced. The 1921 constitution provided for bicameral representative and responsible government. This new approach by the British Imperial government may be considered as a milestone in Malta's constitutional history.

*Teething Problems of Self Government and the Strategic Development of Malta: 1921-1939*

Under the 1921 Constitution, the control of the island was divided between two governments, the Maltese Imperial Government and the Maltese Government. The former was to be under the direction of the Governor, but subject to instructions from London. It was to deal with all matters, such as trade, immigration, defence, foreign relations, and telecommunications – all issues reserved to the Imperial Government under the new Constitution. On the other hand the Maltese Government was to be headed by an Executive Council consisting of seven ministries (including a Head of Ministry). The Executive Council was in turn responsible to a popularly elected Legislative Assembly of thirty-two members and a Senate of seventeen members elected by corporate bodies, such as the Church and the Unions, and by electors possessing special qualifications. Elections for the Maltese Government were to be held every three years. In cases of conflict between the imperial and local governments the matters under dispute were to be referred to the Privy Council. The Privy Council consisted of the Executive Council and the Nominated Council sitting in joint session, or to the Joint Committee of the Privy Council consisting of six members, three from each side. Males, twenty-one years of age or older, who were literate, or enjoyed an unearned income of not less than £5 a year, were eligible to vote for the Legislative Assembly.

English was to be the official language of administration but without prejudice to the use of Italian, the official language of legal record and culture. Debates in the legislature were to be conducted in the two languages and Maltese. But English and Italian were to be recognized as equal languages of culture in education from the higher classes of elementary school onwards. Enrico Mizzi's party, the clergy and the Chamber of Advocates were opposed to these articles in the constitution and urged that knowledge of English and Italian should be made a qualification for membership in the legislature. They were hoping that such a measure would bar members of the emerging Labour Party from standing as electoral candidates in the forthcoming elections. Not surprisingly, the Imperial Workers Union at the dockyard, which strongly supported the labour movement, stressed that Maltese should be retained.

The general elections under the new Constitution were held in early October 1921. Three of the political parties which contested the elections of 1921, the first to be held under self-government, represented all the old divisions which had until then characterized Maltese political development, in terms of personalities, policies and language. The Partito Democratico Nazionalista (PDN) led by Enrico Mizzi, was staunchly pro-Italian. The Unione Politica Maltese (UPM) led by the prelate Mgr. Ignazio Panzavecchia (1855-1925) – essentially the party of the Church – was pro-Italian but more moderate than the PDN in its opposition to English. The Constitutional Party (CP), led by Sir Gerald Strickland, the former Chief Secretary to the Government of Malta, was fervently pro-British. Then there was the fledgling, rather pro-British, Labour Party (LP) – originally known as La Camera del Lavoro, under the leadership of Col. William Savona, son of Sigismondo Savona. The major difference in the pro-British stance between the Labour Party and the Constitutional Party was that the Labour leaders favoured English only because they thought that it would be more beneficial to workers seeking employment.

The only matters common to all contesting parties were the intense party passions and the violent views. When the votes were counted Mizzi's PDN won all four seats of the Gozo constituency but none in Malta. The LP won seven, Strickland's CP seven and Panzavecchia's UPM, won fourteen out of the thirty-two seats in the Legislative Assembly. The new government was inaugurated with great pomp by the Prince of Wales on 2 November 1921. The UPM governed as a minority government under Joseph Howard, a local businessman, as Head of Ministry. In accordance with the constitution, Howard appointed six of his colleagues as ministers. He appointed ministers for Justice, Education, Public Works (which included the departments of transport, water and electricity), Commerce and Agriculture, and Health. Joseph Howard reserved the Ministry of Finance for himself.

The alignment between Panzavecchia and the Mizzi party enabled the Nationalists to win the elections of 1921 and 1924. But the formation of a compact between Strickland's Constitutionalists and the Labour Party permitted a change in government in 1927 and Strickland became Prime Minister. A number of factors – particularly confrontation between Strickland's government and the Catholic Church – led to the breakdown of the existing constitution and in 1930 the self-government constitution was suspended. In 1928, Strickland had expected the Bishops to take a stand against the participation of ecclesiastics in local politics and to direct the ecclesiastics representatives in the Senate to support the government.

According to Joseph Bezzina 'this was the crux of the Church-State confrontation that exploded in 1928'. There were several anti-clerical demonstrations fanned by the Constitutionalist papers and on 15 August the Archbishop of Malta, Dom Mauro Caruana, condemned anti-clericalism and announced the setting up of a Church weekly newspaper in Maltese the *Leħen is-Sewwa* which was meant to counter-act these attacks. The Apostolic Delegate, Mgr. Robinson, sent purposely by the Vatican to analyse the situation, declared that Strickland wished

at all costs to make the church subservient to the State and to reduce the Bishops and priests to the position of mere employees of the Government... [showing] no regard whatever for the law, nor for the rights and feelings of the clergy and of the Catholic people.

It seems that although Strickland was a practising Catholic he was attempting to introduce some Anglican principles – such as that whereby the Sovereign is the Head of the Church – to the practice of Catholicism in Malta.

The situation was further marred by the Carta incident. The Provincial of the Franciscan Conventual Friars, Father Felice Carta had ordered the transfer of Father Guido Micallef to a Sicilian convent. Since Father Micallef was known to sympathize with Strickland's party his transfer was considered by Strickland as a banishment for political motives and Strickland's government intervened to put off the departure. Church-State relations became worse when three Anglican bishops, on a visit to Malta, were allowed to organize a conference in the Throne-Room of the Governor's Palace.

It was only thanks to a recommendation by the Royal Commission of 1931 that self-government was restored. In the following year the Nationalists won a landslide victory. Soon after the elections of 1931 it became clear that the verbal abuse and other incorrect manoeuvres that characterized the general elections were to characterize the debates of both the Legislative Assembly and the Senate. This was partly due to the social and cultural set-up of tiny Malta where the political sympathies and allegiances of individuals and whole family groups are at best known, or at least suspected. Godfrey Pirotta refers to the case of two teachers, Mr Borg and Mr Cachia, who were suffering from the same medical condition and applied for a special permission to travel to England to undergo treatment.

However while the request filed by Mr Borg was immediately acceded to on the basis of his personal physician's medical certificate, that of Mr Cachia was subjected to the scrutiny of a medical board which reported only after the ship on which he was booked had sailed. The issue was discussed at the Legislative Assembly and it was alleged by the opposition that a different treatment was meted out to the two gentlemen in question because while Mr Borg was a supporter of Panzavecchia's party the latter was a supporter of Strickland's party.

Patron-client relationships permeated through society at all levels and, indeed, have continued to be a pronounced feature of society until the present. Having the right contacts, who could mitigate the inertia and inefficiency of the bureaucracy, was all-important, while the reciprocal dispensation of favours, was the essential lubricant of a cumbersome and unresponsive state machine. Laws, which the Council of Government, and later parliament, spewed out in large quantities, were there essentially to be got around rather than obeyed.

Patronage, which had originally developed under the knights as a way of economic and social advancement had, under the British become a kind of defence mechanism against the harshness, and particularly the arbitrariness, of the system of government which was geared towards the running of the fortress-colony. During the middle years of British rule many Maltese began to regard the impositions of the colonizing country as rather more oppressive than those of the later phase of the Hospitallers. Patronage thus became so much ingrained in society that with the installation of the first Maltese parliament in 1921 it proved wholly compatible with the formal institutions of British colonial rule. The local parliamentary deputy saw it not only as an obligation but also as the indispensable precondition of political survival to secure favours for his voters.

In 1924 the Governor himself reported that ministers were involved in political patronage. On the eve of the 1927 elections the Governor reported that Government ministers, sensing defeat, had employed several hundred labourers with the public service. One must admit that in the period 1921-1926, neither the UPM, nor the CP or the PN, all of which had been in government at one point or another, had done anything to eradicate the patronage system inherited from the Imperial Government. Prominent politicians were even reputed to have had a multitude of god-children, many of whom had to be found jobs when they came of age.

This method of patronage was extended to the local Police Force. It should be mentioned that although the Police Force had never really been an efficient and effective body it had nonetheless been strengthened after the *Sette Giugno* riots of 1919. Such improvements were however lost since ministers of the various ruling political parties strove to recruit persons on whose personal loyalty they could depend. The net result was that those appointed did not consider themselves as civil servants but as party henchmen.

Opponents to the ruling party in turn threatened these police officers, making it clear to them that once the ruling party was

Anti-Italian caricature in the pro-British Maltese daily *Il-Berka* criticizing the speech of Italian fascist minister Giunta during his visit to Malta in April 1932.

not re-elected to office they would be dismissed from service. Such conditions induced the Secretary of State for Colonies to send a Royal Commission in 1931 to reappraise the working of responsible government and to recommend methods to improve it. The Royal Commission recommended that unless matters improved, responsibility for the police should be transferred to the Imperial Government. Undoubtedly there was a considerable divergence between the outward form of politics and the substantive practice. The political world may have been something of a self-perpetuating oligarchy but few avenues of advancement were closed off on grounds of social origins alone. The demands on the politicians were such that few prospered at the public expense. In addition, all political figures were expected to, and did, make themselves available to the humblest supplicant.

New elections for both the Senate and the Legislative Assembly were held in June 1932. Political meetings were accompanied by disturbances while threats and violence were not lacking. The Nationalist Party, which had made revocation of the language provisions one of its electoral platforms, won a landslide victory. The Nationalists gained twenty-one seats as against ten by Strickland's Constitutionals and one by Labour.

Immediately, Enrico Mizzi set about restoring the status of Italian. But rather unwisely, Italian influence, including Fascist propaganda, was allowed to increase and several Italian schools, most notably the Umberto Primo College, began to function. It was obviously not the best time for initiating such policies, considering the complex international relations and strained relation of Britain with Italy. British imperial policy was dominated by the strategic interests of the Island Fortress and everything had to be subordinated to those interests. It was argued that 'a calm civil population unexcited by political controversy' was at that point necessary. Despite British warnings to the Nationalist ministers to modify their agenda this policy went unheeded.

In 1933 the British revoked Malta's self-government constitution and the entire cabinet was dismissed. The Governor took full control of the police and gave an ultimatum to the

Maltese government but the ultimatum was rejected. The Governor proceeded to dismiss the government, dissolve parliament and suspend the constitution. Malta was thus reduced to a veritable fortress. Political meetings were banned, the press was placed under stringent controls, and a spate of sedition cases were brought before the Law Courts. In 1934 the function of jurors in sedition trials was abolished and it was decreed that sittings of this kind were to be held behind closed doors while the sentence and its motivations were to remain secret. Judges known for their pro-British sentiments were elevated to the judicial bench, evidence that the British Imperial government had no faith in the pro-Italian judges, including the Chief Justice, Sir Arturo Mercieca. It was claimed that the changes were carried out in order to protect the legitimate interests of British Imperial policy. The subsequent constitutions of 1936 and 1939 were non-representative and most unwelcome for all politically-conscious Maltese.

As it turned out self-government not only failed to repay the early optimism displayed by all parties in Malta but proved to be an anti-climax, for instead of leading towards the major goal of the Nationalist Party – that of Dominion Status – it served to revert the island to the position of a Crown Colony. This gives strength to Frendo's view that in British Malta

constitutions were putty in the hands of their makers and takers... pieces of paper that passed for basic laws for as long as Big Brother thought fit.

Language played an inevitable part in this retrogression. The rise of Fascism in Italy, and Mussolini's frequent reference to Malta as part of Italia Irredenta, together with his claim to the Mediterranean, as Italy's Roman *mare nostrum*, tended to make Britain increasingly nervous about Italian influence in Malta. But even before the rise of Fascist Italy, the British had inserted provisions in favour of the English language in the 1921 constitution. According to this constitution, the English language was, with Italian, to be one of the official languages of Malta and the language of administration. Nothing was allowed to undermine the position of the English language. J.J. Cremona specifies that both Italian and English were to be

recognized as equal languages of culture in the University, in secondary
schools and in the higher classes of elementary schools as subjects of study.

In 1932 Enrico Mizzi, as Minister of Education, had tried to
restore the Italian language to what he considered as its rightful place in the Maltese educational system. He received several
warnings from London which, according to Dennis Austin, was
the reason why the constitution was suspended in 1933. The
final blow to Italian was delivered by the Imperial Government
in 1936 when legislation was passed which formally annulled
the Letters Patent of 1921 in favour of the *pari passu* of English and Italian. Malta reverted to a colonial administrative rule
until 1947, when self-government was restored.

By 1935 Malta had drifted into an undeclared state of emergency. The Italian language was pronounced *lingua non grata*
and Italian influence in Malta was attacked with vigour and
resolve. Godfrey Pirotta remarks that 'public servants, known
for their pro-Italian sympathies were dismissed from the public service and British officers were brought in to supervise
the civil service'. When war broke out others, including some
high ranking officials, were arrested, interned and finally deported.

In September 1939, after the invasion of Poland by the Nazis,
Britain and France declared war on Germany. By June 1940
France was defeated and British troops were everywhere on the
retreat. German victory seemed assured and Italy was expected
to enter the war as its ally. The British knew well enough that
if this were to happen Malta would certainly be attacked.

In expectation of this attack scores of staunch Nationalist
supporters, including the leader of the Party and member the
Council of Government, Enrico Mizzi, were arrested and interned on suspicion of disloyalty or as a precautionary measure.
When the attack finally came, on 11 June 1940, the Governor
put into operation the instruction sent to him from London a
week before. Civil servants suspected of disloyalty to the Crown
were arrested and interned, the most prominent among them
being the Chief Justice, Sir Arturo Mercieca. Eventually those

arrested, including Mizzi himself and Mercieca, were later deported to Uganda without trial or charge, under special emergency powers, until the end of the war. The Nationalist member of the Council of Government Sir Ugo Mifsud spoke in defence of the right of innocent citizens to live in their own country, and for those presumed guilty to be first tried. He collapsed during his speech, in the Council, and died shortly afterwards. The only other Maltese councillor who supported Sir Ugo Mifsud was Dr Giorgio Borg Olivier.

These measures against a group of Maltese did not stir any popular opposition. As war loomed larger the anti-Italian sentiments of the working classes became more manifest. In reality British policy after 1933 was clear and unmistakable. It was to prepare the fortress colony for the events of war with Italy. In 1939 the elective element in the Council of Government was reintroduced replacing that of 1933 which consisted of the Governor and a number of nominated officials. The new Council was to consist of the Governor, eight officials, two nominated members, and ten elected representatives. In the elections that followed, the Nationalists were defeated by the staunchly pro-British Constitutionalists. In itself it represents a significant departure from the past. It was definitely the greatest British victory against Italian – the tongue which had served as the official language of Malta since the Middle Ages. After years of forcible imposition of the English language over the Italian language as an act of Imperial force majeur, the Italian language was finally 'rejected' by the Maltese themselves.

Harshly subjected to Britain's strategic priorities, Maltese constitutional history lacked dynamic evolutionary development. Malta's special position in the empire was eloquently summed up in the observation report of the Malta Royal Commission of 1931. The report pointed out that it was almost impossible 'to plot a graph' of constitutions, 'modelled alternatively on the principle of benevolent autocracy and that of representative government'. Thus, as a British possession and a fortress, Malta did not have the characteristics to develop as a nation-state in the full political sense. On the other hand, unlike several other British colonies – divided by race, religion, tribe, or cultural factions – the Maltese were a homogeneous community, deeply attached to their ethnic traditions.

In short British policy sought to strengthen its authority over Malta in defence of its wider strategic interests. The Imperial government thus strove to strengthen its rule by drawing on the local patriotism of the ordinary people – hence the elevation of Maltese, the language of the masses, rather than Italian the language of the middle classes. Thus from then on Maltese was given equal status with English and priority over Italian. As World War Two was to show, British imperial policy was to reap its reward. The result was an intense local patriotism which resisted both the Italian and Nazi German onslaught, and a closer relationship with Britain which directed and sustained that resistance.

# 6

## World War II and its Legacy

### The Second World War

Malta was endowed with superb harbours and dockyard facilities, an unsinkable fortress strategically situated in the central Mediterranean, a vital link with the two nearest bases a thousand miles away at Gibraltar and Alexandria. Malta's proximity to Sicily made it extremely susceptible to direct air attack and to naval blockade should Italy decide to enter the war on Germany's side – a possibility that had existed ever since the creation of the Berlin-Rome Axis. British rearmament plans, intensified after the Munich crisis of September 1938, but envisaged no serious defence of the island.

The decision not to defend Malta reflected the predominant views of the British Army and Air Force. On the other hand the Admiralty, in particular Admiral Cunningham, Commander-in-Chief of the Mediterranean fleet, knew that the fall of Malta would mean the end of British naval supremacy in the Mediterranean. It was thus with great reluctance that Cunningham agreed to employ a large part of his fleet to Alexandria in Egypt which was to remain its principal base for the first half of the war. Besides the responsibilities of defending and supplying the British garrisons in Egypt, Palestine, Cyprus and Malta, the navy also had the task of maintaining communications with Greece and Turkey in the event of an attack by the Axis powers.

Here lay the importance of Malta as a base for the British Mediterranean fleet.

Thus the problems confronting Admiral Cunningham were complex but since Italy had remained neutral, in the first few months of the war, Admiral Cunningham gave in. Already in September 1939, the naval forces in Malta were minimal so that when the admiral returned to his headquarters in Malta it was to control a much reduced Mediterranean fleet. The ground defences of the island amounted to a few light anti-aircraft batteries and the defensive guns of the Grand Harbour. There were also four British infantry battalions and a newly-formed Maltese battalion. No aircraft were stationed in the three airfields while the only available planes were four Gladiators packed in crates and meant to serve as spares for an aircraft-carrier which was then stationed in British waters.

The failure to provide Malta with adequate means of defence and attack must be regarded as one of the most costly omissions of British pre-war defence policy. The lightning German campaign in France and the evacuation of British and French troops from Dunkirk convinced Mussolini that the time was ripe to enter the war on the side of the Axis. Within a few hours of his declaration of war against Britain and France, Italian planes were dropping their first bombs on Malta. Malta's struggle for survival had began. From then on, and for the next three years, Britain's key link in the Mediterranean was to face the combined wrath of the Italian and German air forces. Major-General Sir William Dobbie, Governor and Commander-in-Chief of Malta had anticipated the Italian move by ordering essential elementary precautions. These included earthwork defences for the airfields, and an attempt to persuade the Maltese to disperse during air raids and take refuge in caves and rock shelters. The Gladiator fighters were uncrated and assembled, one of them crashed but the other three constituted the island's only fighter protection. Conscription was introduced for able-bodied Maltese men, and two regiments – one infantry and one artillery – were formed.

On the first day of hostilities on 11 June, eight air-raids were conducted against the airfields and the dockyard. Two British warships responded with anti-aircraft fire and shot down three enemy planes. The first raids killed twenty-three civilians and seven soldiers. During the first week thirty alerts were recorded. The Maltese soon adjusted themselves to this pattern of high level bombing. Malta's fighter defences and air-striking power remained pitifully inadequate until the end of 1940. This situation made it difficult to keep the movements of Italian merchant ships under observation. It is hardly surprising that out of the 690,000 tons of shipping that the Italians sent to Libya between June and December 1940, only just above two per cent was sunk while 47,000 troops were landed without loss. On the other hand the Italian bombers did not prove as effective as anticipated. Malta had withstood the bomber attacks and would, without any doubt, be in better shape when reinforcements arrived.

The island entered the first phase of a long struggle for survival in January 1941. This struggle was to severely tax the courage and endurance of Malta's defenders and civilian population. Extensive convoy operations, known as 'Excess' managed to bring some relief to the hard-pressed island. On 8 January, five hundred troops and airmen arrived from Alexandria on two cruisers while two Operation 'Excess' ships entered the Grand Harbour with ammunition, seed potatoes, a cargo of twelve Hurricane fighters and eight hundred soldiers.

In the meantime an important target for the Luftwaffe's attention arrived in Malta. On 10 January the air-craft carrier HMS *Illustrious*, which had been severely damaged by German dive-bombers operating from Sicily, limped into the Grand Harbour for repairs. By 15 January the Luftwaffe decided to destroy the carrier and sent reconnaissance planes to explore the Grand Harbour. The following day some eighty Stuka dive-bombers flew over the Grand Harbour in successive waves, aiming their bombs at the *Illustrious* and the dockyard. In this attack the dockyard, together with several public buildings and churches were severely damaged. Nearly one hundred men, women and children, mostly in the Cottonera area, lost their lives during this first German raid. The anti-aircraft guns of the carrier and of the dockyard defences and the fighters had managed to shoot down ten dive-bombers.

The Germans returned on 18 June directing their attacks towards the airfields of Luqa and Hal Far, when six aircraft were destroyed on the ground, and many others were damaged. The next day the Stukas once again concentrated their efforts on the still floating *Illustrious*. Repairs on the carrier were pursued in earnest in order to get her clear of the island in the shortest possible time. The *Illustrious* managed to sail to Alexandria on the night of 23 January. During the following days the crippled and outnumbered air force in Malta had to fight against the Luftwaffe whose numbers varied from forty to eighty planes at any one time. Nonetheless the fighter and anti-aircraft defences managed to shoot down sixteen German planes. Meanwhile Admiral Cunningham became convinced that unless a minimum fighter protection could be provided the passage through the Mediterranean by ships of Operation 'Excess' had to be suspended. Malta's air defences had to be vastly strengthened if the British wanted to keep Malta especially since it became obvious that the Germans were more determined, very accurate and definitely more dangerous than the Italians. The British capture of Cyrenaica and the advance to El Agheila on 8 February 1941 resulted in a slight reduction of the *Luftwaffe* forces in Sicily, as these had gone to bolster up those in North Africa. But by the end of the month Malta was again under heavy attack which began to occur almost daily. By March a one-hundred-plane attack on Hal Far caused extensive damage to the planes and airport buildings of that airfield.

In the meantime food stocks and other essentials fell lower by the hour and real hardship began to creep in on the islanders. No further supplies reached Malta until late March when a small convoy arrived from Alexandria. During the first ten months of hostilities Malta stood in the forefront of the Mediterranean struggle. The island had managed to defend itself with great determination against far superior forces. There is little doubt that in the opening months, when the garrison and the ground and air defences were quite inadequate, a more resolute and enterprising opponent would have successfully invaded and taken the island. But the Italians had let this unique opportunity slip by thus enabling Malta to survive.

After the fall of Crete in June 1941, Malta was a thousand miles from its nearest help. Fortunately the supply lines were still open, food was not yet scarce, and since the Italians were still in control in Sicily, air-raids were few and inaccurate. Italian bombers never learned the German dive-bombing technique. However in July 1941, the Italian Decima Flottiglia Mas made a bold attack upon the Grand Harbour in order to sink a convoy that had just arrived. Some months before the Italians had successfully launched explosive motor boats against British shipping in Crete and put a British cruiser out of action. These small boats carrying an explosive charge were so small that there was space only for the engine and the pilot who sat on an ejector seat which he could dislodge to shoot himself away before the moment of contact with the target.

Eleven such boats participated in this attack on Malta. The attackers were unaware that as soon as they left Augusta in Sicily they had already been detected by the Malta radar, and the coast defence was alerted. It had been intended to bomb Malta during the course of the operation and obscure the noise of the seaborne attack. However the air raid did not take place and the noise of the engines could be heard by the batteries of the Malta Grand Harbour. The long breakwater at the entrance of the Grand Harbour forced the small flotilla to pass through the narrow passage close to the shore. The passage had been blocked by steel netting but the Italians proposed to breach it by using a small torpedo. The explosive boats attempted a forced entry but although some of the boats blew up the netting failed to be dislodged. One of the boats hit and exploded part of the iron bridge over the breakwater bringing part of it down. The remainder of the small flotilla soon realized that the operation had to be abandoned and escaped for Sicily. However by this time the searchlights were picking up the remaining vessels and the boats were blown up by the shore batteries. As dawn approached a Hurricane squadron went in search of any remaining boats but all of them were either sunk or badly damaged. It was a courageous operation in which brave men had died uselessly.

The Maltese were disgusted and annoyed at their Italian neighbours for bringing the war at home. But the worst had still to come and the authorities continued to ignore the advice to build underground hangars into the easily workable limestone cliffs. Then in September 1941 German aircraft arrived in Sicily from the Russian front – the advent of Field-Marshal Kesserling as Commanding Officer of the *Luftwaffe* in Italy. At first his raids coincided with convoys of supplies being sent from Italy to North Africa, but as his power grew, the attacks became more aggressive and unpredictable. By the end of February 1942 it was estimated that he had managed to command a formidable Air Force of nearly a thousand planes.

The last weeks of 1941 were, for Britain, the beginning of the blackest six months of the war – a period during which British fortunes everywhere reached their nadir and the worst for the British fortunes in the Mediterranean laid still in store. The fleet was at its lowest strength, the Axis dominated the air, and Malta was hard pressed to survive, let alone act as a base for offensive operations. Field-Marshal Kesserling, commanding the assault on Malta, had assured Hitler that the *Luftwaffe*, with the aid of the Italian Air Force, would 'wipe Malta off the map'. Supply convoys had therefore to be forced through. Repeated attempts failed since the ships which managed to get through were destroyed in the harbour when only partly unloaded. Such a state of affairs went on for quite a long time until, in an act of desperation, it was finally decided to run convoys simultaneously from both ends of the Mediterranean. But even then out of seventeen supply ships, with an escort of eighty-two warships, which sailed on Operations 'Harpoon' and 'Vigorous' only two merchant ships managed to reach their destination safely. Malta's fortunes were at their lowest ebb.

The real bombing on Malta began during the first week of March 1942. The island anti-aircraft defence, though strong, was not enough and since Egypt could not supply any fighter aircraft, they had to come from Britain by air-craft carrier. The situation was made more difficult since there was a large stretch of open sea separating Gibraltar and Malta. At the end of March the full fury of the *Luftwaffe* had descended on the dockyards. Luckily all ships that could propel themselves out of the yards were evacuated but two destroyers which could not make it were destroyed. By the end of April, on account of the increasing difficulty of keeping channels swept clear of mines, it became necessary to evacuate the surviving submarines. In April 1942 more than 6,700 tons of bombs were dropped on or around the island. During that month of destruction Valletta and the docks were hit in practically every raid. The Maltese provided the labour force in and around the docks but as the raids increased and civilian workers were forced into the shelters for longer periods, the time spent clearing and repairing became negligible and it became impossible to find workers to work at the docks. It was the same with the workers on the airfields. By Herculean efforts a few defending Hurricanes and Spitfires were kept flying, and during April these shot down some thirty-seven German and Italian planes. For the time being Malta had ceased to exist as a naval base while the people and the defending garrison were left to eke out a miserable ration. The Maltese would have to surrender through starvation unless some providential convoy came to its rescue.

The early disgust the Maltese had felt for the Italians increased, and then soured into a pent-up hysterical hate, further increased by the anti-Italian propaganda campaign waged in the local press and on the radio. The old British dream to alienate the Maltese completely from their Italian neighbours had finally been achieved. While the hatred of the Maltese for the

Italians increased, their fears of the Germans spread and deepened and their only hope lay in their prayers to Heaven. They prayed for help from Britain, which by now was overdue. At this time Axis strategy saw it necessary to capture Malta before any further advance was made in North Africa.

The definitive siege of Malta was about to commence. By the beginning of April, however, the progress made by the British in regrouping and reinforcing the army in eastern Cyrenaica was giving Field Marshal Rommel doubts as to his ability to hold out much longer against the growing concentration of British force. He wished to forestall any British offensive and was luckily able to convince Hitler and Mussolini to agree to a limited offensive designed primarily to capture Tobruk. The assault on Malta was thus postponed until 20 July.

Meanwhile the Maltese sheltered themselves in whatever cliffs they could find. Whole families dug the limestone and made shelters-homes. Natural caves became shelters, others were dug. The bulk of the population lived in these shelters. Within the confined space of double or triple-tiered bunks, whole families existed on the meagre rations. There they took with them the few belongings they were able to rescue from their homes, now destroyed by the bombs. Many of the inhabitants preferred to remain below during this period of heavy bombardment, rarely ever coming up into the daylight. Since ventilation was inadequate these shelters were stifling hot, and the air inside them was heavy and rank.

By the first week of August, the situation in Malta was so bad that official calculations showed that food and fuel would be completely exhausted within three or four weeks. If help did not reach Malta by the end of that time the Maltese would have no alternative but to surrender. The last major attempt to replenish the island had been made in June. The only hope was an immediate transfusion of supplies by sea. Operation 'Pedestal' was carried out when a convoy was sent form Gibraltar. Despite heavy losses, the convoy got through – and Malta was able to hold out until the Allied offensive in Africa forced the Axis to abandon their hopes of neutralizing Malta. The ships of 'Pedestal' entered the Mediterranean through the straits of Gibraltar during the night of 10-11 August. Fifteen Axis submarines were waiting for them, at the straits, along with motor torpedo boats, and the heavy ships of the Italian navy. There was also an air fleet of nearly eight hundred Axis aircraft. By the 13 August the convoy was reduced to three ships which managed to reach Malta the following day. On the 15 – the feast of the Assumption – the *Ohio* reached Malta with a vital cargo – oil. The fact that these three ships succeeded in reaching their destination meant that this great attempt to revive Malta had been a qualified success. The Maltese attributed the safe arrival of the four vessels to the Assumption and began to refer to this convoy as the 'Santa Marija Convoy'.

Although under the most difficult conditions Malta was able to, somehow, hold out until the beginning of December 1942. Maltese rations at the toughest period of the siege were less than those allotted by the German authorities to the people of occupied Greece. During this period Maltese rations had gone down to 1,690 calories a day for men and 1,500 for women and children. In Britain rations never fell below 2,800 calories.

When the Allied victories began in North Africa in October/ November 1942, there was still no sign of relief for Malta. One more convoy, known as 'Stoneage', consisting of four merchant ships sailed from Port Said to Malta on 17 November. The new convoy profited enormously from the advance of the 8th Army along the Libyan coast. Tobruk fell on 13 November and Benghazi on 20 November. As the ships unloaded their cargoes it became apparent that the Axis threat to Malta was fast diminishing and enemy action against the Harbour was minimal.

The balance had shifted towards the western Mediterranean, where the Allies were sending their armies to speed up their advance in Algeria towards Tunis. Malta was thus no longer the prime target of the Axis. This was confirmed on 5 December, when another convoy – the 'Portcullis' arrived in Malta from Alexandria. The 'Portcullis' – which delivered 56,000 tons of

Kingsway, the main street of Valletta, during the war.

supplies, besides a vital oil supply – was not attacked either in
transit nor during the unloading operations. The 'Portcullis' extended Malta's supply reserves to March/May 1943. By early
1943 Malta was therefore out of the theatre of hostilities. From
then on Malta was to be supplied from Alexandria only so that
the Allies could concentrate on a speedier concentration against
the Axis in Tunisia and thus ensure a more rapid conclusion
in the African war.

Malta was the operational headquarters during the Allied
assault upon Sicily. The island was largely used as a fighter base
to give air cover to the main body of the attack since the island
was too small to hold the entire invasion force which mainly
attacked from Tunisia and other parts of North Africa. Once
Sicily fell to the allies the strategic value of Malta declined, since
the Axis powers could no longer contest the passage of the central Mediterranean which was now firmly in the hands of the
allies. By June 1943 Malta was thus out of war.

During the few years of the battle for Malta the island had suffered some of the heaviest bombing of the war. The civilian casualties alone reached 1,409 if one excludes those who died during service with the British forces. Damage was particularly extensive especially in the dockyard and the harbour towns. In all 35,000 homes had been destroyed while large areas of Vittoriosa, Senglea and Cospicua were flattened during the air raids. The damage was so extensive that the British government decided to grant £30 million to finance reconstruction. The reconstruction fund helped to improve the economic conditions of Malta and increased the wealth of the island. Nonetheless Malta was still almost wholly dependent upon British military spending.

One important result of the war had been to make the Maltese much more sympathetic towards the British. The British had greatly valued the role of Malta and by 15 April 1942 King George VI decided to grant the George Cross to Malta. On 7 July 1943, the Governor of Malta announced that the British government intended to restore internal self-government at the end of hostilities. In the following year, on his return from the Teheran conference, the United States President Roosevelt, called at Malta and praised the Maltese for their stand in the war. Malta's stand during the war was thus being valued on the international scene. The time was ripe to reconsider the constitutional development of Malta. A National Assembly was formed in 1944 and prepared a draft constitution which was presented to Sir Harold MacMichael, the representative of the Secretary of State for the Colonies, on 17 July 1946. MacMichael had instructions to propose ways of implementing the promise of 1943.

*Changing Political Demands in Post-War Malta*

The 1947 constitution, known as the MacMichael Constitution, remained in force until 1958. It was prepared in the spirit of the post-1919 *Sette Giugno* riots and followed closely the pattern of that of 1921. It provided for a single chamber Legislative Assembly of forty members. The major difference from the 1921 lay in the quantity and quality of voters. Universal suffrage was extended to women and British subjects beyond the age of 21 who were resident in Malta for a period of not less than one year. The education, sex and property qualifications – which had previously made very few people eligible to vote – disappeared and there were now over 150,000 voters. Political power slipped from the hands of the middle-classes, landed proprietors and educated classes as even the blue-collar workers and the uneducated had the right to vote.

Other important changes from the 1921 Constitution was that the maximum number of ministers was raised from seven to eight. Moreover English and Maltese became the official languages of Malta. Likewise debates and discussions had to be conducted in either English or Maltese. Similarly bills and laws were to be printed in the two languages. The MacMichael Constitution ensured that any traces of Italian culture, among some of the elected members, had to be eliminated.

As in the 1921 Constitution, in the 1947 Constitution no power was reserved to the Crown to revoke the Constitution by prerogative rights. The ruling political party was expected to run the government of Malta through an Executive Council which advised the Governor who represented the British sovereign for a period of four years. But as in 1921, power was reserved to amend certain important sections of the Letters Patent mainly dealing with reserved matters and with special subjects related to emergency laws. Section 59 of the Letters Patent saw that the Governor alone, as head of the imperial government in Malta had executive and legislative power in the 'reserved matters touching the public safety of defence'. An amendment of 1953 revoked section 59 which was re-enacted in a different form. Full power was now reserved for the British Sovereign who, by Order-in-Council, could make such provisions if it appeared to be necessary, for maintaining or securing public safety, or if the Secretary of State for Colonies believed that a public emergency existed in Malta, or else in order to provide, maintain, or secure supplies and services in Malta during any such period. By any Order made under this section the Governor, as representative of the Sovereign, had the power to enact laws which were entitled 'Emergency Ordinances' as might appear to be necessary to him for any purposes mentioned above.

These new measures were opposed by the Maltese Government. But diarchical constitutions, like those of 1921 and 1947 included complicated mechanisms were the line of demarcation between the Maltese and the Imperial spheres are not clear. In spite of the elaborate general structure the boundary between reserved and non-reserved matters, as in the case of the defence policy, was often blurred. One may tend to concur with J.J. Cremona that 'the insufficiency or inadequacy of the machinery for consultation between the two governments' may be considered an 'unfortunate imperfection' of the 1947 Constitution.

The election which followed was won by the Labour Party with an absolute majority of seats and Dr Paul Boffa became Prime Minister. The Labour Party's term of office was however terminated during the summer of 1949 when a serious split occurred within it and rapidly brought about its downfall. In June 1950 Boffa's party was defeated over the budget vote and the Governor Sir Gerald Creasy (1949-1954) dissolved Parliament on 23 June of that year. During its short period in power the Labour Party had been able to introduce Income Tax and Old Age Pensions.

The split of 1949 led to the election of Dom Mintoff as leader of the Labour Party. Boffa withdrew from the party and formed the Malta Workers Party. A general election was held in September 1950 in which no party managed to obtain an overall majority. However since the Nationalist Party obtained a numerical majority, they were obliged to form a minority government composed of Nationalist-elected members under the premiership of Dr Enrico Mizzi. Unfortunately Mizzi died in December of that year, after being in power for only three months, and was succeeded by Dr Giorgio Borg Olivier as Prime Minister and leader of the Nationalist Party. Nevertheless Borg Olivier himself was soon defeated on a vote of no confidence so that a General Election had to be held by May 1951. Once again no party contesting the election obtained a clear majority of votes and in June 1951 the nationalists formed a coalition government with Boffa's Malta Workers Party under the premiership of Dr Borg Olivier. The Nationalist proposals for Dominion Status and the transfer of responsibility for Maltese affairs to the Commonwealth Relations Office was rejected by the British government which proposed instead the transfer of Maltese affairs to the Home Office.

The coalition government was defeated on a budget motion in October 1953 and new elections were held in 1953. Once again the Nationalists managed to join forces with Boffa's Workers Party and formed a new Coalition government under Borg Olivier. However this new government lasted less than a year due to a split within Boffa's Workers Party. In the new elections held in February 1955, the Malta Labour Party, under Dom Mintoff, won an overwhelming majority of votes. Labour had fought the elections on the assumption that if elected they would start negotiations for integration with Britain. They proposed the gradual integration of Malta into the political, financial and social structure of Britain while retaining its local autonomy and legislature. It was thought that this political integration with Britain would bring about a general improvement in the living standards.

Events moved rapidly and in July 1955, the British Prime Minister, Sir Anthony Eden, appointed a Round Table Conference composed of members of the British Labour, Conservative and Liberal parties to

> consider constitutional and related questions arising from closer association between Malta and the United Kingdom and in particular from the proposal that Malta should in future be represented in Parliament at Westminster.

This new idea began to find favour with the members of the Round Table Conference and formed the subject of a referendum held in Malta in February 1956.

In the meantime a Pastoral letter, issued conjointly by the bishop of Malta and the bishop of Gozo, made it clear that whatever the constitutional changes, the status quo of the Church had to be guaranteed in writing. On its part the Nationalist Party carried out a campaign to boycott the integration plan of the Malta Labour Party. The outcome bears witness of the fierce campaign fought by the political parties over the referendum: 67,607 voted in favour of integration; 20,177 voted against. There were 2,559 invalid votes and 62,480 abstentions. The referendum result created a controversy inducing the British Prime Minister, Sir Anthony Eden, to declare in the House of Commons that

representation of Malta in the house of Commons will be brought in operation only if and when the Maltese people have shown their decision for it in a general election.

Nonetheless the referendum appeared destined to come to fruition, so much so that by October 1957, the elaboration of the Integration project by the Labour Government was nearly complete.

At this point difference arose over the proposed change in the British defence policy in which it was decided that some overseas bases, including Malta, were to be less heavily manned and equipped than previously. In the immediate post-war period Malta had played an important role at a time when post-war colonial troubles were adding further stress to the already strained and proven economies of the erstwhile great European powers. In particular Malta had been useful for Britain in the growing tensions of the Middle East and the island had played a vital role in the major attack on the Suez. However, notwithstanding all this, it was thought necessary to progressively run down the British military forces in Malta and consequently sharply cut the financial expenditure.

The local government realized that this measure would have a deleterious effect on Malta's economy. Matters came to a head particularly over the future of the Malta Drydocks where around 6,000 skilled industrial workers, mostly staunch supporters of the Labour party, were gainfully employed. Relations between

Malta and Britain were so bad that the Maltese Parliament unanimously passed a resolution threatening to severe all ties with Britain. Attempts to avoid this deadlock proved useless and in April 1958 Mintoff's Labour government resigned and declared that from then on it was to work in favour of a politically independent and neutral Malta.

The resignation of the Labour Party in April 1958 led to widespread riots and demonstrations. Since the Nationalist Party refused to form a government and reaffirmed their policy in favour of Dominion Status within the Commonwealth, the Governor, Major-General Sir Robert Laycock (1954-1959), proclaimed a state of emergency and in February 1959 the 1947 Constitution was suspended.

Once again Malta was placed under a colonial government and a new Constitution came into operation by April 1959. The Constitution was the first one for Malta to be granted by Order-in-Council. Among other things, provisions were made in this Constitution for the setting up of a Public Service Commission and a Judicial Service Commission. Other measures concerned financial provisions which were tightened up. It was stipulated that expenditure could only be authorized if charged on public funds by the Constitution. However an ordinance was made for making money available, in advance of appropriation, for the purpose of unforeseen expenditure, or to cover a period not exceeding three months. Malta's constitutional status had been reduced to that of insignificant British colonies.

Nonetheless the British government was not happy with this situation and considered this Constitution an ad interim one. In July 1960 a constitutional commission was set up under Sir Hilary Blood and recommendations for the basis of a new constitution were published in February 1961. The new Constitution, popularly known as the Blood Constitution, was approved in November 1961. It provided for a Legislative Assembly of fifty members with full legislative and executive powers. From then on judges and magistrates were to be appointed by the Governor, acting on the advice of the Prime Minister. On his part the Prime Minister had to keep the Governor fully informed on the running of the Malta Government. He also had to pass on to the Governor, Commissioner papers which in the Prime Minister's opinion concerned the responsibility of the British government for defence and external affairs. Thus defence and external affairs were to be run concurrently with the British government. The salient feature of this Constitution is the disappearance of the old diarchical concept in which several matters were considered to be imperial reserved matters, which could therefore not be discussed by Maltese elected members of Parliament. Nonetheless defence and external affairs remained precariously undefined.

Six parties contested the general elections held in February 1962 and electoral programmes varied from complete independence for Malta to closer ties with Britain. The Nationalist Party won the elections with twenty-five seats and on 3 March 1962 Dr Giorgio Borg Olivier was sworn in as Prime Minister. On 20 August of that year, Borg Olivier formally demanded independence for Malta within the Commonwealth. Several meetings were held with all Maltese political parties in question, the most important being the one held at Marlborough House in London in 1963. On that occasion the parties formally stated their basic positions especially with regards to internal freedom, defence and foreign policy issues which hinged on Malta's ability to pull through economically and politically.

The two major parties, the Nationalist Party and the Malta Labour Party, were both in favour of independence. At the same time the smaller parties represented at the Conference – the Christian Workers Party led by Toni Pellegrini (an off-shoot from the Malta Labour Party); the Democratic Nationalist Party led by the lawyer and war internee Dr Herbert Ganado (a breakaway from the Nationalist Party); and the Progressive Constitutional Party (a post-war reformed Constitutional Party under Mabel, daughter of Sir Gerald Strickland) – were against an imminent independence proposal. They feared, like thousands of Maltese, lest the Maltese would lose their jobs with the

British Services. Eventually, however, the Secretary of State for Colonies Duncan Sandys, accepted the argument that, since the two major parties polled seventy-six per cent of the votes in the 1962 elections and both had included independence in their election manifestos, then independence should be granted. The conference concluded with the announcement that Malta would become independent on 21 September, 1964. A referendum was held in May 1964 amidst fears of a run down of the British Forces and an economic collapse.

An agreement between Malta and Britain on financial aid and defence was reached but it was evident that a new economic set-up had to be initiated. During the conference Mr Sandys pointed out that Britain had no longer 'an absolute need for a military base in the central Mediterranean'. Nevertheless he expressed the British government's wish to retain facilities for the British forces if this was 'acceptable' to the Maltese government.

Giorgio Borg Olivier waving the Independence Constitution to the public on 21 September 1964.

The Malta Independence Constitution, which was presented to the House of Commons by Duncan Sandys in July 1964 was the first liberal and democratic constitution which guaranteed fundamental human rights and at the same time provided every means for legal and constitutional redress. It endorsed the red and white flag as Malta's national flag, and the Maltese hymn – written by Malta's national poet Dun Karm Psaila to the music of Robert Samut – was to become Malta's national anthem. The Maltese and English languages were to be the official languages of Malta. Other languages could be introduced as official languages by Parliament by at least a two-thirds majority. It even specified that the language of the law courts had to be Maltese. Despite fears that Malta would be reduced to a Third World country the Malta Independence Act was enacted. Malta achieved independence on 21st September 1964.

*The Position of the Catholic Church*

The insularity and historical experience of Malta managed to preserve a rigid and strict application of Catholic rules of conduct. During the period of the knights relations between the Order of St John and the local diocese were not very amicable. However in a situation where the local gentry was virtually absent it was possible for the village priest to play a dominant position as teacher, legal advisor and spiritual mentor of the local community. He was also the main link with the outside world particularly since he had to pass through seminary and to keep in touch with the Bishop's curia. It was considered a great honour to be a relative of the priest. This new position acquired by the parish priests enabled the Church to gain complete ascendancy, particularly among the rural sectors of Maltese society which, until the late eighteenth century comprised approximately two-thirds of the total population. In short the Church became the social meeting place and the basis of institutionalized activity.

During the nineteenth century an uneasy *modus vivendi* was established between the Church and the British Protestant rulers. During this period, the Church played an important role as it was a time when the British and the local political leaders were battling over the Language Question, and the demands of a reasonable self-government constitution. It was a time when the Maltese Church was able to enforce very strict rules of conduct on the population by strengthening the role of traditional values. The British found it fruitful to offer the local Church a measure of protection in exchange for the Church's promotion of the loyalty of the ordinary folk to the British crown. Accordingly the Church concentrated its interests on religious symbolism – which fostered collective pride and satisfaction – as can be evinced in the decadent neo-baroque religious values of the British period. Thus, according to the precepts of the Roman Catholic Church, it was not only important to save one's soul by leading a good life and by participating in the Church's ritual, but it was important to contribute one's share to the parish church's physical aspect. Thus at face value the omnipresence of the Church could best be understood in the way the village

Popular Fair at the Boschetto gardens, limits of Rabat, Malta, in the 1920s. Oil on canvas by Edward Caruana Dingli (1876-1950).

*festa* (feast) had developed during this period. The feast was essentially a time for exuberance, fire-works, and carnivalesque. Yet the feast reached its culmination during the procession in which the whole congregation would walk behind the statue of the patron saint of the village.

By the 1860s non-religious band clubs started to appear – the first one in Rabat. But these not only became identified with the parish they hailed from but even with parish rivalries which were already very strong in the 1920s. By that time the Band Club had become a major feature of social life in both town and village of Malta. Class conflicts and political rivalries were therefore sublimated under an unending competition between parties celebrating the feast of different patron saints within the same village.

It is worth noting that Malta's independence (1964) coincided with the conclusion of the Second Vatican Council (1965). Malta was at the time an archdiocese divided into forty-nine parishes and Gozo a diocese with fifteen parishes. Only five of the Maltese parishes were run by religious orders. At the same time the Gozo parishes were all run by diocesan clergy. Once appointed, the *kappillan* (parish priest) was relatively independent in parochial matters and his position was technically for life unless persuaded to accept a larger parish or, in old age, promoted to the rank of Monsignor of the Cathedral Chapter. The latter rank gave the priest the right to wear a mitre.

The parish priest had to supervise the work carried out by the relatively numerous local clergy. He used to frequent the local government schools and was involved in the appointment of officials of the lay organizations within the village precincts. He was also in charge of local charities and was heavily involved in organizing the village *festa*. Finally he also served as the moral guardian of the parish in question. Consequently he wielded great power which naturally put those living 'in sin', or who were not particularly fervent in their religious practices, in a difficult position. Parishioners were routinely checked by the parish priest on whether they were still performing their religious duties by means of a system of tickets (*bollettini*). These were distributed to all family members during the annual home-blessing and each practicing Catholic had to hand over the new ticket the first time he went to church and received Holy Communion. One may argue that the pre-independence parish priest fulfilled many functions of both a religious and secular nature. Furthermore he was encouraged by the secular administration of British Malta to fulfil such duties and thus he could wield considerable authority and influence within his community.

Due to the absence of local councils he normally served as the representative of the parish and its parishioners. He thus served as public registrar issuing birth, marriage, and death certificates.

It was thus possible for the Church in Malta to discourage secular trends, such as for example the decline of family size. Perhaps this mentality is best explained in family patterns. In the traditional rural communities, where the precepts of the Church are most conscientiously regarded, large families remained normal until the late 1950s. In the more heterogeneous and urbanized harbour area large families were already on the decline during the same period. Writing in 1961 H. Bowen-Jones, B.W. Beeley and W.A. Charlton opined that while the Church had

> succeeded in adjusting herself to nineteenth century changes [it] has been faced
> in the twentieth with the consequences of those changes. The traditional society
> in which it was virtually omnipotent and omnipresent is changing into a new
> society in which the individual does not have to lean so much on the priest.

Naturally the mass emigration of the post-war period further helped to alter the religious habits of the Maltese. In consequence by the 1950s there was already a growing community of agnostics mostly hailing from the urbanized centres. The Church reacted in two different ways to this new situation. It took official action by imposing a rigorous film and book censorship, as well as by the issue of edicts against the use of certain types of clothing and modes of behaviour like the use of sleeveless clothes, bikinis, lip stick and tight clothes by women.

Studies of a sociological nature, like the one by the Abbé Houtart – which was published in Brussels in 1960 – were also carried out on behalf of the Maltese diocese.

At the same time Catholic lay organizations were strengthened. Some of these, like the M.U.S.E.U.M. and Catholic Action, had been in existence well before the Second World War. The M.U.S.E.U.M. is a Maltese lay organization comprising of male and female members who have to remain celibate. Their main task is that of teaching catechism to children. This society was founded by a diocesan priest – Dun Ġorġ Preca – before World War One (1909).

New organizations, like the Cana Movement, the Legion of Mary, Social Action Movement, the Holy Name of God Society and many others of foreign and Maltese origin began to appear after the war. They were strongest in the urbanized and fast-developing areas and helped to minimize the challenge against the Church, especially in places where this challenge was at its strongest.

But perhaps the worst threat the Church had to face since the times of Strickland's premiership in the late 1920s was the ascendancy of Dom Mintoff as Labour Party leader and Prime Minister. Lord Strickland had become engaged in a fierce struggle with almost the entire clergy when he sought to curtail their influence in secular matters. On that occasion Lord Strickland had to give in as the Church threatened to ruin his political career. Early in his career Mintoff tried to develop a distinction between secular and spiritual matters. Matters came to a head between 1955-1958 when Mintoff, as Prime Minister, proposed plans for an integration of Malta with the United Kingdom. The Church obstructed Mintoff's plans and declared that unless the church authorities were given the required assurances – that is that the Catholic religion would remain protected – their position would forever be against integration. When in 1958 Mintoff dropped the integration project and instead proposed independence from Britain, the Church condemned the violent behaviour of Mintoff's supporters.

Mintoff had formulated proposals for state-church relations which envisaged the separation of church and state. He proposed the recognition of civil marriage; the abolition of mandatory religious education; the inspection by state-officials of subsidized, mainly Catholic, private schools; the dispensation of social services to all inhabitants without any sort of favouritism; financial restrictions to be placed on the church; the exclusion of church intervention in the state censorship of books and films; the limitation of the *privilegium fori* (thanks to which the Bishop could not be taken to a government court); and lastly the end of meddling in politics by ecclesiastics. During this dispute Church goers were advised to refrain from voting for Mintoff's party. Refusal to do so would mean interdiction. It became a mortal sin to vote Labour. Mintoff's proposals for church-state relations were not implemented in the Independence Constitution of 1964, in which, thanks to the intervention of the British, the dominant position of the Church was safeguarded.

The archdiocese of post-independent Malta was still reflecting the mentality of a triumphant, wealthy Baroque Catholic Church. Evidence of this is its financial position which remained

Dom Mintoff addressing a mass meeting during the1971 electoral campaign.

very strong. Thus until the advent of independence the Church still owned around nineteen per cent of agricultural land and a large amount of urban property. Politically the Church continued to rest its hold over the minds and hearts of the people. It was until recently the strongest entity in Malta.

## British Outlook and Policy

Conditions in Malta generally changed for the better in the course of the last twenty years of British rule. Nevertheless, the British continued to consider the island first and foremost as a fortress-colony. This was the main and constant theme of British occupation from the dawn of the nineteenth century right up to the late 1950s. British interest in Malta was thus limited to its strategic value. Once this had been safeguarded Britain was not really interested in Maltese domestic affairs. Thus social and religious institutions were usually run on a highly self-conscious system of patron-client relations.

It is often said that, Britain was slow at first, to appreciate Malta's strategic value. Lord Nelson is reported to have considered it as 'a useless and enormous expense'. In actual fact, Britain later considered Malta the first line of defence of its grand Indian empire and did her best to consolidate her position in the Mediterranean by stationing troops and a fleet in Malta. During the early years of occupation, Britain strengthened her legal claims on Malta. This was indispensable in order to establish herself securely on the island and to secure greater stability for her position. Malta was thus to prove to be of utmost importance as a fortress in the imperial defence system.

In the course of the ninteenth century, Malta's utility as a naval base grew constantly, especially during the Crimean War (1854-1856). This in part explains why in the opinion of Hilda Lee, it did not suit the British to allow much liberty to the Maltese; in fact the natives were excluded 'from all but the lowest offices' in government making them feel 'like strangers in their own country'. The Maltese were excluded from high positions even in the Armed Forces and the dockyard, and this caused constant friction and resentment among the more ambitious.

British outlook is nowhere better expressed than in the speech
Joseph Chamberlain made to the House of Commons in 1902:

> We hold Malta solely and entirely as a fortress essential to our position in the
> Mediterranean. Not as an ordinary colony but as a fortress… In a fortress any-
> thing like open agitation against the government is a thing that cannot be tol-
> erated on the face of it.

The British were in Malta for its strategic value and they
adapted a 'mild apartheid' in their dealings with the Maltese.
To prove this point, the lawyer journalist Herbert Ganado
cites an event which took place in the early twentieth century.

Ganado reports that when Sir Adrian Dingli, who was perhaps the most influential of the Maltese of the time, was excluded from membership of the Union Club, it was felt as a
national insult by all Maltese. The decision irritated King
Edward VII himself and his brother, the Duke of Connaught,
Admiral of the British Mediterranean Fleet. In fact, both resigned from the Club on the announcement.

Gradually, however, a new middle class of educated Maltese,
accustomed to the British style, came to accept British rule and
developed pronounced pro-British loyalties. These were relied
upon to carry out 'acceptable policies' and most administrative
posts in the civil service were entrusted to them. British influence took popular root among the populace in the early part
of the twentieth century partly thanks to the stationing of
troops in all parts of the islands. British families took to coming to Malta to enjoy the good weather. Meanwhile more Maltese were becoming dependent on the British in various ways.

The local administration of the civil service was thus entrusted to Maltese personnel who readily followed the patronage pattern. The bureaucrat patrons joined the ranks of the
traditional professional, clerical and other influential persons.
To the clients, patronage became a tangible way of coping with
a generally-difficult situation where personal intervention with
power holders was needed as this was the only way in which
the powerless could survive in a system wherein they depended
upon the inadequacy of formal institutions to provide for their
needs.

For the British the widespread resort to patronage offended their declared principles and official policies but they acknowledged that it served an important function in their drive to strengthen a paternalistic policy which would enable them to strengthen their hold on people's minds.

During the colonial period, the Maltese were powerless in tackling their own problems but they often lacked any alternative solutions of their own and often had no other option but to abide by the rules imposed on them by the British rulers. Malta was essentially reduced to a client-state which was economically and politically dependent upon the 'mother country'.

In the post-war period, when the British came to realize that their great imperial days were over, there were various attempts to reduce, and possibly eliminate, Malta's dependence upon paternalism and client-patron relations. This policy went hand in hand with a series of new investment and industrialization programmes which were aimed at transforming Malta's economy. These programmes suggested ways of diversifying the economy – a task which became necessary in view of a succession of anticipated rundowns of British service establishments in Malta. Such measures brought about a heavy loss of exchange, employment and other economic setbacks on Malta. The need to create alternative employment for those who were losing their jobs with the British Services presented a constant challenge to successive local governments between the late 1950s and the immediate post-independence years. However it helped to induce the Maltese to restructure their local economy.

The British colonial experience had seriously affected the attitude of the Maltese among themselves. Maltese English trained politicians like, Sigismondo Savona and Gerald Strickland, were often inclined to be 'outrageously tyrannical' in order to pursue their reformist ends, often in line with British imperial policy, when they attained positions of power. At one time Savona had even recommended the abolition of representative government in favour of the autocratic rule of the governor. On the other hand Strickland, who believed in the Darwinian principle of the 'survival of the fittest', hindered the path to self-government and when it was attained in 1921 his obstructive methods impeded its proper functioning. At the same time the Nationalist obsession to cling to traditional values, induced them to suspect any move towards modernization and were often unable to distinguish a progressive policy from attempts at despotic rule.

Finally the Nationalists remained essentially a middle-class party which had a very limited rapport with the working classes. They never tried to speak their language and they never really managed to get their message heard at that end. It was thus understandable that the mass of the workers was more appreciative of Strickland's 'reformist' and 'progressive' views which could guarantee their daily existence.

After the Second World War, Strickland's pro-British policy was to a certain extent adapted by the Malta Labour Party that had attracted the allegiance of many working-class sympathizers, former supporters of Strickland, after the latter's demise in 1940. *Italianità* ceased to be a dominant motif in Maltese post-war politics, even when, after the Second World War, Enrico Mizzi returned to power and was succeeded, on his death, by G. Borg Olivier, both as leader of the Nationalist Party and as Prime Minister in 1950. Between the wars, the place reserved for Italian was taken up by Maltese, originally strongly opposed by the Nationalists, since it had been paradoxically instrumentalized by the British as a medium of instruction to favour the spread of English faster and easier.

Until 1931, Maltese had no standard orthography and it only came to be accepted as the official language of Malta with the adoption of the Independence Constitution of 1964. English thus became officially a second language, while Italian influence has been retained mainly through cultural ties and the diffusion of Italian T.V. channels that have a strong following among the better-educated sections of the Maltese community. Thus, as Henry Frendo puts it, in the post-war phase,

> the acrimonious language battle, which mostly caused the formation of, and gave character to, Maltese political parties, had been fought... 'with borrowed weapons', but with Malta serving as a casting mould.

# 7

## Epilogue

After the attainment of independence Malta joined a number of international organizations apart from the British Commonwealth of Nations. In 1965 Malta became a member of the United Nations and the Council of Europe. In 1968 the new state became a member of the International Monetary Fund. The Malta Nationalist government of Dr Giorgio Borg Olivier applied to join the European Economic Community (E.E.C.) and became an associate member in 1970. Although a very small state Malta's representatives have suggested a number of initiatives in international affairs. The most notable example is perhaps the suggestion made in 1967, by Arvid Pardo, Maltese delegate to the United Nations. Pardo proposed the elimination of possible conflicts concerning the sovereignty of the sea-bed. His proposal incorporated a plan for using wealth derived from the sea-bed to finance development in the poorer countries of the world.

During the early stages of the post-independence stage the government felt the need to implement a co-ordinated development plan to diversify Malta's economy which had so far relied excessively on sources of income and employment tied to the British colonial policy. The basic objectives of successive plans by Maltese governments of different ideologies were essentially that of making Malta a viable economic unit, which by its own efforts would provide jobs for the Maltese. To achieve this aim measures were originally taken to diversify the economy away from defence occupations to manufacturing, tourism, and agriculture. However since Malta's internal market is very small, industrial expansion had to depend heavily on the export market. It was thus natural to stress the importance of competitiveness. So far all plans were directed on the need to adapt attitudes and methods of production to the changing structure of the Maltese economy.

The major differences between the planning approaches under the Nationalist and Labour governments from the 1960s until the early 1990s were related to the role of the state in directing productive activities. The Nationalist government believed that the state should only take a backing role in such activities, whereas Labour held that the state should participate directly, especially in areas where the private sector failed to take the initiative.

In a discussion on Labour Party social policy Godfrey Pirotta argues that the creation of a welfare state in the 1970s was a logical consequence of Labour politics at the time. He adds however that the maintenance

> of such a state requires in a consistent manner enormous public funding which neither Malta's economic capacity nor fiscal potential could ever provide.

Labour tried to offset this by

> rapidly decoupling Malta's economy from its dependency on a declining British defence budget, wresting Malta from the jurisdiction of NATO and actively promoting a neutral and non-aligned status for the Islands.

It was a policy which aimed to open Malta to new markets, investments and financial aid from hitherto untapped sources. It led to the signing of treaties with the satellites of the Soviet Communist bloc like Romania and Bulgaria, as well as North Korea, and a protocol with Communist China. The Malta-China protocol, signed in 1977, centred around the building of the Red China Dock in the Grand Harbour and a breakwater at Marsaxlokk harbour.

It was not uncommon for the Labour Prime Minister Dom Mintoff to distinguish between the Europe of Abel (the countries behind the Iron Curtain) and those of Cain (the corrupt capitalist western countries) even though relations with West

Germany, Italy and France were improved and strengthened. It is worth noting that during this period Labour also improved Malta's relations with the oil rich Arab states especially Libya.

The Labour government went out of its way to champion the Arab cause in the international scene. The Maltese were projected as partly Arab and partly European, and the teaching of Arabic became compulsory in Maltese secondary schools. This move served to open an issue over Maltese ethnic identity indicating that the search for an identity is far from a dead issue in tiny Malta. A natural consequence of this new approach was the proclamation of Malta as a republic on 13 December 1974.

In 1979 when Malta had just ceased to serve as a British base Prime Minister Mintoff was reported to have referred to the Libyans as 'blood brothers', clearly combining the two elements implicit in this construction, namely, language and descent. However, it is worth noting that the term 'brother' in Semitic languages is a classificatory term often used strategically to reduce distance. In reality, Mintoff's discourse contributed towards closer relations between Malta and Libya at a time when the Maltese depended, almost totally, on Libyan oil for their energy consumption.

The major economic problem introduced by the Labour government between the late 1970s and the early 1980s was the introduction of tariffs imposed on commodity exports. The system was intensified after the closure of the British base in Malta in 1979. Taxes imposed on imported goods were levied to increase government revenue at a time when Malta ceased to receive revenue from abroad. The result was that it soon became part of a policy to discourage imports by making them more expensive. The introduction of quotas further reduced the limit on imports and gave rise to an excessive demand for the product in question and this also resulted in an increase in the price of the goods produced locally. Since domestic prices were also controlled, quota restrictions gave rise to black markets.

A distinguishing feature of the Maltese economy is its size. The agricultural sector is very small, while the manufacturing sector contributes to about thirty per cent of the gross domestic product. Malta has a large manufacturing sector in relation to the gross domestic product. In terms of population and land area, Malta is one of the smallest nations of the world. Malta cannot be compared to the rich developed countries of North America, Western Europe, or Australasia but it would be misleading to classify Malta with the poor underdeveloped countries of Asia, Africa or Latin America. In 1988 Lino Briguglio described the Maltese economy as 'an intermediately developed economy'. He explained that the countries normally classified as developing, such as Malta, are in an intermediate stage of development. Countries which joined the European Union like Spain, Greece and Portugal would also fit in this category.

Since 1964 Malta has become increasingly interested and concerned with international trade and finance. Due to the relatively large volume of local savings, banking has long been an important service industry on the islands. A number of local and British banks began to offer a wider range of financial services in the late 1960s. But perhaps the most important event in Maltese banking history was the setting up of the Central Bank of Malta in 1968. Another important event was the cessation of operations of the bank known as BICAL (Bank of Industry, Commerce, and Agriculture Limited) in 1972, following a run on the bank. BICAL had started operating in Malta a few years before.

The banking law was changed with the change of government in the early 1970s. Maltese commercial banks, some of which had been in existence since the nineteenth century, had been amalgamated some time after World War Two to form the National Bank of Malta. Another major development in the mid-1970s was the nationalization of the two major commercial banks namely the National Bank of Malta which became known as Bank of Valletta and the Barclays Bank which was renamed Mid-Med Bank. A change in legislation not only encouraged private companies from Europe, the USA and Turkey but it even led to the development of the APS bank and the strengthening of Lombard Bank. At the same time the two major commercial banks were once again privatized by the late 1990s and Mid-Med Bank was even integrated into the HSBC (Hong Kong and Shanghai Banking Corporation) group by 1999.

Banking activity encouraged by the liberal legislation of the late 1960s enabled Malta to develop some of the characteristics of an off-shore financial centre. There were even hopes that the island could develop into a centre for Mediterranean trade. Yet although plans for a free port containing warehousing, manufacturing units, and various other ventures were planned it was only in the late 1990s that a free port was developed. By 1999 it had already managed to gain the rank of third busiest free port in the Mediterranean.

During the last forty years the birth rate has shown a tendency to decrease. From about thirty per thousand population in the early 1950s it decreased to about seventeen per thousand in the 1970s. Death rates have remained relatively stable, averaging just under ten per thousand so that the natural increase of the Maltese population – defined as the difference between the birth and the death rates – decreased to about seven per thousand during the 1980s. At the same time the number of migrants tended to be higher than the number of emigrants. Current trend in birth, death and migration rates considered together would seem to indicate that the growth tendency of the Maltese population is around one per cent per annum. At the same time the Maltese population is an ageing population with the mean age rising from 27 years in 1948 to 33 years by 1985 a tendency which continued to increase during the 1990s.

There has also been a change in the geographical distribution. Between 1957 and 1967 the population of the outer harbour area increased at the expense of the inner harbour area. After 1967 changes in the distribution of population was more dramatic. Thus while the inner harbour area population continued to decrease the outer harbour area continued to increase dramatically resulting in the building of a large number of spaces which had previously served as public land. The development of housing estates has meant that a 'lumpenproletariat', which had previously been concentrated in a few specific areas of Malta, has now been dispersed all over the island with the result that exclusive areas of residence have practically ceased to exist. Nonetheless the price of land continued to increase to such an extent that those with a middle of the range salary have now to make do with inferior accommodation when compared to their counterparts living in western European countries.

In just over a decade after the attainment of independence the economy of the island was no longer dependent upon the British services. Maltese economy became more than ever dependent upon the tertiary sector notably the tourist and manufacturing industries. Economic developments brought a demand for improved standards and a continual rise in the cost of living. The advantages that Malta enjoyed, in the immediate post-independence period, in the form of skilled and cheap labour force as a natural corollary to attracting new industries, gradually began to disappear. Similarly the assets of the tourists industry are finite and there is a limit to the number of visitors that can be attracted to visit Malta. The island's original charm has in fact been marred in several areas due to excessive building, especially along the coastline. Thus erstwhile tranquil fishing villages like St Paul's Bay with nearby Qawra, Buġibba and Xemxija in the north and Marsascala in the south have been radically transformed by a multitude of hotels, restaurants and apartments. But perhaps the worst kind of development took place in the Sliema/St Julians area. A careless use of land has been allowed to go on for far too long before a proper Planning Authority was devised. Furthermore a misuse of land and a mishandling of rent laws has engendered the problem of landownership due to the excessive price of land for the building of first homes.

Finally one must admit that the planning process in Malta has been beset by a series of difficulties related to the island's dependence on the international scene. During Malta's early years as an independent state, the greatest worry of the Nationalist government included the successive and even unexpected decreases in the British defence expenditure. In the early 1970s the Labour government had to face unprecedented inflationary pressure due to the international energy crisis. By the early 1980s the same Labour government had to deal with international recession which was a major problem the Nationalist government, elected again in 1987, had to face.

Furthermore the absorption of labour in the public sector and government-owned industry has created an artificial economic structure which ever since 1987 successive governments have stated that it must be dismantled before a steady economic improvement could be achieved. In more recent years overspending largely made in order to upgrade the infrastructure inherited from colonial days created financial problems which neither the Nationalist government (1987-1996) nor the Labour government (1996-1998) after it, were able to solve.

Among Malta's achievements one can boast of the new telecommunications system which has been hailed as the most advanced in Europe. A satisfactory measure of development has also been achieved in the Maltese economy as can be evinced by the growth in the number of gainfully occupied, the expansion of industry and the manufacturing sector as well as a steady rise in real national income.

Since independence Malta's economy has been closely linked to the European Union (previously known as the European Economic Community and more recently European Community). A very large percentage of exports are in fact directed towards the major partners of the union while most of the island's imports come from these same countries. Foreign-owned firms are also largely European including the more successful electronics firms like the ST Electronics – previously SGS Thomson. Malta is therefore already tied to Europe and in July 1990 it applied to join as full member.

Those who are against the Union, as is the Malta Labour Party, cite, as a major disadvantage, the fact that import controls against EU member states would have to be dismantled with full membership and this would naturally give rise to a loss of output and employment in firms enjoying protection. Another disadvantage associated with full EU membership is the price increase on basic commodities particularly food products. Local farmers may also suffer hardship because they will have to compete with better-organized European farmers. At the same time full membership may be beneficial to Maltese agriculture through grants for farm modernization and better prices for products grown in Malta. The loss of revenue resulting from the dismantling of the system of import duties is also another problem put forward by those against the union. This problem was however seen to by the Nationalist government with the introduction of (value-added tax) VAT. The anti-unionists have so far argued that VAT has pushed up prices. Nonetheless the abolition of duties on imports from Europe could help to reduce prices on superior quality products originating from EU member states. Finally the anti-unionists insist that as a full EU member Malta would cease to be able to act independently in major political and economic issues. This became more of a reality after the completion of The Union's internal market and the creation of a monetary union. Moreover, the Labour party insists that Malta's influence in the EU would be next to nil in a Union which is dominated by Germany, France, Britain and Italy.

Those in favour of joining the Union as a full member – an option fervently presented by the Nationalist Party – argue that it would be a great disadvantage if, in the future, Malta were to remain out of the EU. They argue that the reduction of import controls is likely to promote efficiency in local industry. An increasing trade harmonization within the community has already made matters more difficult for Malta to penetrate the Union market. This has become more evident since the 1980s when Greece, Spain and Portugal joined the Union. At the same time the Global Mediterranean Policy of the European Union has made trade with non-EU countries more difficult. One must bear in mind that the Maltese economy is very small and it has to rely on exports if its manufacturing industries are to produce on a sufficiently large scale. At the same time imports make up for its lack of any sort of natural resources.

The smallness of the island's economy renders it completely vulnerable to international affairs which explains why the international recession of the early 1980s had such a large impact on the Maltese economy. The high import requirements further makes Malta dependent on foreign markets. The Maltese governments of the 1970s and 1980s imposed controls in order to encourage import substitution. But the strict import controls most often encouraged inefficient production and many manufacturing firms were only able to survive thanks to the protectionist policy of the government which gave rise to inferior quality products, and the wasteful use of human, physical and financial resources. In the late 1990s successive governments struggled hard to introduce a work ethic and to try to achieve efficiency at work.

One may assume that young people's attitude to work is largely the outcome of Malta's educational system which is quite high when compared to the normal standard of the Mediterranean but which is definitely below the standards of central Europe at both the secondary vocational training and university level. Indeed the educational system is riddled with problems. E.P. Delia mentions, for instance, the high drop-out rate after the age of 16; the low proportion of students who follow technical and further educational courses; the general lack of interest in apprenticeship schemes by both employers and students; the low proportion of university students following engineering and science subjects. This condition has resulted in what Delia calls 'skill bottlenecks' largely 'attributed to the absence of an industrial tradition and culture'. Indeed the shortage of skilled workers is often considered to be the 'single most important obstacle in the transition of Malta's economy... towards higher productivity levels' and the generation of wealth. Efforts are still being carried out by the Education Division and, to some extent, the local university in order to entice more students to continue their studies at a vocational school.

One can envisage that economic survival could only come about if there is a general improvement of managerial and supervisory skills both in the industrial sector and the tourism accommodation sector. The tourist industry in particular has long felt the need to employ highly-qualified staff since hoteliers are continually being compelled to diversify their operations and are often induced to offer a wider range of facilities making the inadequacy of personnel even more evident. Irrespective of whether Malta joins the EU or not the technical and managerial skills of the local labour force have become a prerequisite for the island's future economic and social development. High quality training programmes and a streamlining of public sector employment must be coupled with a more cost-effective management in public corporations and a selective recruitment policy which would ensure that only the more reliable hardworking employees get the top administrative jobs.

In conclusion one notices that the fulcrum of Malta's political, economic and social strategies are intimately related to the issue of political modernization, namely its democratic character. It appears that during the British period when Maltese politicians were largely absorbed by the acquisition of self-government and self-determination, there had been a total disregard for values and attitudes which should form an integral part of a modern democracy. Values such as political and religious tolerance, freedom of expression, the right to agree or disagree without direct or indirect coercion have not been completely upheld by those in power. Unfortunately well meant policies are sometimes hindered by the widespread tendency, at all levels of the administration, to favour patron-client relationships. This tendency may have started as a response to British colonial arrogance and may even have deeper roots going back, at least, to the period of the Knights of St John. It was, and still is, officially condemned as a corrupt practice since it gives unfair advantage to a few over others. Yet everyone admits that it is arguably the most effective way to secure scarce resources ranging from a job to more simple matters. The underprivileged masses of Maltese are often reminded that what counts is not how much you know (meaning one's level of education, ability, or work experience) but whom you know thus: '*Mhux kemm taf, imma lil min taf*'.

The situation became worse after independence when a small oligarchic group of families began to dominate the local scene without effectively being challenged not only in politics, but even in the economic and the educational scene of Malta. This state of affairs often works against the national good for it often favours the less competent at the expense of the more capable citizens who lack a patron's support. The same condition probably dominates the political arena which, due to partisan mobilization, those in power often lose sight of the commonly-valued goals of a state which claims to be a modern democratic European country. After all the pursuit of a European dimension cannot proceed without a parallel concern for European values.

On its part the Maltese electorate seems conscious of the need for a change in the mentality of their political leaders as the rapid change in successive elected governments has shown during the late 1990s.

# Appendix 1

## Grand Masters of the Order of St John in Malta

| | |
|---|---|
| L'Isle Adam, Philippe Villiers de | 1530-1534 |
| (L'Isle Adam had been elected Grand Master in Rhodes in 1521) | |
| Ponte, Pierino del | 1534-1535 |
| Saint Jaille, Didier de | 1535-1536 |
| Homedes, Juan d' | 1536-1553 |
| Sengle, Claude de la | 1553-1557 |
| Valette, Jean Parisot de la | 1557-1568 |
| Monte, Pietro del | 1568-1572 |
| Cassière, Jean l'Evêque de la | 1572-1581 |
| Verdalle, Hughes Loubenx de | 1581-1595 |
| Garzes, Martino | 1595-1601 |
| Wignacourt, Alof de | 1601-1622 |
| Vasconcellos, Luis Mendez de | 1622-1623 |
| Paule, Antoine de | 1623-1636 |
| Lascaris Castellar, Jean Paul | 1636-1657 |
| Redin, Martin de | 1657-1660 |
| Chattes Gessan, Annet Clermont de | 1660 |
| Cotoner, Rafael | 1660-1663 |
| Cotoner, Nicolas | 1663-1680 |
| Carafa, Gregorio | 1680-1690 |
| Wignacourt, Adrien de | 1690-1697 |
| Perellos y Roccaful, Ramon | 1697-1720 |
| Zondadari, Marc'Antonio | 1720-1722 |
| Vilhena, Antonio Manoel de | 1722-1736 |
| Despuig, Ramon | 1736-1741 |
| Pinto de Fonseca, Manoel | 1741-1773 |

| Ximenes de Texada, Francisco | 1773-1775 |
| Rohan Polduc, Emmanuel de | 1775-1797 |
| Hompesch, Ferdinand von | 1797-1798 |

# Appendix 2

## British Civil Commissioners and Governors

### Civil Commissioners

| | |
|---|---|
| Ball, Captain Alexander, R N | 1799-1801 |
| Pigot, Major-General Henry | 1801 |
| Cameron, Sir Charles | 1801-1802 |
| Ball, Rear-Admiral Sir Alexander | 1802-1809 |
| Oakes, Lieutenant-General Sir Hildebrand | 1810-1813 |

### Governors

| | |
|---|---|
| Maitland, Lieutenant-General Sir Thomas | 1813-1824 |
| General the Marquess of Hastings | 1824-1826 |
| Ponsonby, Major-General Sir Frederic | 1827-1836 |
| Bouverie, Lieutenant-General Sir Henry F | 1836-1843 |
| Stuart, Lieutenant-General Sir Patrick | 1843-1847 |
| More O'Ferrall, The Right Honourable Richard | 1847-1851 |
| Reid, Major-General Sir William | 1851-1858 |
| le Marchand, Lieutenant-General Sir John Gaspard | 1858-1864 |
| Storks, Lieutenant-General Sir Henry | 1864-1867 |
| Grant, General Sir Patrick | 1867-1872 |
| Straubenzee, General Sir Charles T | 1872-1878 |
| Borton, General Sir Arthur | 1878-1884 |
| Simmons, General Sir Lintorn | 1884-1888 |
| Torrens, Lieutenant-General Sir Henry D | 1888-1890 |
| Smyth, Lieutenant-General Sir Henry A | 1890-1893 |
| Fremantle, General Sir Arthur J L | 1893-1899 |
| Grenfell, Lieutenant-General Lord | 1899-1903 |

| | |
|---|---|
| Mansfield Clarke, General Sir Charles | 1903-1907 |
| Grant, Lieutenant-General Sir Henry F | 1907-1909 |
| Rundle, General Sir Leslie | 1909-1915 |
| Methuen, Field-Marshal Lord | 1915-1919 |
| Plumer, Field-Marshal Viscount | 1919-1924 |
| Congreve, General Sir Walter N | 1924-1927 |
| Du Cane, General Sir John P | 1927-1931 |
| Campbell, General Sir David G M | 1931-1936 |
| Bonham-Carter, General Sir Charles | 1936-1940 |
| Dobbie, Lieutenant-General Sir William G S | 1940-1942 |
| Gort, Field-Marshal Viscount | 1943-1944 |
| Schreiber, Lieutenant-General Sir Edmond C A | 1944-1946 |
| Douglas, Sir Francis (later Lord) | 1946-1949 |
| Creasy, Sir Gerald H | 1949-1954 |
| Laycock, Major-General Sir Robert | 1954-1959 |
| Grantham, Admiral Sir Guy | 1959-1962 |
| Dorman, Sir Maurice | 1962-1964 |

Governors General

| | |
|---|---|
| Dorman, Sir Maurice | 1964-1971 |
| Mamo, Sir Anthony | 1971-1974 |

# Appendix 3

## Maltese Prime Ministers

| | |
|---|---|
| Howard, Mr Joseph | 1921-1923 |
| Buhagiar, Dr Francesco | 1923-1924 |
| Mifsud, Sir Ugo | 1924-1927 |
| Strickland, Sir Gerald (later Lord) | 1927-1932 |
| Mifsud, Sir Ugo | 1932-1933 |
| Boffa, Dr (later Sir) Paul | 1947-1950 |
| Mizzi, Dr Enrico | 1950 |
| Borg Olivier, Dr Giorgio | 1950-1955 |
| Mintoff, Mr Dominic | 1971-1984 |
| Mifsud Bonnici, Dr Carmelo | 1984-1987 |
| Dr Eddie Fenech Adami | 1987-1996 |
| Sant, Dr Alfred | 1996-1998 |
| Fenech Adami, Dr Eddie | 1998- |

# Appendix 4

## Presidents of Malta

| | |
|---|---|
| Mamo, Sir Anthony | 1974-1976 |
| Buttigieg, Dr Anton | 1976-1981 |
| Barbara, Ms Agatha | 1982-1986 |
| Xuereb, Mr Paul (Acting President) | 1987-1989 |
| Tabone, Dr Vincent | 1989-1994 |
| Mifsud Bonnici, Dr Ugo | 1994-1999 |
| de Marco, Professor Guido | 1999- |

# Appendix 5

Coinage under the Order of St John: 1530-1798

6 dinari = 1 grano
5 grani = 1 cinquina
2 cinquine = 1 carlino (or 10 grani)
2 carlini = 1 tarì (or 20 grani)
12 tarì = 1 scudo
30 tarì = 1 oncia (or 2½ scudi)


Coinage under British rule and early Post-Independence Years: 1800-1972

3 grani = 1 farthing
4 farthings = 1 penny
12 pence = 1 shilling
5 shillings = 1 crown
20 shillings = 1 pound sterling (sovereign)
21 shillings = 1 guinea

# Bibliography

## General

Bradford, E., *Mediterranean. Portrait of a Sea*, London, 1971.

Braudel, F., *The Mediterranean and the Mediterranean World in the Age of Philip II*, 2nd edn 2 vols. Eng. trans. London, 1972-73.

Horden, P. & Purcell, N., *The Corrupting Sea. A study of Mediterranean History*, Oxford, 2000.

## The Land and Its People

Anderson, P.W. & Schembri, P.J., *Coastal Zone Survey of the Maltese Islands*, Malta, 1989.

Aquilina, J., *Papers in Maltese Linguistics*, Malta, 1961.

Attard, L. E., *The Great Exodus, 1918-1939*, Malta, 1989.

Azzopardi, J. (ed.), *St. Paul's Grotto, Church and Museum at Rabat, Malta*, Malta, 1990.

Blouet, B., *The Story of Malta*, London, 1967.

Boissevain, J., *Saints and Fireworks. Religion and Politics in Rural Malta*, London, 1965.

——————, *Hal Farruġ, A Village in Malta*, New York, 1969.

Bowen-Jones, H., Dewdney, J.C., & Fisher, W.B. (eds), *Malta, Background for Development*, Durham, 1961.

Buhagiar, M., 'The St. Paul Shipwreck Controversy. An Assessment of the Source Material', *Proceedings of History Week 1993*, Malta, 1997.

Cassar, C., 'U Mulu di Malta: The Maltese Trade in Donkeys and Mules', *Storja 1996*, Malta, (1996), 12-21.

——————, 'Nutrition in a Central Mediterranean Island Community: Malta in Medieval and Early Modern Times', *Rivista di antropologia*, Supplemento al volume 76 (1998), Italy, 153-162.

Cassar Pullicino, J., 'Pirates and Turks in Maltese tradition', *Scientia*, vol. xiv (1948), 164-190.

—————, 'The Order of St. John in Maltese folk memory', *Scientia*, vol. xv (1949), 149-75.

—————, 'Malta in 1575, Social aspects of an Apostolic Visit', *Melita Historica*, vol. ii (1956), 19-41.

—————, *Studies in Maltese Folklore*, Malta, 1976.

Chetcuti, D., Buhagiar, A., Schembri, P.J., & Ventura, F., *The Climate of the Maltese Islands*, Malta, 1992.

Dudley-Buxton, L.H., 'Malta, An anthropogeographical study', *The Geographical Review*, vol. xiv (1924) 75-87.

Freller, T., *St Paul's Grotto and its Visitors. Pilgrims, Knights, Scholars and Sceptics*, Malta, 1996.

Fsadni, M., *The Girna. The Maltese Corbelled Stone Hut*. Malta, 1992.

Koster, A., *Prelates and Politicians in Malta, Changing Power-Balances Between Church and State in a Mediterranean Island Fortress*, The Netherlands, 1981.

Luke, H., *Malta. An Account and Appreciation*, 2nd revised ed., London, 1960.

Marshall, D., *History of the Maltese Language in Local Education*, Malta, 1971.

Quintin D'Autun, J., *Insulae Melitae descriptio*, Lyons 1536, edited with translation in H.C.R. Vella, *The Earliest Description of Malta*, Malta, 1980.

Sant-Cassia, P.,'History, anthropology and folklore in Malta', *Journal of Mediterranean Studies*, vol.iii (1993), 291-315.

## Ancient History

Blagg. T., Bonanno. A., & Luttrell. A., *Excavations at Hal Millieri*, Malta, 1990.

Bonanno, A., 'A Socio-Economic Approach to Maltese Prehistory. The Temple Builders', *Mid-Med Bank Ltd., Malta, Studies of its Heritage and History*, Malta, 1986.

Borg, V., 'Malta and Its PaleoChristian Heritage, A New Approach', *Mid-Med Bank Ltd., Malta, Studies of its Heritage and History*, Malta, 1986.

Busuttil, J., 'Diodorus Melitensis', Busuttil, J., 'Diodorus Melitensis', *Melita Historica*, vol. v (1968), 32-35.

Evans, J.D., *Malta*, London, 1959.

—————, *The Prehistoric Antiquities of the Maltese Islands*, London, 1971.

Frendo, A., 'Religion in the 'prehistoric phases' of Phoenician Malta', in Waldren, I., Ensenyat, W.H., Kennard, J.A. (eds), *Ritual, Rites and Religion in Prehistory*, Oxford, 1995.

Gouder, T., 'Malta and the Phoenicians', *Lombard Bank (Malta) Annual Report 1991*, Malta, 1992.

Stoddart , S., Bonanno, A., Gouder, T., Malone, C., & Trump, D., 'Cult in an island Society, Prehsitoric Malta in the Tarxien Period', *Cambridge Archaeological Journal*, vol. 3 no. 1 (1993), 3-19.

Trump, D.H., *Skorba. Research Reports of the Society of Antiquaries of London*, London, 1966.

—————, *Malta, An archaeological Guide*, London, 1972.

## Medieval Period

Brincat, J.M., *Malta 870-1054, Al-Himyari's Account*, Malta, 1991.

Dalli, C., 'Capitoli, The Voice of an Élite', *Proceedings of History Week 1992*, Malta, 1994.

Luttrell, A.T., 'Malta and the Aragonese crown, 1282-1530', *Journal of the Faculty of Arts*, The Royal University of Malta, vol. iii (1965), 1-9.

—————, (ed.), *Medieval Malta. Studies on Malta Before the Knights*, London, 1975.

—————, (ed.), *Hal Millieri, A Maltese Casale, its Churches and Paintings*, Malta, 1976.

—————, 'Giliberto Abbate's Report on Malta, Circe 1241', *Proceedings of History Week 1993*, Malta, 1997.

Wettinger, G., 'The distribution of surnames in Malta in 1419 and the 1480s', *Journal of Maltese Studies*, no. 5 (1968), 25-48.

—————, 'The militia list of 1419-1420, A new starting point for the study of Malta's population', *Melita Historica*, vol. v (1969), 80-106.

—————, 'Concubinage among the clergy of Malta and Gozo, 1420-1550', *Journal of the Faculty of Arts*, The University of Malta, vol. vi (1977), 165-188.

—————, 'Looking back on the "cantilena" of Peter Caxaro', *Journal of Maltese Studies*, no. 12 (1978), 88-105.

—————, 'The pawning of Malta to Monroy', *Melita Historica*, vol. vii (1978), 265-283.

—————, 'The militia roster of watch duties of 1417', *The Armed Forces of Malta Journal*, no. 32 (1979), 25-42.

—————, 'Agriculture in Malta in the late Middle Ages', *Proceedings of History Week 1981*, Malta, 1982.

—————, *The Jews of Malta in the Late Middle Ages*, Malta, 1985.

—————, 'The Arabs in Malta', *Mid-Med Bank Ltd., Malta, Studies of its Heritage and History*, Malta, 1986.

—————, Plurilingualism and cultural change in Medieval Malta'. *Mediterranean Language Review 6-7* (1993), 143-159.

—————, & Fsadni, M., *Peter Caxaro's Cantilena, a Poem in Medieval Maltese*, Malta, 1968.

## The Hospitaller Order of St. John, 1530-1798

Balbi di Correggio, F., *The Siege of Malta 1565*, English trans., Copenhagen, 1961.

Blondy, A., 'La France et Malte au XVIIIè siècle, Le problème de la double nationalité', Fiorini S. & Mallia-Milanes V. (eds), *Malta - A Case Study in International Cross-Currents*, Malta, 1991.

Bradford, E., *The Great Siege, Malta 1565*, London, 1961.

Callus, P., *The Rising of the Priests*, Malta, 1961.

Cassar, C., 'The Reformation and sixteenth century Malta', *Melita Historica*, vol. x (1988), 51-68.

—————, *Sociey, Culture and Identity in Early Modern Malta*, Malta, 2000

Cassar, P., *Medical History of Malta*, London, 1964.

Cavaliero, R., *The Last of the Crusaders*, London, 1960.

Chritien, A., 'The foundlings under the Order and after', *Scientia*, vol. xv (1949), 3-19.

Ciappara, F., *Marriage in Malta – In the Late Eighteenth Century*, Malta, 1988.

Cutajar, D. & Cassar, C., 'Malta and the sixteenth century struggle for the Mediterranean', *Mid-Med Bank Report and Accounts*, Malta, 1985, 23-59.

—————, 'Malta's role in Mediterranean affairs, 1530-1699', *Mid-Med Bank Ltd., Malta, Studies of its Heritage and History*, Malta, 1986, 105-140.

—————, 'Budgeting in 17th century Malta', *Mid-Med Bank Ltd., Malta, Studies of its Heritage and History*, Malta, 1986, 141-149.

Debono, J., 'The cotton trade of Malta 1750-1800', *Archivum, Journal of Maltese Historical Research*, vol. i, (1981), 94-125.

Earle, P., *Corsairs of Malta and Barbary*, London, 1970.

Fava, P., 'A reign of austerity, Economic difficulties during the rule of Grand Master Ximenes', Frendo, H. (ed.), *Storja 78*, Malta, 1978.

Fiorini, S., '"Status Animarum I", A unique source for 17th and 18th century Maltese demography', *Melita Historica*, vol. viii (1983), 325-343.

Fiorini, S., 'The resettlement of Gozo after 1551', *Melita Historica*, vol. ix (1986), 203-44.

Grima, J.F., '"Gente di Capo" on the galleys of the Order in the first half of the seventeenth century', *Hyphen – A Journal of Melitensia and the Humanities*, vol. ii (1979), 51-70.

Hoppen, A., 'The finances of the Order of St John of Jerusalem in the sixteenth and seventeenth centuries', *European Studies Review*, vol. iii (1973), 103-119.

—————, *The Fortification of Malta by the Order of St. John 1530-1798*. 2nd ed., Malta, 2000.

—————, 'The fortification of Malta 1530-1798, The impact on the Maltese', *Hyphen – A Journal of Melitensia and the Humanities*, vol. ii (1980), 103-114.

Lochhead, I.C., & Barling, T.F.R., *The Siege of Malta 1565*, London, 1970.

Luttrell, A.T., 'The Christianization of Malta', *The Malta Year Book 1977*, 415-426, Malta, 1977.

—————, 'Girolamo Manduca and Gian Francesco Abela, Tradition and invention in Maltese historiography', *Melita Historica*, vol. viii (1977), 105-132.

—————, 'Eighteenth century Malta, prosperity and problems', *Hyphen – A Journal of Melitensia and the Humanities*, vol. iii (1982), 37-51.

Mallia-Milanes, V., 'The Order of St. John 1793-1798, Impending collapse of a glorious heritage. The despatches of Antonio Miari, Venetian minister in Malta', *Hyphen – A Journal of Melitensia and the Humanities*, vol. iii (1982), 89-115.

—————, 'Valletta, 1566-1798. An epitome of Europe', *Bank of Valletta Annual Report and Financial Statements*, Malta, 1988.

—————, *Descrittione di Malta anno 1716, a Venetian Account*, Malta, 1988.

—————, (ed.), *Hospitaller Malta 1530-1798. Studies on Early Modern Malta and the Order of St. John of Jerusalem*, Malta, 1993.

Mahoney, L., *A History of Maltese Architecture from Ancient Times up to 1800*, Malta, 1988.

Mangion, G. (ed.), *Maltese Baroque*, Malta, 1989.

Schermerhorn, E.W., *Malta of the Knights*, London, 1929.

Vassallo, C., *Corsairing to Commerce. Maltese Merchants in XVIII Century Spain*, Malta, 1997.

Wettinger, G., 'Early Maltese popular attitudes to the government of the Order of St. John', *Melita Historica*, vol. vi (1974), 255-278.

## The French Period

Denaro, V., *The French in Malta*, Malta, 1963.

Fiorini, S., 'From the diary of a priest in Senglea during the French blockade', *Melita Historica*, vol. viii (1982), 234-260.

Testa, Carmel, *The French in Malta 1798-1800*, Malta, 1997.

## The British Fortress Colony, 1800-1939

Bartolo, P., 'British Colonial Budgeting, The First Formative Decades 1800-1838', *Melita Historica*, vol. viii (1980), 1-22.

Bezzina, J., *Religion and Politics in a Crown Colony 1798-1864*, Malta, 1985.

Bonnici, A, 'The church and the freedom of the press in Malta', *Melita Historica*, vol. ii, (1957), 103-121.

—————, 'The oath question', *Melita Historica*, vol. iv, (1964), 14-26.

Chircop, J., *The Left within the Maltese Labour Movement*, Malta, 1991.

Cremona, J.J., *An Outline of the Constitutional Development of Malta*, Malta, 1963.

—————, *The Maltese Constitution and Constitutional History since 1813*, Malta, 1994.

Fiorentini, B., *Malta rifugio di esuli e focolare ardente di cospirazione durante il risorgimento italiano*, Malta, 1966.

Frendo, H., *Ir-Rivoluzzjoni Maltija tal-1919*, Malta, 1970.

—————, 'Language and nationality in an island colony, Malta', *Canadian Review of Studies in Nationalism*, vol. iii (1975), 22-33.

—————, *Party Politics in a Fortress Colony, The Maltese Experience*, Malta, 1979.

—————, *Malta's Quest for Independence, Reflections on the Course of Maltese History*, Malta, 1989.

—————, (ed.), *Maltese Political Development 1798-1964. A Documentary History*, Malta, 1993.

Harding, H.W., *Maltese Legal History Under British Rule 1801-1836*, Malta, 1980.

Hull, G., *The Malta Language Question. A Case Study in Cultural Imperialism*, Malta, 1993.

Laferla, A.V., *British Malta 1800-1921*, 2 vols, Malta, 1946.

Lee, H.I., *Malta 1813-1914, A Study in Constitutional and Strategic Development*, Malta, 1972.

Mallia-Milanes V. (ed.), *The British Colonial Experience 1800-1964, The Impact on Maltese Society*, Malta, 1988.

Pirotta, G.A., *The Maltese Public Service 1800-1940, The Administrative Politics of a Micro-State*, Malta, 1996.

Pirotta, J.M., 'Enrico Mizzi's Political Integrity, Fact or Fiction?', *Proceedings of History Week 1986*, Malta, 1992.

Price, C., *Malta and the Maltese, A Study in Nineteenth Century Migration*, Melbourne, 1954.

Smith, H., *Britain in Malta*, 2 vols, Malta, 1953.

Smith, H. & Koster, A., *Lord Strickland, Servant of the Crown*, Malta, 1986.

York, B., *Empire and Race. The Maltese in Australia 1881-1949*, Kensington, Australia, 1990.

## World War II and Its Legacy, 1940-1964

Austin, B., *Malta and the End of Empire*, London 1971.

Bradford, E., *Siege, Malta 1940-1943*, London, 1985.

Dobie, E., *Malta's Road to Independence*, Oklahoma, USA, 1967.

Koster, K., 'The kappillani, the changing role of the parish priest in Malta', Wolf, E.R. (ed.), *Religion, Power and Protest in Local Communities. The Northern Shore of the Mediterranean*, Berlin, New York and Amsterdam, 1984.

Micallef, J., *When Malta Stood Alone, (1940-1943)*, Malta, 1981.

Pirotta, J.M., *Fortress Colony, The Final Act 1945-1964*, 2 vols, Malta, 1987 & 1991.

## Post-Independence

Abela, A.M., *Transmitting Values in European Malta, A Study in the Contemporary Values of Modern Society*, Malta, 1991.

Busuttil, S., *Malta, the EU and You, A Practical Guide*, Malta, 1999.

Mizzi, E., *Malta in the Making 1962-1987*, Malta, 1995.

Frendo, H., *Origins of Maltese Statehood*, Malta,1999.

Polacco, C., *Malta – EEC Relations*, Malta, 1992.

Tabone, C., *The Secularization of the Family in Changing Malta*, Malta, 1987.

Vassallo, M., *From Lordship to Stewardship, Religion and Social Change in Malta*, The Hague, 1979.

Zammit, E.L., *A Colonial Inheritance, Maltese Perceptions of Work, Power and Class Structure with Reference to the Labour Movement*, Malta, 1984.

# Index

# Society, Culture and Identity in Early Modern Malta

## Carmel Cassar

*Society, Culture and Identity in Early Modern Malta* seeks to explain how Maltese society, its culture and identity, evolved in the crucial years following the Ottoman Siege of Malta of 1565. It shows how the Order of St John managed to govern effectively through the closer interaction between state and society. The book discusses two broad themes the first of which concerns the dramatic success of the Order of St John in its ability to govern Malta more effectively than its predecessors. The second relates to the development of an ethnic identity.

Basing itself on original archival research the book shows how the Order of St John acted as an impetus to help transform Malta from an isolated post of the Kingdom of Sicily into a minor entrepôt of the Mediterranean thanks to the development of a system of sea-communications, migration, and changing demographic and social patterns.

The book shows that it was only under the rule of the Order that a 'Maltese' culture really came into being, and that this 'Maltese' culture was largely based on three constituents namely language, religion and the emergence of a Maltese polity.

It offers a comprehensive and persuasive discussion of the structural features of economy and society in Malta, showing how effectively the author has learned from Braudel's example. That discussion is based on extensive use of archival sources, and makes a valuable contribution to our understanding of Malta's place within the early modern Mediterranean economy. The discussion of orality, literacy, cultural symbols, social memory and ethnic identity contains a great deal of new and fascinating material, and the author has made excellent use of a wide range of recent work in social anthropology and cultural history.

*Robert W. Scribner*

# Witchcraft, Sorcery and the Inquisition in Early Modern Malta

## Carmel Cassar

*Witchcraft, Sorcery and the Inquisition in Early Modern Malta* attempts to reconstruct the complexities of witchcraft, astrology and various sorts of popular magic at the turn of the seventeenth century in a central Mediterranean island society. The analysis is restricted to a few basic Malta Inquisition Tribunal case-studies at a time when the witch craze was raging throughout Europe. In Malta, as in the case of the Italian peninsula, the inquisitors – who retained jurisdiction over witchcraft cases – were far milder than the secular judges of continental Europe. Many suspects were either released or else condemned to relatively minor punishments.

This study provides a vivid portrayal of popular mentality and beliefs at a time of great religious intolerance, when Malta served primarily as a Christian base for defence against Islam, while the Tribunal of the Roman Inquisition worked incessantly to reform traditional society in line with the precepts of the Council of Trent. Finally the book shows that the knowledge of witchcraft was not only widespread, but oral traditions interacted with elite culture.

## Hospitaller Malta 1530-1798:
### Studies on Early Modern Malta and the Order of St John of Jerusalem
Edited by V. Mallia-Milanes

This collection of sixteen original research papers, each written in a vivid and authoritative manner, seeks to understand Malta's position in its broader Mediterranean context, its gradual social and political transformation, its mental habits, aspects of its urban and economic developments, its military and architectural reality, its varied artistic life, the effects of the Enlightenment on its Church-State relations, and the place it held in the complex politics of revolutionary France.

There is no doubt that behind the changes which early modern Malta progressively experienced from 1530 to 1798 lay the powerful dynamism and resources of the Hospitaller institution of the Order of St John. But, on the other hand, was not the nature of the island itself and its geographical location an equally powerful force which during the course of over two-and-a-half centuries of history was partly to determine the direction of the Order's own development and decline? This volume is therefore as much concerned with early modern Malta as it is with the Order of St John.

## The British Colonial Experience 1800-1964:
### The Impact on Maltese Society
Edited by V. Mallia-Milanes

This book, in the form of a collective work, has drawn together a team of 17 specialists, including contributions from Great Britain, Holland, and Australia. Together they seek to explore, through their essays, the extent to which Maltese society, in some of its major aspects, has been modified by the impact of its long British colonial experience – the 164 years that separated the end of the revolutionary upheaval in 1800 (against the French Administration of General Vaubois) from the island's attainment of Independence in 1964.

Change is therefore the overall theme of the book – the slow departure from old habits, a small Mediterranean island society yielding, in imperceptible stages, to a perhaps unintended process of Anglicization. The topics discussed range from the origins of Maltese nationalism to the structure of everyday life and patterns of behaviour at various stages; from Church-State relations and the nature of the local economy to the question of identity and nationhood; from Malta's fate within the British imperial decolonization to her developing art, literature, architecture, and other dimensions.